Consumer Behaviour and Promotional Strategies

Consumer Behaviour and Promotional Strategies

B. Rameshwaran

SERIALS PUBLICATIONS
NEW DELHI (INDIA)

First Published – 2011

ISBN: 978-81-8387-440-3

Published by

SERIALS PUBLICATIONS
4830/24, 1st Floor, Ansari Road
Darya Ganj, New Delhi-110002 (India)
Phone : 23245225. Fax : 91-11-23272135
E-mail : serials@sify.com
serialspublications.india@gmail.com
Website: www.serialspublications.com

This book is dedicated to

My beloved Parents, My wife
and My beloved daughters RITU and RIMA.

Contents

Foreword

This book titled "Consumer Behaviour and Promotional Strategies" is a published work of the doctoral thesis undertaken by B.Rameshwaran in the Department of Management Studies, Kannur University under my supervision and guidance.

The book covers the analysis of the social, cultural, economic and behavioural aspects of the car owners and potential consumers in the car market in Kerala. Modern research methods and techniques like factor analysis, KMO, ANOVA and Chi-square tests have been used to arrive at meaningful conclusions from the findings of the study. It throws open several challenges and opportunities not only to the marketers in the car industry but also to researchers, teachers, consumers in the car market and to management professionals at large.It also throws light on various promotional strategies used by marketers in the small car market in Kerala. Sufficient charts, tables and relevant examples have been stated to substantiate the study.

I heartily congratulate Dr. B.Rameshwaran for his painstaking efforts in bringing out this comprehensive book. I am sure the book will serve as reference to marketers in the car industry, students, research scholars, teaching faculty and management professionals at large.

Dr. P.T. Raveendran,
Professor,
Department of Management Studies,
KannurUniversity, Thalassery Campus,
Palayad. 670 661.

Preface

This book is written with the purpose of blending both concepts and applications from the field of consumer behaviour and marketing research. No special assumptions have been made regarding student preparation for this text. The motivation for writing this book has arisen from the feeling that research has now reached a stage of development where traditional research methods and techniques require synthesis and application. I believe this book is novel in the aspect of providing information about the promotional strategies used by marketers in the car industry and the nuances in consumer behaviour in the car market in Kerala, whose output is a potential value for management decision.

The book emphasizes, relatively, the importance of modern analytical tools such as factor analysis, KMO, ANOVA and Chi-square test to analyse the primary data collected for the purpose of arriving at meaningful conclusions with regard to consumer behaviour and promotional strategies in the small car market in Kerala.

Considerable effort has been made to present the material clearly and in a style that is readable, lucid, interesting and motivating to students, researchers and management professionals.

The book is presented in five chapters. The first chapter highlights the introduction to the study, scope and importance of the study, objectives of the study, research problem, methodology of the study, limitations of the study and scope for further study.

The second chapter throws light on the review of literature of the study. It expatiates various research studies carried out by researchers and management professionals in the field of consumer behaviour and promotional strategies in the car industry.

The third chapter presents an overview of the automobile industry both global and Indian, and is devoted to the historical perspective of the automobile industry.

The fourth chapter illustrates the analysis and interptetation of the buyer behaviour and promotional strategies in the small car market in Kerala.

The fifth chapter highlights the findings, conclusions and recommendations of the study and puts forth suggestions for future research.

B. Rameshwaran

1 Introduction

INTRODUCTION

The study of buyer behaviour has assumed paramount importance in the car industry in general and in the small car market in particular. It has thrown open several challenges to the car manufacturers and car dealers in formulating effective and competitive promotional strategies for growth and market acceptance. It fosters the process of understanding why a customer or a buyer makes a car purchase. Without such an understanding the car industry will find it very difficult to respond to the needs and wants of the customers. It is challenging to understand how customers respond to the plethora of promotional tools used by marketers in the marketing of cars. If car manufacturers and car dealers could understand these customer preferences and perceptions better than their competitors then it is potentially a significant source of competitive advantage for the car makers. Hence car makers spend considerable time, money and effort to learn consumer behaviour. The term consumer behaviour is defined as the behaviour that consumers display in searching for, purchasing, using, evaluating and disposing of products and services that they expect will satisfy their needs.[1] Thus consumer behaviour focuses on how individuals make decisions to spend their available resources like time, money and effort on consumption related items. That includes what they buy, why they buy it, when they buy it, where they buy it from, how often they buy it, how often they use it, how they evaluate after the purchase and the impact of such evaluations on future purchases, and how they dispose of the products and services.

The wave of globalization which has swept across the country since 1991 has paved way to witness an unprecedented growth and competition in all the sectors of our economy. The deregulation of the licensing regime, delicensing of several industries, tariff cuts, abolition of import and export restrictions, removal of trade barriers have made tremendous impact on the industrial growth of the nation in terms of increased capacity of utilization, easy access to state of the art technology and free flow of foreign capital to India. All these measures have solved the supply side of the problem of our economy to a great extent. But the demand side of the problem is still looming large. In the current market scenario where cut throat competition among business houses prevail, a marketer has to chalk out effective promotional strategies to rule the roost. In today's competitive world where miniaturization is the buzzword, Shumacher's wisdom of 'small is beautiful' stands in good stead in the car market of Kerala where car makers are trying to bring out tailor-made small cars that suit the needs of the buyers appropriately, both in terms of economy and size of the car.

SCOPE AND IMPORTANCE OF THE STUDY

The study of the buyer behaviour and the promotional strategies in the small car market is geographically limited to the state of Kerala and the coverage of the study is limited to small cars only. The mid segment cars and the large segment cars (premium cars) do not fall under the purview of the study. The models of the cars that have been studied are Maruti 800, Maruti Alto, Maruti Zen, Maruti WagonR, Maruti Swift, Maruti Zen Estilo, Hyundai Santro and Tata Indica.

The promotional tools have been confined to advertising, sales promotion, direct marketing, personal selling, publicity, public relations and word of mouth.

The study is very important from the angle of the car manufacturers, car dealers, car owners and the potential car buyers in the small car market in Kerala. The study throws light on the important factors on which consumers base their car purchase decisions. The different promotional tools have been ranked according to the preferences, tastes and perceptions of the car buyers in Kerala. This will help car manufacturers and car dealers to evaluate and reformulate their promotional strategies, which in turn will churn out better sales and profit and subsequently will lead to better market acceptance.

The ultimate beneficiaries of the study are the potential car buyers and the society at large. It will offer several opportunities and challenges for other car manufacturers to deliver quality cars at affordable prices which will throw open several employment opportunities in Kerala and in turn will augur better standard of living and portend a great place to live in.

The study provides a theoretical framework under which the manufacturers and dealers of small cars can formulate appropriate promotional strategies for their cars which will give a fillip to their market performance and growth, and ultimately bring customer satisfaction for the car buyers.

So far no serious attempt has been made to analyse the promotional activities undertaken by the manufacturers and dealers of small cars in Kerala. This study has a wide scope in serving as an eye opener to many researchers and marketers to explore the promotional aspects of the car industry and come out with better research findings.

The study also helps in understanding the perception of consumers towards small cars and the factors that are responsible for the purchase decision of cars. This will help the car manufacturers and dealers in formulating appropriate promotional strategies and in turn pass on the benefits of promotion to the consumers.

OBJECTIVES OF THE STUDY

Primary Objective

To study the buyer behaviour in the small car market in Kerala and to identify the various promotional tools that influence the car purchase decision and to recommend the most effective promotional strategy in the small car market in Kerala.

Secondary Objectives

1. To identify various promotional strategies those influence the car purchase decision in Kerala.
2. To identify the social factors those influence the car purchase decision in Kerala.
3. To analyse the importance of various factors like safety, economy, comfort, performance, design and style in the small car market in Kerala.
4. To identify the reasons why car owners in Kerala replace their previous cars and choose another car.
5. To identify the reasons why people shift from two-wheelers to cars in the small car market in Kerala.
6. To study the customer satisfaction of car owners with regard to after sales service of the car dealers in Kerala.
7. To identify the economic factors those influence the car purchase decision in Kerala.

HYPOTHESES

The following is the main hypothesis constructed by the researcher for the study.

There is no significant difference in the purchase behaviour of the sample units and the various promotional tools used by the small car manufacturers and dealers with respect to the region, area, gender, age and the income groups.

In order to validate the main hypothesis it may be tested with the help of the following sub hypotheses.

1. The car purchase decision is independent of the promotional strategies used by car marketers among

the region, gender, age and income groups in the small car market in Kerala.

2. There is no significant difference in the social factors and the car purchase decision among the region, gender, age and income groups in the small car market in Kerala.
3. There is no relationship between the importance of factors like safety, economy, comfort, performance, design and style, and the car purchase decision among the region, gender, age and income groups in the small car market in Kerala.
4. There is no significant difference in the reasons why car owners in Kerala replace their previous cars and choose another car among the region, gender, age and income groups in the small car market in Kerala.
5. There is no significant difference in the reasons why people switch from two-wheelers to cars among the region, gender, age and income groups in the small car market in Kerala.
6. Customer satisfaction of the car owners is independent of after sales service of the car dealers among the region, gender, age and income groups in the small car market in Kerala.
7. There is no significant difference in the economic factors those influence the car purchase decision among the region, gender, age and income groups in the small car market in Kerala.

These hypotheses were tested using Chi-square test.

DEFINITION OF CONCEPTS

Promotion

Promotion is the means by which firms attempt to inform, persuade, and remind consumers–directly or indirectly–about the products and brands that they sell. In a sense, promotion represents the 'voice' of the brand and is a means by which it can establish a dialogue and build relationships with consumers. Promotion performs many functions for consumers. Consumers can be told or shown how and why a product is used, by what kind of person, and where and when; consumers can learn about who makes the product and what the company and brand stand for; and consumers can be given an incentive or reward for trial or usage. Promotion allows companies to link their brands to other people, places, events, brands, experiences, feelings, and things.[2]

Strategy

Michael Porter defines strategy as "the creation of a unique and valuable position involving a different set of activities". A company can claim that it has a strategy when it "performs different activities from rivals or performs similar activities in different ways". Strategy is a game plan for achieving the goals of an organization.[3]

Strategy can be seen as a normative matter concerning what an organization would like to achieve. As such it:

- Guides the organization in its relationship with its environment;
- Affects the internal structure and processes of the organization;
- Centrally affects the organisation's performance.

Small Car

A small car means a car of length not exceeding 4000 mm and whose width is less than 1600mm and whose height should not be more than 1600 mm. A small car can have a maximum engine capacity of 1500 cc for diesel cars and 1200 cc for petrol cars. The pricing of small car will range from 1 lakh to 4.5 lakhs.[4]

Buyer Behaviour

Buyer behaviour is defined as the behaviour that buyers display in searching for, purchasing, using, evaluating and disposing of products and services that they expect will satisfy their needs.[5]

BUYER DECISION MAKING - AN OVERVIEW

The process of buyer decision making can be viewed as three distinct but interlocking stages viz., the input stage, the process stage and the output stage. The input stage influences the buyer's recognition of a product need and consists of two major sources of information viz., the firm's marketing efforts (the product itself, its price, its promotion and where it is sold i.e. place) and the external sociological influences on the buyer (family, friends, neighbours, other informal and noncommercial sources, social class, cultural and subcultural memberships). The cumulative impact of each firm's marketing efforts, the influence of family, friends, neighbours and society's existing code of behaviour, are all inputs that are likely to affect what buyer's purchase and how they use what they buy.

The process stage focuses on how buyers make decisions. The psychological factors inherent in each individual (motivation, perception, learning, personality and attitudes) affect how the external inputs from the input stage influence the consumer's recognition of a need, pre-purchase search for information, and evaluation of alternatives. The experience gained through evaluation of alternatives, in turn, affects the consumer's existing psychological attributes.

The output stage of the buyer decision-making model consists of two closely related post-decision activities: purchase behaviour and post-purchase evaluation. Purchase behaviour for a low-cost, nondurable product may be influenced by a manufacturer's coupon and may actually be a trial purchase; if the buyer is satisfied, he or she may repeat the purchase. The trial is the exploratory phase of purchase behaviour in which the buyer evaluates the product through direct use. A repeat purchase usually signifies product adoption. For a relatively durable product, the purchase is more likely to signify adoption.

Buyer Behaviour in Making Purchase Decision

It is very important for any marketer to study how individuals and organization make purchase decisions and the influence of various factors in their buying decisions. Buyer decision making is influenced by both external and internal factors. The external factors that influence the purchase decisions are social factors, cultural factors, demographic factors, social class and family. The internal factors that influence the purchase decision are the psychological characteristics like motivation, learning, personality, attitudes and perception. The external factors which influence the buyer decision making are social factors, cultural factors, demographic factors, social class and family.

Social Factor

The social factors are family members, friends, relatives, neighbours, social class and social status. There are other social groups like contactual groups, aspirational groups and disclaimant groups. The comments of a friend, an editorial in the newspaper, usage by family member, an article in a journal, the views of experienced consumers participating in a special interest discussion groups on the internet are all non-commercial sources of information which form part of social factor. The influences of social class, culture and subculture, although less tangible are important input factors that are internalized and affect how consumers evaluate and ultimately adopt products. The cumulative impact of each firms marketing efforts; the influence of family, friends and neighbours; and society's existing code of behaviour are all social factors that are likely to affect what consumers purchase and how they use what they buy.

Cultures and Sub-cultures

The sum of learned beliefs, values and customs that regulate the behaviour of members of a particular society is called culture. The three components of culture are beliefs, values and customs. Belief is proposition that reflects a person, particular knowledge and assessment of something. Values are general statements that guide behaviour and influence beliefs and attitudes. It has been stated that the function of a value system is to help a person to choose between alternatives in everyday life. Marketers have a special interest in values, because values are influenced shaping one's behaviour.

Practical consideration force the marketer to be more interested in cultural values than personal values. If a culture begins to value family and personal health and relaxation over achievement and material success, this cultural trend would be of interest to many marketers. Customs are overt modes of behaviour that constitute culturally approved ways of behaving in specific situations. Customs do vary from region to region, from country to country and even from family to family.

The emergence of sub-cultures is a natural evolution that occurs in any culture. Although, the core values in culture are held by virtually the entire population, secondary values are not. Sub-culture refers to a subgroup of the people who share a set of secondary values. According to Philip Cateora, the factors that can place an individual in one sub-culture are material culture, social institutions, belief systems, aesthetics and language.

Demographic Factor

Demographic traits such as age, sex and income obviously mould values and behaviour. Changes are occurring constantly in the demographic make up of the people of every country. These changes are often dramatic and the adjustments they require are far reaching. The demographic environment with important implications for promotion include the baby boomers (born between 1946 and 1964 in USA), senior citizen, migration patterns, education and occupation, the employed women, distribution of income and ethnic surge. Most of these elements are easily monitored and should be watched by promotion managers. Promoters have to design advertising campaigns, discounts, off season reductions, contests, free test drives, exchange melas/loan melas for different segments of the population.

The demographic environment of every country is subject to change. The promoters have to watch constantly the changes occurring in the demographic environment of the country and to formulate promotional strategies in accordance with these changes. For example a baby boom occurred during the period from 1946 to 1964 in the United States of America. Seventy six million babies were born during this period. 70 million of them are still alive. They are now between 45 and 63 years of age and make up about one third of the total population. The point is that this largest group in the American population will go through predictable stages, and wise managers will be sensitive to these patterns.

High mobility and migration rates also suggests problems for the promotion managers. For example, a car dealer or a car manufacturer may customize its promotional campaigns or promotional offers for different regions. People who move from one region to another may become confused when they see different promotion messages.[6] Likewise, direct marketing is extremely difficult to maintain accurate mailing lists.

Continually rising level of education is another change of considerable significance to marketers. The educational gap between men and women is narrowing. While the share of young men with four or more years of college has dropped since 1980, the share of young women with four or more years of college has grown.[7]

The prevalence of working women has been one of the key economic and social development of our times. The overall percentage of working women will continue to increase, with 61% expected to be in the workforce by 2010.[8] In USA, women now head 28% of America's 91 million households. For the promotion manager, the increase in working women offers problems as well as opportunities. Sales promotion tools like discounts, free insurance, free road tax, free accessories are found appealing to working women.

Distribution of income and wealth is another factor to be considered by marketers while formulating promotional strategies. For example, a few years ago, middle income consumers could be counted on to go for lower end models of cars which are priced low for their car purchase. However, as they have become more astute in their purchase decisions, they are more likely to purchase higher end models of car of high price, without compromising on the quality of the car.

Nowadays consumers are seen to be more demanding. They need qualitative improvement in the case of every product they use. Producers and marketers should try to understand the demands of the consumers so that necessary changes and improvements can be made by them on their products.

The emergence of credit loving consumers is another problem faced by the marketers. Consumers prefer purchasing cars on loans and repay the amount in installments. The middle income and the lower income people are reluctant to pay the price in full at the time of purchase of a car. This problem is tackled by having tie up with banks and such other financial institutions like State Bank of India, Mahindra & Mahindra, Kotak Mahindra, Canara Bank, HDFC bank, ICICI bank, Magma Finance, Axis bank, Sriram Finance and Sundaram Finance.

Above all these, the spurt of several car dealers and foreign car manufacturers in Kerala has made the consumers more selective and choosy. Hence, every marketer, in order to have an edge over his competitors has to be very meticulous in the formation of promotional strategies and also in the quality of the product.

Marketing of Small Cars

Marketing, as defined by Philip Kotler, is a social and managerial process by which individuals and groups obtain what they need and want through creating offering and freely exchanging goods and services of value with others.[9]

In the small car market, the aim of marketing is to make selling superfluous. The aim of marketing is to know and understand the customer so well that the car or service suits him appropriately and sells itself. Ideally, marketing of a car should result in a customer who is ready to buy one. All that should be needed then is to make the product or service available.[10]

The American Marketing Association offers the following definition:

Marketing is the process of planning and executing the conception, pricing, promotion and distribution of ideas, goods, services to create exchanges that satisfy individual and organizational goals.[11]

In the marketing of small cars, the marketer should take competition into consideration. With several domestic and foreign players in the car market, marketing of small cars can pose a great challenge to marketers because competition includes all the actual and potential rival offerings and substitutes that a buyer of a small car might consider. We can broaden the marketing picture of small cars by distinguishing four levels of competition, based on the degree of car substitutability.

Brand Competition

A company sees its competitors as other companies offering a similar product or service to the same customers at similar prices. Maruti Udyog Ltd. might see its major competitors in the small car segment as Hyundai Motors, Tata Motors and other manufacturers of small cars. It would not see itself as competing with Mercedes or Audi.

Industry Competition

A company sees its competitors as all companies making the same product or class of products. Maruti Udyog Ltd. would see itself as competing against all other automobile manufacturers.

Form Competition

A company sees its competitors as all companies manufacturing products that supply the same service. Maruti Udyog Ltd. would see itself competing against not only other automobile manufacturers but also against manufacturers of motorcycles, bicycles and trucks.

Generic Competition

A company sees its competitors as all companies that compete for the same consumer rupees (currency). Maruti Udyog Ltd.

would see itself competing with companies that sell major consumer durables, foreign vacations and new homes.[12]

Promotion of Small Cars

Promotion is concerned with effectively communicating the results of the marketing strategy to the largest audience.

In the small car market, promotion plays a very important role in communicating the product features, quality, design, style, brand name, services, warranties, credit terms, discounts and price of the car to the target audience. Thus promotion is an active and explicit form of marketing communication. Promotion highlights the marketing elements in order to increase the odds that consumers will buy and become committed to the product. It is the marketing function concerned with persuasively communicating to target audiences the components of the marketing programme in order to facilitate exchange between the car manufacturers/car dealers and the potential customers to help them satisfy the objectives of both.[13]

The promotion mix consists of six major modes of communication which provide the key tools to attain the goals of promotion.

Advertising

It is any paid form of non-personal communication and promotion of ideas, goods or services by an identified sponsor. Although some advertising is directed at specified individual, most advertising messages are tailored to a group and use mass media such as radio, television, newspapers, magazines, booklets, brochures, billboards and other outdoor displays.

Personal Selling

Face to face interaction with one or more prospective purchasers for the purpose of making presentations, answering questions and procuring orders. It is the interpersonal communication with one or more prospective purchases for the sake of making sales. Examples include sales calls to business organizations by a field representative, in-store assistance of a salesman and representative calling at homes (door to door selling).

Sales Promotion

A variety of short-term incentives to encourage trial purchase or purchase of a product or service is called sales promotion. Sales promotion consists of marketing activities that add to the basic value of the product or service for a limited period and directly stimulate consumer purchasing, for example, coupons, contests, sales meetings, discounts, free accessories, free insurance, free road tax and free test drives.

Public Relation and Publicity

A variety of programmes designed to promote or protect a company's image or its individual products. It is a co-ordinated attempt to create a favourable product image in the minds of the public by supporting certain activities or programmes, publishing commercially significant news in a widely circulated medium or obtaining favourable publicity, that is, favourable presentations on radio, television or stage that are not paid by the sponsor.

Direct Marketing

Use of mail, telephone, fax, e-mail or internet to communicate directly with or solicit a direct response from specific customers and prospects is called direct marketing.

Word of Mouth

The image of a product, the benefits, the positive or negative aspects of a product can be promoted by word of mouth by way of passing on the message of a product from one person to another and subsequently percolating to the target audiences. The word of mouth promotion has a tremendous impact in brand building and market acceptance of a product.

The above six modes of promotion mix are the most common active forms of marketing communication. Clearly, both productive and reactive forms of communication are crucial. Thus promotion brings the consumer to the threshold of the car showroom who is completely equipped with brand awareness, product knowledge, a positive attitude and an extra incentive to buy.

METHODOLOGY

This is a descriptive study of the buyer behaviour and promotional strategies in the small car market in Kerala. The study is based on both primary and secondary data which are analysed using appropriate statistical tools to draw conclusions.

Sources of Primary Data

Since most of the information necessary to fulfil the objectives of the study were not available from secondary sources, the researcher mainly based his study on relevant primary data which were collected by conducting a field survey from the selected sample units in Kerala.

Sources of Secondary Data

The secondary data necessary for the study were compiled from published and unpublished sources.

Accounting Records

The 'Sales Invoice' of the car dealers and manufacturers is sought. The sales invoice includes the name of the customer, address, accessories and other items ordered, quantities, discounts and date of sale.

Sales Force Reports

The Sales Force Reports represent a rich source of marketing information. This is given by the sales personnel of car dealers and manufacturers.

Miscellaneous Reports

The previous marketing research studies and special audits form the miscellaneous reports.

Internal Experts

An internal expert is any one employed by the firm who has special knowledge related to the question in hand. This knowledge is stored in the individual's mind rather than on paper or computer disk.

The researcher used the following external sources of secondary data:

Computerized Database

A computerized database is a collection of numeric data or textual information about the car industry and promotion strategies that were made available in the internet.

Bibliographic Database

A number of bibliographic databases were available for a wide variety of marketing strategies including the promotional strategies of cars which the researcher used. Marketing and Advertising Reference Service (MARS) was used as secondary data.

Numeric Databases

The Census-based numeric database provided by the Census of India especially on population figures was a good source of secondary data which was used by the researcher.

Syndicated Services

Syndicated services collect data by conducting periodic market surveys and sell them on a subscription basis. A.C. Nielsen Market Survey is a syndicated service, which the researcher used in the study.

Associations

There are several associations that frequently publish detailed information on the car industry or the automobile industry. Society for Indian Automobile Manufacturers (SIAM) publishes several reports on the car industry. Automotive Car Manufacturers Association (ACMA), Federation of Automobile Dealers Association (FADA) also publishes information on car industry. The reports of these associations were used by the researcher as secondary data.

Government Agencies

The different departments of the government, the DIC (District Industries Centre), Census of India and NSSO (National

Sample Survey Organisation) serve as reliable sources of secondary data which the researcher used.

Stock Exchange

Stock Exchanges provide data on the financial characteristics, product line sales, joint ventures and competitor analysis, which the researcher used as source of secondary data.

Directories

Industry directories, trade show directories and telephone directories were useful in collecting secondary data by the researcher.

External Experts

External experts were individuals outside the organization who provided expertise knowledge on the car industry and the study undertaken. Central and State government officials associated with the study, trade association officials, editors, writers for trade and business publications, university researchers were all reliable and good sources of secondary data.

The following sources of secondary data were also used by the researcher:

1. The published records from the Ministry of Industries, Government of India.
2. Publications of Ministry of Industries, Government of Kerala.
3. Journal of Marketing Research
4. Journal of Advertising Research
5. Journal Consumer Research
6. Journal of Marketing
7. Data published by Marketing Research Organisations like MARG, ORG, AC Nielsen and TNI.
8. Gartner Report
9. Harvard Business Review
10. Economic and Political Weekly
11. Indian Journal of Marketing

12. IIMB Management Review
13. Vikalpa
14. Published records from SIAM, FADA and ACMA
15. THE HINDU Survey of India.
16. Department of Motor Vehicles, Government of Kerala.

Unpublished sources of secondary data include:

1. Ph.D. Theses
2. M. Phil Dissertations

Research Problem

A car purchase decision is based on several external and internal factors. The external factors that influence the car purchase decision are social factors (like family, friends, neighbours, other informal and noncommercial sources and social class), cultural factors and demographic factors.

The cultural factors that influence the car purchase decision are the psychological characteristics like motivation, learning, personality, attitudes and perception.

The research problem is to investigate into those factors that are responsible for the influence of a car purchase decision and to determine the most important factor among them, which a car buyer thinks would influence his or her car purchase decision.

Furthermore, there are several promotional strategies used by car manufacturers and car dealers who use them as promotional tools to influence the car purchase decision in the small car market in Kerala. The various promotional tools used by car manufacturers and dealers are advertising, sales promotion, personal selling, direct marketing, word of mouth, public relation and publicity.

Thus the researcher would further like to investigate into those promotional tools that are crucial in the influencing of a car purchase decision in the small car market in Kerala and to study if there is significant difference in the promotional strategies used and the influence of socio-cultural factors among the different income levels, gender and the three regions of Kerala viz., northern, central and southern.

Sample Frame

The present study pertains to car manufacturers, car dealers and the car owners in Kerala. There are altogether three car manufacturers viz. Maruti Udyog Ltd ,Hyundai Motors Ltd and Tata Motors Ltd operating at their regional levels in Kerala. There are eighteen company authorized dealers in Kerala, out of which nine are of Maruti Udyog Ltd, five are of Hyundai Motors Ltd and four are of Tata Motors Ltd. As it was not possible to cover all the dealers in Kerala due to the constraints of time and money, it was decided to conduct a sample study on the basis of a cross section of the dealers in Kerala. It was decided to select a representative sample of 50 per cent of the dealers from each region. Three dealers from each region viz., northern, central and southern regions of Kerala were selected. Thus nine dealers were selected from all the three regions of Kerala. It was decided to select a sample of 675 car owners from the 3 regions of Kerala viz., northern, central and southern. Out of the 675 car owners selected, 225 car owners were decided to be selected from the northern region, 225 car owners from the central region and 225 car owners from the southern region. After scrutiny, it was observed that out of the 675 car owners selected, only 602 car owners were subject to statistical analysis. This was because there were partial responses and inconsistencies observed in the responses given by 73 car owners. Thus, response rate was only 89.19 per cent in the survey conducted by the researcher. Table 1 reveals the region-wise break-up of the sample car owners selected.

Table 1
The Region-Wise Break-up of the Sample Car Owners

	Number of Car Owners		
Region	*Urban*	*Rural*	*Total*
Northern	100	103	203
Central	99	100	199
Southern	100	100	200
Total	299	303	602

Thus, a sample comprising 3 car manufacturers, 9 car dealers and 602 car owners was selected from the sample frame of the study.

Sample Design

The study adopts a multistage stratified random sampling method for sample selection.

First Stage

The state was divided into three regions for the purpose of the study viz., northern, central and southern. The northern region comprises five districts viz., Kasargode, Kannur, Kozhikode, Wyanad and Malappuram. The central region consists of Palakkad, Trichur, Ernakulam and Idukki districts and the southern region covers the remaining districts in the state viz., Kottayam, Alappuzha, Kollam, Pathanamthitta and Thiruvananthapuram.

Second Stage

From each region one district each was selected at random by way of simple random sampling method. From the northern region the researcher selected Kozhikode district, from the central region, Ernakulam district was selected and from the southern region, Thiruvananthapuram district was selected.

Third Stage

Having selected one district each from the three zones of Kerala the researcher divides each district thus selected into two categories. The areas of jurisdiction of corporations and municipalities will be categorized as urban and the area of jurisdiction of panchayaths will be categorized as rural. Then using simple random sampling technique the researcher selected 100 small car owners from the population living within the corporation and another 100 small car owners from the population living within the panchayaths. From Thiruvananthapuram district, Thiruvananthapuram corporation and Pangode panchayath were selected. From Ernakulam district, Kochi corporation and Thevara panchayath were selected. From Kozhikode district, Kozhikode corporation and Mukkom panchayath were selected.

In this way there are 3 corporations and 3 panchayaths selected for the study. Thus the researcher altogether selected 675 sample units (car owners) from the three corporations and three panchayaths in Kerala. Thus altogether, 602 sample units (car owners) were selected for the study.

In the case of car dealers and car manufacturers which form part of the sample frame, 9 company authorised car dealers were selected at random from 18 company authorised car dealers (which were established before 2004) spread across the three regions of Kerala viz., northern, central and southern regions. From the southern region, 3 dealers were selected viz., Popular Automobiles of Maruti Udyog Ltd., Kulathingal Motors of Tata Motors and Hilton Hyundai of Hyundai Motors Ltd. From the central region, 3 dealers were selected viz., Indus Motors of Maruti Udyog Ltd., RF Motors of Tata Motors and MGF Hyundai of Hyundai Motors Ltd. From the northern region, 3 dealers were selected viz., Indus Motors of Maruti Udyog Ltd., Koyenco of Tata Motors and KTC Hyundai of Hyundai Motors Ltd.

Altogether, 9 company authorised car dealers (which were established before 2004) were selected for the study. In the case of the three car manufacturers viz., Maruti Udyog Ltd., Tata Motors Ltd. and Hyundai Motors Ltd., the regional offices of the car manufacturing companies situated in Kerala were visited by the researcher and the regional managers were interviewed about their opinions of the study.

Thus altogether, the study comprised a sample of 602 car owners, 9 car dealers and 3 car manufacturers to study the buyer behaviour and promotional strategies in the small car market in Kerala.

Type of Study

The type of study undertaken by the researcher is a descriptive study. The researcher studied the buyer behaviour and the various promotional strategies in the small car market in Kerala.

Area of the Study

The state of Kerala has been chosen by the researcher as his area of the study. The state of Kerala comprising 14 districts has been classified into three zones viz., northern zone, central zone and southern zone. The northern zone comprises the following five districts viz., Malappuram, Kozhikode, Wayanad, Kannur and Kasaragode. The central zone comprises four districts viz., Ernakulam, Thrissur, Palakkad and Idukki. The remaining five districts viz., Thiruvananthapuram, Kollam, Pathanamthitta, Alleppey and Kottayam would come under southern zone.

Period of Study

The study covered a period of six accounting years from 2002 to 2008.

Period of Survey

The survey was conducted during the six months period from July, 2008 and continued up to December, 2008. The 203 car owners in the district of Calicut were surveyed first, next 199 car owners in the district of Ernakulam, and finally the 200 car owners in the district of Thiruvananthapuram were surveyed for information. The car dealers of Maruti Udyog Ltd., Tata Motors and Hyundai Motors of Thiruvananthapuram, Ernakulam and Calicut were also surveyed for obtaining information about the buyer behaviour and the promotional strategies in the small car market in Kerala.

Tools for Collection of Primary Data

The primary data were collected from 602 car owners through an interview schedule. The schedule had 80 questions divided into two broad sections viz., information regarding the purchase behaviour and promotional strategies in the small car market in Kerala, and the personal information of the respondents. The questions on purchase behaviour and the influence of promotional tools were asked to the car owners, car dealers and the car manufacturers.

The schedule was pre-tested on 60 car owners in Calicut district and based on the pre-test information, 10 irrelevant questions were dropped from the total of 100 questions.

Ernakulam is situated in the centre of Kerala, Thiruvananthapuram the southern part of Kerala and Calicut is situated in the northern part of Kerala and hence they ensure a fairly geographically scattered sample.

Pre-testing of Interview Schedule

Keeping in mind the objectives of the study, an interview schedule covering all aspects of the study was developed taking into account the valuable suggestions of experts in this field. It was pre-tested on a small trial group, consisting of 60 sample units from the district of Kozhikode, to check the variability in the perception of the car owners and to ensure the validity and reliability of the questions in the interview schedule. On the basis of response to the pilot study, necessary modifications were made in the interview schedule and the modified interview schedule was used for the collection of primary data. The interview schedule contained 90 questions in two sections A and B. Section A deals with the questions relating to the factors influencing the car purchase behaviour and the influence of promotional strategies in the car purchase decisions in the small car market in Kerala. Section B deals with the personal profile of the respondents. Each part of the interview schedule contained many questions and sub-questions. A copy of the interview schedule is appended.

Tools Used for Analysis

The primary data collected were finally analyzed by classifying, tabulating and applying statistical tools such as percentage analysis, Chi-square test, ANOVA and Factor analysis. Chi-square test was used for testing of hypotheses. Chi-square is used as a test for independence and also to know the significant difference among the variables used in the study.

Variables Used for the Study

To fulfil the objectives of the study, the researcher has used 90 variables in the study. Ten variables pertain to the personal profile of the respondents and the rest 80 variables pertain to the buyer behaviour and promotional strategies in the small car market in Kerala.

LIMITATIONS OF THE STUDY

This study is not free from limitations. The following are the limitations that the researcher could find in his study.

1. The study could not unearth the inner psychological characteristics that determined the cause for the opinions given by the respondents with regard to the influence of promotional tools in the car purchase decision.
2. The Likert scale used by the researcher could not precisely examine by what degree the respondents agreed or disagreed to a particular statement or remark made by the researcher with regard to the car purchase decision. The study could not quantify the responses or opinions made by the respondents.
3. A few car owners hesitated in giving accurate information regarding their income, and the car dealers hesitated in revealing their sales figures from their sales outlets. However, effort had been taken to verify the income of car owners and sales figures of car dealers by cross checking with other related variables.

SCOPE FOR FURTHER RESEARCH

The study brings out a number of behavioural characteristics of car owners and the promotional tools used by dealers and manufacturers in the state of Kerala. However, the following areas need further research.

1. To study the problems in the society and examine how far corporate social responsibility of the car dealers and car manufacturers is effective in solving these problems.

2. Cars have now become a necessity more than a luxury. Therefore, research should be conducted to know to what extent government measures like subsidies and cut in excise duty for cars can help a common man afford a small car.
3. To study the effectiveness of using environment friendly and economical fuels to reduce pollution in Kerala.

CHAPTER SCHEME

The study is presented in five chapters. The first chapter highlights the introduction to the study, scope and importance of the study, objectives of the study, research problem, methodology of the study, limitations of the study and scope for further study.

The second chapter throws light on the review of literature of the study.

The third chapter presents an overview of the automobile industry -Global and Indian, and is devoted to the historical perspective of the automobile industry.

The fourth chapter illustrates the analysis and interpretation of the buyer behaviour and promotional strategies in the small car market in Kerala.

The fifth chapter highlights the findings, conclusions and recommendations and puts forth suggestions for further research.

REFERENCES

Nelson, Philip, "Information and Consumer Behaviour", *Journal of Political Economy,* Vol. 78, No. 2, pp. 311-329.

Burnett, John J. (1998), "Promotion Management", 1st ed., McGraw Hill.

Wilson, Richard M.S. and Collin Gilligan (2005), "Strategic Marketing Management", Butterworth Heinemann, 2nd ed., Oxford, p. 35.

Levitt, Theodore (1960), "Marketing Myopia", *Harvard Business Review,* August, pp. 45-46.

Howard, John A.. (1977), "Consumer Behaviour: Application of Theory", McGraw Hill, New York.

2 Review of Literature

As there have been only few studies conducted in the area of car industry, the availability of literature has been very scant. Yet, the researcher has been able to manage in reviewing the available literature from reliable sources which are as follows:

Newman Joseph W. and Richard, Staelin[1] (2002) conducted a study on *Pre-Purchase Information Seeking for New Cars and Major Household Appliances*. Their objective was to know how much information seeking precedes purchase of consumer durables and what factors are related to the differences among buyers? This study focuses on these questions for new cars and major household appliances. It discussed the related measurement problem and presented the results of multivariate analyses of measurements based on survey data. The findings supported the hypothesis that the purchase and use of a product result in learning which later influences buying behaviour.

Bucklin Randolph E. and George, Silva Risso[2] (2008) conducted a study to develop a new method to assess how changes in the intensity of mature distribution networks in the automotive industry will affect consumer choice. The study revealed that the buyers were more likely to select cars whose dealer networks had shorter distances to the closest outlet (accessibility), more dealers within a given radius from the buyer (concentration) and locations that skewed towards the buyer (spread).

Michel, G. Mueller and Peter, de Haan[3] (2008) conducted a study on the *Impact of Incentives on Car Purchase in Agent Based Micro Simulation of Consumer Choice of New Cars.* They presented an agent based micro simulation capable of forecasting the effects of policy decisions that influence individual choices of new passenger cars. The conclusion of the study was that the approach is useful for the assessment of policies that influence purchase decisions of new passenger cars. It allows accounting for a highly resolved car fleet and differentiated consumer segments.

Geoffrey, C. Kiel and Roger, A. Layton[4] (2000) conducted a study on *The Behaviour and Correlates of Information Seeking by New Car Buyers.* Here the authors examine three dimensions of information seeking – a source of information dimension, a brand dimension and a time dimension. Cluster analysis is used to develop consumer taxonomies of search behaviour based on measurements of each of the dimensions. The finding of the study was that after examining the correlates of the individual search dimensions, only certain predictors of search behaviour are related to the different search dimensions.

Another finding was about the time dimension. Two consumers may visit the same number of car dealers and will be exposed to the same number of advertisements but will be different in aggregate search behaviour if one consumer undertakes this search activity in a short period of time (e.g. a week) and the other takes a much longer period of time (a year).

Johnson, Chang[5] (2001) conducted a study on *the Comparison of Car Buying Behaviour between American and Chinese People Living in North America.* It was an exploratory study. The objective of the study was to compare the behavioural pattern in purchasing a car among American and Chinese. His finding was that American considered *fuel efficiency* of the car as the important factor that influenced the car purchase and *economy* of the car was given the least preference. The Chinese considered economy of the car (mileage) as most important and after sales service as least important factor.

The study uses the wheel of consumer analysis model to explain how cultural differences between American and Chinese consumers affect car buying decisions.

Aurangazeb[6] (2007) conducted a study on the *Impact of Colour on Consumer Buying Behaviour among the Car Buyer*. The objective of the study was to understand the colour on the strategy, i.e. to study the impact of colour on the consumer buying behaviour among the car dealers. He conducted a descriptive study using questionnaires and interview methods. He concluded that occupation, age and gender influence car buying attitudes. The study uses the wheel of consumer analysis model to explain how cultural differences between states can affect the car buying decision. The wheel of consumer analysis consists of three elements: (1) environment, (2) behaviour, (3) affect/cognition and is useful model for explaining buyer behaviour in general and car behaviour in particular.

Thomas, Andrews and Cynthia, Benzing[7] (2007) conducted a study on *The Determinants of Price in Internet Auctions of Used Cars*. This study analyses how auction, seller and product factors influence the price premium in a used car auction market. The important finding of the study was that cars had a greater probability to selling if the seller had a better reputation. Also, for auctions that resulted in a sale, cars with clear title and dealers were able to secure significantly greater price premiums, but seller reputation had significant effect.

Shang Chan Yung[8] (2007) conducted a study on *The Relationship between the Service Quality Elements and Customer Satisfaction with Reference to the Car Industry*. The study is based on the theory of SERVQUAL proposed by Parasuraman, Zeithmal and Berry (1988) and it discusses each service quality element and analyse the differences between a customer, expectations and the perceived service and further understand the real needs of a customer and the reasons affecting his/her satisfaction. The result of this study shows that what a customer really cares about is the basic aspects of car maintenance, professional knowledge and technical skills.

A study was conducted by Jim Gilbert and Jamie Lee[9] (2005) on the topic *Consumer Behaviour of Automobile Enthusiasts: Their Automotive Leisure Related Pursuits*. The sample frame was an automobile enthusiast association consisting of owners of restored vehicles, street roads and muscle cars. The objective of the study was to (1) measure the enthusiast's depth of involvement in the car culture hobby, (2) personal interests beyond building, driving and displaying their respective automobiles, (3) the enthusiast's demographics.

They concluded the study stating that technological advances often best reiterate the consumer behaviour of automobile hobbyists on why they do and what they do. Discretionary time and money allows personal choice as to how, what and where to spend it. The car culture is supported by many Americans as a leisure pursuit.

Xuan, Bai and Liu, Dongyan[10] (2008) conducted a study on the *Car Purchasing Behaviour in Beijing: An Empirical Investigation*. The objective of the study was to give an overview on young Chinese consumer car purchase behaviour. The findings of the study showed that car purchasing decision is important for majority of Chinese. Consumers get information from different channels. The results of the study also tells us that Chinese consumers takes *safety* as the most important characteristic and take value for money as the second most important factor, and riding comfort as the third important factor.

Chinese consumers take 'after sales service' and 'exterior design/size' as the fourth most important factor when making the purchase decision. For 'exterior design/size', it indicates that Chinese people are *status seeking* and Chinese people prefer to choose a bigger car with a good appearance (Mian Zi Che) to show their good social status and want to get respect from others. Chinese consumers place the least importance in resale value that is because second hand car market is not well developed in China.

Suresh and Raja[11] (2006) conducted a study on the topic *Measuring Customer Satisfaction for Small Cars – An Empirical Study*. The empirical study on measurement of customer satisfaction was undertaken for four models of small cars viz., Maruti 800, Santro, Tata Indica and Wagon R. The studies were relating: (1) To analyse the responses of customers towards the performance of different models of small cars. (2) To identify the factors of customer satisfaction (Factor analysis). (3) To identify the differences in demographic groups towards factors of customer satisfaction.

The methodology adopted was as follows: The target population was identified as all owners of small cars in Bangalore city. The sample population consisted of 40 small car owners each of Maruti 800, Tata Indica, Santro and Wagon R, making it a total of 160.

The data were analysed using statistical tools like ANOVA (Analysis of Variance) and Mean Score Analysis. Factor analysis was used to measure customer satisfaction. The factors used were sales support, vehicle design, purchase support, cost of ownership and delight features.

Suresh and Raja concluded saying that Santro was rated as the most accepted small car with regard to vehicle design, purchase support and delight features, Wagon R was rated best for sales support and Maruti 800 for cost of ownership.

Urvashi Makkar[12] (2006) conducted a study on the topic *Impact of the Phenomenon of Social Class Mobility on the Consumer Buying and Disposal Behaviour in Indian Perspective: A Case Study of White Goods Markets*. In the study Urvashi says that consumers have a tendency to move from lower social class to the middle social class and from middle social class to the upper social class keeping in view their changing tastes and preferences for better goods and services. Consumers are now going for real, 'life quality' products and services. Consumers of India want a better quality of life for themselves and their children, described in terms of durables that make life better especially in education, health care, transportation and communication.

Social class mobility: Recognising that individual often aspire for the lifestyle and possessions enjoyed by members of a higher social class, marketers frequently incorporate the symbols of higher-class membership, both as products and sops in promotions targeted to lower social class audiences. Consumer's buying behaviour is strongly influenced by the social class to which they belong, or aspire to belong, rather than by the income alone. The class differences are distinctly symbolized by consumption differences. Urvashi concludes saying that the lower upper class families follow a consumption pattern like spending on large homes with flashy and expensive decorations, best education for children, cars for transportation latest household gadget The upper middle class spend on buying 'quality' products, like Colour TV's, DVD players, personal computers, cars like Santro, Zen, Wagon R etc. The lower middle class spend a good deal of time shopping around for the best bargain, they buy consumer durables, like two wheelers, CTV, fridge, Maruti 800, Maruti Alto, etc.

Saraswathy[13] (2006) conducted a study on the topic *CRM - A New Dimension of Marketing*. In this study she has highlighted the significance of CRM (Customer Relationship Management also Customer Relationship Marketing), the pre-requisites of CRM and the constraints of CRM. The authoress says that the traditional marketing practices have not been effective in yielding good return. The four P's of marketing – price, product, promotion and place have to be combined with CRM to retain a customer and to build customer loyalty. She says "it costs 5 times less to retain an existing customer than to acquire a new one". The aim of CRM is to produce delighted and loyal customers. At present, car manufacturers and other companies are designing promotional strategies to retain customers and build long term relationships with them through CRM.

Saraswathy concludes her study stating that the main objective of CRM is building long term, sustaining relations with customers by delivering superior customer values and satisfaction. A customer centric culture is to be adopted in companies and companies should launch loyalty programmes which is indispensable in CRM for retention of customers.

Balachandran and Venkatesh[14] (2006) conducted a study in the topic *Issues in Changes of Global Brands into Domestic Brands*. In this study their objective was to 1) study the influence of brand ambassadors in India. They say that the degree of localization of brands is very high in the Indian market. As the Indian Market is known for its diversities, localization is to be carried out across all the 'P's of marketing mix, i.e. when an MNC (Multi National Company) or a foreign company introduces a brand or a product in the Indian market, it has to consider the tastes, preferences, interests, values and norms of Indians in making a purchase. For this, globalisation has to change to (G) localization. The Korean Car Company called Hyundai Motors Ltd, launched its Korean car in India as 'Santro' Car which suits the Indian road condition and the preferences of the Indians. Pepsi launched 'Pepsi blue', a new colour of soft drink to mark the colour code of Indian cricket team in the ICC world cup. PIZZA Hut, the world's largest PIZZA chain with 55 outlets across India, launched 'Masala Pizza'. This is to make the consumer feel that the product is suitable to the Indian conditions.

Balachandran says about the influence of brand ambassadors in India. He says that promotion is considered to be an important element of marketing mix since it communicates about every other element in the marketing mix. Therefore, (G) localization at this level of promotion starts right from the choice of celebrity or the brand ambassador. For instance, to promote Pepsi, film actor Shahrukh Khan would be a better choice than 'Ricky Martin' a foreigner. This is due to the credibility that the former enjoys in India than the latter. To promote Maruti Versa, Amitabh Bachchan has been made the brand ambassador. To promote Santro car, the brand ambassador is Sharukh Khan and Preeti Zinta.

Balachandran and Venkatesh concludes their study by saying that, it is advisable for MNC's to promote their brands on Indian brands. It should be a 'Local brand' instead of being a 'Global brand'.

Sankaran[15] (2005) conducted a study on the topic *Pure and Applied Research in Business - How Shall the Twain Meet?* One of the objectives of his study was to develop an initial hypothesis using the McKinsey way for introducing an Electric Car in the Market which can be used as research methodology for applied research.

He says, to tackle business situations, consulting firms have developed their own methodologies for applied research. Among these, there is a general agreement that the methodology used by McKinsey consultants, the Initial Hypothesis, or IH method, is a simple yet powerful one. This method has been extensively worked upon by a former consultant at McKinsey and developed into what is called the 'Pyramid Principle'. The basic principle here is that all human thought, all analysis including those in problematic situations, can be represented in a pyramidal fashion. The role of consultants is to transport working ideas from the research level to the organizational level. For this there should be greater collaboration between the research and consultant communities. Theory should go hand in hand with practice to reap the benefits of research in the market place and the shop floor.

Prathap Oberoi and Michael J. Baker[16] (2005) conducted a study on the Topic *International Marketing Strategies in India: An Application of Mixed Method Investigation*. The objective of the study was to examine the sources of competitive advantage in a few selected sectors and firms, including the automobile sector, and to explore the internationalization possibilities and potential. The study is exploratory in nature.

Case research methodology, modeling technique and grounded theory approach have been used in the study. The main weakness of qualitative research methodologies is the ostensibly idiosyncratic and hence perceptibly subjective nature of the research process of data generation, analysis and interpretation.

The international marketing strategies of 12 industrial sector have been explored. They are: automobiles, compact discs (CDs), cement, paints, pharmaceuticals, socks manufacturing, software, syringes and needles, tea, textiles, two wheeler tyres and watch components. The Major findings of the study was that after analyzing the data using multi dimensional mapping technique, the sectors were classified into five different clusters in order to identify the main elements of their international marketing strategies. The research also made the finding that the characteristic of the automobile sector being unique, it is classified as a separate cluster. Unlike the businesses in cluster 2, the auto sector has significant value addition possibilities.

Marketing of cars may necessitate a more direct relationship with customers for prolonged periods of time and post-sale. Logistics capability is also crucial here but not as much as it is with the business in cluster.

Vivek Gupta and Avishek Suman[17] (2005) conducted a study on the topic *Hyundai's Marketing Strategies in India.* The objective of the study was to formulate effective promotional strategies for the cars manufactured by Hyundai Motors (India) Ltd. to be marketed in India. The methodology used was a survey method using questionnaires to collect primary data and also interviews were held for the car owners.

The data were analyzed and tabulated using ANOVA and other statistical tools like Percentage Analysis.

The findings of the study were as follows:

1. To promote 'Santro' brand, advertisement in the T.V. media and the other electronic media including the print media like Newspapers, Magazines were found to be very effective.
2. Santro was a household name. This was due to 'word of mouth' promotion.
3. Santro had increased its sales it repositioned itself as a 'sunshine car' featuring Preity Zinta and Shahrukh Khan as the brand ambassadors.

Sreenivas Cheedi[18] (2004) conducted a study on the topic *Celebrity Endorsement: Risks and Rewards.* The objective was to find out the risks and rewards/opportunities associated with celebrity endorsements for the purpose of brand building. An exploratory study was conducted to study the risks and rewards associated with celebrity endorsements.

The findings of the study were:

1. The values associated with the celebrity are transferred to the brand and therefore, help create an image that can be easily referenced by consumers.

2. A brand should not be promoted using celebrities whose values do not match with the product attributes. E.g. 1) Amitabh Bachchan when endorsed Pepsi, the new generation rejected. (2) When Amitabh Bachchan endorsed Versa Car, it was a failure because; consumers could not accept the idea of a rich and famous star driving around in an ordinary car.
3. Other finding was Image failure. Mike Tyson endorsed Pepsi when he was the world boxing champion. One fine day when Tyson was charged for rape, he was jailed. This tarnished his image and Pepsi lost its sales.

Thus, providing credibility, building awareness, and emotional influence are a few factors that can help in rewarding celebrity endorsements.

Pradeep Krishnaray et al[19] (2005) conducted a study on the topic *Brand Recall of Advertisements on KBC*. The objective was to examine the audience behaviour and the efficacy of communication strategies of the sponsors.

The study also examines which sponsor's advertisements are easily recalled.

A total of 262 respondents were administered a questionnaire the day after the much anticipated marginal episode. Cross tabulation analysis of the data was done using SPSS. The finding showed that Airtel has been successful in its promotion strategies and enjoys a good brand recall whereas the other sponsors of KBC have not been successful as Airtel. The other sponsors were Kotak Mahindra, Max New York Life Insurance.

Amit Banerji and Utkarsh Bandhu[20] (2005) conducted a study on the topic *Challenges Faced in Communication in Advertising through Television*. The objective was to find out the effectiveness of advertisement through Television. The researchers administered two questionnaires, which was filled by two advertising heads of Bicardi Company Ltd and Pepsi Cola Co. Ltd. Both of whom have been able to run extremely successful advertisement campaigning. The question that were being asked included questions like how do you select specific time slots when you wait for your advertisements, how do you choose events such as cricket match etc that you want to sponsor. How do you make your advertisements attractive?

After analysis of these questionnaires, the researchers concluded with the following suggestions:

1. The advertisements must be simple and message that companies want to convey should be very clear for better understanding of the customers.
2. Scientific methods based on the ratio can lead to cost effective advertisement.
3. Customers are much more intelligent and aware than they used to be 10 years ago and so the advertisements and slogans should not be too exaggerated.
4. Companies should not project themselves as anti-consumers.

Paul Nieuwenhuis and Peter Wells[21] (2003) conducted a study on the topic *The Automotive Industry and the Environment.* In the study, the objective was to find out the technical, business and social future of the automobile industry. They also wanted to find out the demand for cars and to find out if there was a market for alternative technology vehicles especially the electric cars.

The authors first discussed the development of the automotive industry and the problems it currently faced. They then considered the solutions the industry can adopt. The study reviews trends in more environmentally- friendly technologies such as the use of more sustainable fuel sources and new types of modular design with built in recyclability. The findings and conclusions of the study is that the environmentally – friendly technologies can be fully exploited only if methods of manufacture change. They also suggest that new models of decentralized production, particularly the micro factory retailing (MFR) model, which provide an alternative to volume production and promise to be both more sustainable and more profitable.

Renganathan[22] (2005) who is a senior lecturer in the School of Management, Sastra Deemed University, Thanjavur has conducted a study on the *Consumer Markets and Buyer Behaviour of Cars*. In his study, the objectives were as follows: To ascertain the customer's opinion regarding the purpose of having a car. To find out customer's perception about a car, ascertain people's awareness about various brands of cars, analyse the pros and cons of various cars present in the industry, to analyse the consumer buying behaviour of cars, provide various suggestions to serve customer better.

The area of the study was Chennai in Tamil Nadu and the sample size chosen for the study was 135, which comprised people who own a car and those who are willing to upgrade from a two-wheeler to four-wheeler.

The methodology he used was a non-probability sampling method, viz., convenience sampling. Since there was a time-constraint of completing the survey within two months from June 2003 to July 2003 he restricted his sample size to 135.

Peter Wells[23] (2004) a Senior Research Fellow in the centre for Automotive Industry Research, Cardiff Business School has conducted a study in *the Automotive Industry*. The researcher remarks that the core problem for the automotive industry is that it is insufficiently profitable, particularly given the capital intensity of the industry. The problem really relates to the growing gap between the production system and market it is intended to serve. The researcher also brings to light the challenges faced by the automotive industry. He says that the automotive industry is faced by the environmental, social and economic challenges. The environmental challenge is the toxic emissions from the automobiles. Hence, hydrogen fuel cells is seen as a panacea for this problem. The researcher also says that alternative fuels, materials and designs are not cost competitive with the industry norm and there is no chance of introducing these alternatives (or atleast that the industry needs massive help in the form of research findings from government, or tax incentives for consumers to purchase 'green' cars. Here 'green' car means a car, which does not pollute the environment during its cruise.

Nieuwenhuis P. and Peter wells[24] (2004) conducted a study on *The Automotive Industry*. Their objective was to find out the impact of the running automobiles on the environment. This was an exploratory study which concluded saying that there have been changes in the nature of market demand, particularly in the saturated markets of the establishment industrialized economies.

Davis G[25] (2003) conducted a study on *The Sustainability of Automobile Industry*. This was an exploratory study concluding that for sustainable development of the automobile industry the demand and supply of automobiles should match appropriately.

Nieuwenhuis P. and Peter Wells[26] (2003) conducted a study on *Automotive Industry and the Environment – A Technical, Business and Social Future*. Their objective was to find out the impact of the automotive industry on the technical business and social future of the industry. They concluded that there was a great relationship (positively skewed) among these three variables viz. technical, business and social aspects in determining the sustainability of the automotive industry.

Nieuwenhuis P.[27] (1994) conducted a study on *Emission Legislations and Motor Vehicles*. His objective was to find out the pollution of motor vehicles in the environment and to determine the components of the pollutants. He concluded that there were many suspended particles in the emission of motor vehicles.

Graedel T.E. and B.R. Allenby[28] (1998) conducted a study on the topic *Industrial Ecology and Automobile*. The study was to find out the impact of the automobile pollution both noise and sound on the effectiveness of the industrial ecology. They concluded that there was a great dependence of the automobile pollution on the structure of the manufacture of the automobile.

Wells P.[29] (1998) conducted a study on *Automotive Material– The Challenge of Globalization and Technological Change*. The study was to find out the different challenges posed by globalization and change in technology and its impact on automotive materials. He concluded that the materials that are to be used in the automotive industry depend largely on the technological changes.

Burns, McCormick and Borron[30] (2002) conducted a study on *Vehicle of Change*. The study was to find out the pattern of change in the modes of transportation. They concluded that it was imperative to adopt modern and new technologies to have development in the automotive sector.

Wells P. and P. Nieuwenhuis[31] (1999) conducted study on *Micro Factory Retailing*. The study was to find out the retailing aspects of the automotive industry. They concluded that micro factory retailing was a radical business concept for the automotive industry.

T.G. Vijaya[32] (2005) conducted a study on the topic *Market Watch–Light Commercial Vehicles, Manifestation of Success and Growth*.

In her study she stated that the industry has shown great advances since delicensing and opening up of the sector to foreign direct investment (FDI) in1993. It has deep forward and backward linkages with the rest of the economy, and hence, has a strong multiplier effect. In India, since the early 1940s when the auto industry rolled out first passenger car, significance in the economy has progressively increased. However, from its early days until the mid 1980s for two-wheelers and LCVs and until the early 1990s for passenger cars, the focus of development of the automotive industry has been on import substitution. In developing market such as India, investment in road infrastructure is enabling efficient road transport, higher road speeds and increasing use of the more payload efficient multiaxled vehicles and semi-trailer combinations.

The researcher concludes that the challenge is:

The country needs to change and improve its present national road system: roads are dangerous; it has been designed many years ago for traffic conditions that differ widely from todays.

Koichi Shimokawa[33] (1985) conducted a study on *the Automobile Industry-Out of the Maturity Age*. He was emphasizing on the importance of structural changes that are necessary in the automobile industry. The Automobile industry is undergoing a process of reorganization putting major focus on scale economy at the global level.

Masataka Ikeda[34] (1999) conducted a study on *Japanese Automobiles and Automobile Component Industry*. He concluded saying that Japanese automobile manufacturers are pursuing flexible production and trying to create flexible production lines to adjust the rate of operations at plants or on production lines. The new production lines at Toyota Shimoyama engine plant are implementing this production plan.

Isabelle Szmigin and Marylyn Carrigan[35] (2001) conducted a study on the topic *Learning to Love the Older Consumer*. Their objective was to find out if subcultural memberships interact to influence the consumer's purchase decisions. They concluded saying that since all consumers simultaneously are members of several subcultural groups, the marketer must determine for the product category how specific subcultural memberships interact to influence the consumer's purchase decisions.

Abhishek Roy[36] (2008) conducted a study on *Consumer Buying Behaviour in Small Car Market*. His objective was to study the consumer buying behaviour in the small car market in India. He concluded saying that, since there is an increase in the per capita income of an average Indian, the purchase rate of buying cars has also risen. People of the country are interested in new models of cars. The old ones are being replaced by the new ones. The social factors like family members, friends, relatives and neighbours play a great role in influencing the car purchase decision.

The Jupiter Research Firm[37] (2008) conducted a study on the topic *To What Extent Online Research Influences the Offline Purchase*. He concluded saying that 0.5 per cent of all new car sales in the U.S. were transacted online in 2004; around 65 per cent of those shopping for a new car do some research online before buying offline. Thus Jupiter Research says that consumers use web research to help them decide on brand-make and model, but not a particular place to buy.

Simon Alias[38] (2008) conducted a study on *New Car Buyer Behaviour*. The overall aim of the study was to assess the nature of demand for short lead times for new cars and to provide a reliable understanding of private new car buyers' behaviour and attitudes, particularly in relation to the length of time that is taken in the various stages of the new car buying process. He concluded saying that with over 1000 new car buyers surveyed, the results indicate that the dealer has an important role in supplying facts and figures to the public. Friends and relatives are also relied upon for advice, especially by younger buyers.

Paul A. Harbig and Hugh Kramer[39] (1994) conducted a study on the topic *The Effect of Information Overload on the Innovation Choice Process.* They concluded that there is an overload of information on the innovation choice process exercised by consumers. The decision of choice is done made by consumers on the basis of information that they get about the product, service, ideas, events and experiences. A product choice is made on the basis of the diffusion of information from influences made by gatekeepers, buyer, influencer and the consumer.

Thomas Guinn and L.J. Shrum[40] (1997) conducted a study on the topic *Role of Television in the Construction of Consumer Reality.* His objectives were to find out the role of television in the formation of opinions about the impact of culture and the influence on the consumers behaviour across different regions in a country. It was concluded that when people are exposed to the public with different cultural values or customs the people become aware of how culture has moulded his/her behaviour.

The television industry brings out several advertisement messages, which is far from reality. Consumers form opinion about the several characteristics of advertisement copy of a product shown on televisions for a consumer response. Thus he concluded that the role of television in the construction of consumer reality has a profound impact.

Dennis Rook[41] (1985) conducted a study on the topic, *Ritual Dimension of Consumer Behaviour.* In this study he explained the different dimensions of consumer behaviour which affects the purchase, evaluation, disposing of products and services that will satisfy the needs of the customer. The ritual dimension of consumer behaviour has directly impact on the value system. He found that consumers become active members of the environment that they are living. Rook was interested to know how consumers select, interpret and organize the stimuli from the environment to make meaningful picture of the world. He concluded that the ritual dimension of consumer behaviour does not depend on norms and customs alone but also the rites and rituals of the society in which he lives.

Richard Bagozzi and Utpal Dholakia[42] (1999) conducted a study on *Relationship Marketing and Goal Setting in Consumer Behaviour*. Their objective was to find out the goal of an organization, which it sets for itself and its employees and thriving for achieving the objectives of the organizations. Richard Bagozzi, established relationship marketing programmes to foster usage loyalty and commitment to their company's product and services. The objective of relationship marketing was to create strong, lasting relationships with core group of customers. To develop long term bonds with customers and to make them interact with the business was the secondary objective of the study. He concluded saying that although direct marketing, sales promotion, general advertising may be used as part of relationship marketing strategy, relationship marketing stresses long term commitment to the individual customer.

Barbera Stern[43] (1997) conducted a study on the topic *Advertising Intimacy: Relationship Marketing and the Services Consumer*. His objective was to study the different characteristics of services viz., (1) tangibility, (2) heterogeneity, (3) perishability, (4) ownership and (5) simultaneous production and consumption. He opined that in a positive vein, businesses have been finding that the Internet is an inexpensive, efficient, and more productive way to extend customer services. He concluded that relationship marketing could be strengthened by understanding the basic characteristics of services.

REFERENCES

1. Joseph, W. Newman and Richard Staelin (2002), "Pre-purchase Information Seeking for New Cars and Major Household Appliances", *Journal of Marketing Research*, Vol. 9, No. 3, August, pp. 249 - 257.
2. Randolph, E. Bucklin and Silva Risso George (2008), "Distribution Intensity and New Car Choice", *Journal of Marketing Research*, Vol. 45, No. 4, August, pp. 473-486.
3. Mueller, Michel G. and Peter de Haan (2008), "The Impact of Incentives on Car Purchase in Agent Based Micro Simulation of Consumer Choice of New Cars", *Energy Policy*, Vol. 37, No.3, March, pp. 1072-1082.
4. Kiel, Geoffrey C. and Roger A. Layton (2000), "Dimensions of Consumer Information Seeking Behaviour Among New Car Buyer", *Journal of Marketing Research*, Vol. 18, No. 1, May, pp. 233-239.
5. Chang, Johnson (2001), "The Comparison of Car Buying Behaviour between American and Chinese People Living in North America: An Exploratory Study", *Journal of Marketing Research*, Vol. 18, No. 7, August, pp. 180-189.
6. Aurangazeb (2007), "Impact of Colour on Consumer Buying Behaviour Among the Car Buyers in India", *Indian Journal of Marketing*, Vol. 27, No. 3, June, pp. 12-22.
7. Andrews, Thomas and Cynthia Benzing (2007), "The Determinants of Price in Internet Auctions of Used Cars", *Atlantic Economic Journal*, Vol. 35, No. 1, March, pp. 43-57.
8. Yung, Shang Chan (2007), "A Study on the Relationship between the Service Quality Elements and Customer Satisfaction with Reference to the Car Industry", *Journal of International Management*, Vol. 7, No. 2, March, pp. 129-149.
9. Gilbert, Jim and Jamie Lee (2005), "Consumer Behaviour of Automobile Enthusiasts: Their Automotive Leisure Related Pursuits", *Unpublished Thesis*, August, pp. 10-84.
10. Bai, Xuan and Dongyan Liu (2008), "Car Purchasing Behaviour in Beijing: An Empirical Investigation", *Unpublished Thesis*.
11. Suresh, A.M. and Raja K.G. (2006), "Measuring Customer Satisfaction for Small Cars - An Empirical Study", *Indian Journal of Marketing*, Vol. 36, No. 2, February, pp. 3-8.

12. Makkar, Urvashi (2006), "Impact of the Phenomenon of Social Class Mobility on the Consumer Buying and Disposal Behaviour in Indian Perspective; A Case Study of White Goods Markets" *Indian Journal of Marketing*, Vol. 36, No. 2 February, pp. 20-26.

13. Saraswathy, B.C. (2006), "CRM-A New Dimension of Marketing", *Indian Journal of Marketing*, Vol. 36, February, pp. 9-11.

14. Balachandran, V. and J. Venkatesh (2006), "Recent Issues in Changes of Global Brands into Domestic Brands", *Indian Journal of Marketing*, Vol. 36, February, pp. 33-37.

15. Sankaran, K. (2005), "Pure and Applied Research in Business - How Shall the Twain Meet?" *IIMB Management Review*, Vol. 17, No. 3, September, pp. 115-124.

16. Oberoi, Prathap and Michael J. Baker (2005), "International Marketing Strategies in India: An Application of Mixed Method Investigation", *Vikalpa*, Vol. 30, No. 4, December, pp. 11-23.

17. Gupta, Vivek and Avishek Suman (2005), "Hyundai's Marketing Strategies in India" *Marketing Mastermind*, Vol. 5, No. 5, May, pp.69-81.

18. Cheedi, Sreenivas (2004), "Celebrity Endorsement: Risks and Rewards", *Marketing Mastermind*, Vol. 4, No.11, November, pp.7-9.

19. Krishnaray, Pradeep et al. (2005), "Brand Recall of Advertisements on KBC 2", *Marketing Mastermind*, Vol. 5, No.11, November, pp.57-60.

20. Banerji, Amit and Utkarsh Bandhu (2005), "Challenges Faced in Communication in Advertising through Television." *Marketing Mastermind*, Vol. 5, No.7, July, pp. 21-24.

21. Nieuwenhuis, P. and Peter Wells (2003), "The Automotive Industry and the Environment: A Technical, Business and Social Future", Woodhouse Press, Cambridge.

22. Renganathan, R. (2005), "Consumer Markets and Buyer Behaviour of Cars", *Indian Journal of Marketing*, April.

23. Wells, Peter (2004), "Automotive Industry", *Management Review*, Vol. 16, No. 4, December, p. 15.

24. Nieuwenhuis, P. and Peter Wells (2004), "The Automotive Industry - A Guide", Cardiff: CAIR and BT.

25. Davis, G. (2003), "Materials for Automotive Bodies", *Society of Motor Manufacturers and Traders*, Elsevier, Amsterdam .

26. Nieuwenhuis, P., and Peter Wells (2003), "The Automotive Industry and the Environment: A Technical, Business and Social Future", Woodhouse Press, Cambridge.

27. Nieuwenhuis, P. (1994), "Emissions Legislation and Incentives in the USA and Europe", John Wiley, Manchester, pp. 97-112.

28. E., Graedel T. and B.R.(1998), Allenby, "Industrial Ecology and the Automobile", Prentice-Hall, NJ.

29. Wells, P. (1998), "Automotive Materials: The Challenge of Globalisation and Technological Change", *Financial Times Automotive*, London.

30. Burns, L.D., J.B. (2002), McCornick and C.E. Borron's-Bird, "Vehicle of Change," *Scientific American*.

31. P., Wells and P. Nieuwenhuis (1999), "Micro Factory Retailing: A Radical Business Concept for the Automotive Industry," *Automotive Marketing Review*, Vol. 5, pp. 3-7.

32. Vijaya, T.G. (2005), "Market Watch-Light Commercial Vehicles, Manifestation of Success and Growth" *Indian Journal of Marketing*, Vol. 35, No.4, April, p. 3.

33. Shimokawa, Koichi (1985), "Automobile Industry, Out of Maturity Age", *Japanese*, Yuhikaku Publisher, Tokyo, pp. 131-132.

34. Ikeda, Masataka (1999), "Japanese Automobiles and Automobile Component Industry", *Japan Automobile Industry Association*, August, pp. 7-8.

35. Isabelle, Szmigin and Marylyn Carrigan (2001), "Learning to Love the Older Consumer", *Journal of Consumer Behaviour*, June, pp. 22-34.

36. Roy, Abhishek (2008), "Consumer Buying Behaviour in Small Market", *Journal of Consumer Research*, January, pp. 31-34.

37. Jupiter Research Firm (2008), "To what Extent Online Research Influences the Offline Purchase", *Journal of Marketing Research*, January, p. 20-22.

38. Elias, Simon (2008), "New Car Buyer Behaviour", *Journal of Marketing Research*, February, pp. 18 -22.

39. Herbig, Paul A. and Hugh Kramer (1994), "The Effect of Information Overload on the Innovation Choice Process", *Journal of Consumer Marketing*, Vol. 11, No. 2, pp. 45–54.

40. Guinn, Thomas and L.J. Shrum (1997), "The Role of Television in the Construction of Consumer Reality", *Journal of Consumer Research,* Vol. 23, March, pp. 278–295.

41. Rook, Dennis (1985), "The Ritual Dimension of Consumer Behaviour", *Journal of Consumer Research,* Vol. 12, December, pp. 251–264.

42. Bagozzi, Richard and Utpal Dholakia (1999), "Relationship Marketing and Goal Setting in Consumer Behaviour", *Journal of Marketing,* Vol. 63, pp. 19–32.

43. Stern, Barbera (1997), "Advertising Intimacy: Relationship Marketing and the Services Consumer", *Journal of Advertising,* Vol. 26, pp. 7–19.

3 | Automobile Industry–An Overview

AUTOMOBILE INDUSTRY: A GLOBAL SCENARIO

The evolution of the automobile industry sparked off from the rudimentary origins of transportation. Before the invention of the automobiles, the main mode of man's travel was on foot. He had attempted to find out some mechanical device for his transport. The first of such attempts is recorded to be in 3500 B.C.

It is on record that the Sumerians who lived in the river basins of Tigris and Eufretis had travelled by a mode of transport made on wheels. Later on, Kings and others used palanquins borne by men; and chariots pulled by horses and other animals, for their travel. Domestic animals like cows, donkeys, horses and elephants were made use of for pulling cartloads. References to such vehicles are galore in the epic works of literature. The horse-carts and bullock-carts are still in force in certain places.[1]

Automobiles are those motor vehicles that can move on their own, and motor vehicles are meant to be machines carrying men and materials from one place to another.

It was Nicholas Jacob Cugnot, a French Captain, who built the oldest known automobile car.[2] In 1769, he built a three-wheeled car working on steam. This car, moving at a speed of 6 kilometre per hour had been used by the French army to carry cannons; but was not used widely. In the same year 1769, he produced more cars. In 1771, one of these cars met with an accident, which is on record as the first motor vehicle accident.

By the 19th century, "Steam Engines" had their say in the industrial field. This paved way for new experiments in the sphere of motor vehicles.

Steam Engine

Steam engines are machines which work by converting the energy obtained on cooling, expanding steam into mechanical energy. The energy evolved from water vapour maybe used for raising a piston to rotate the wheels of some machines. The heat energy evolved from steam is helpful in the functioning of a good number of machines like generators, pumps, etc.

In 1765, James Watt designed the first steam engine with a separate condenser connected to it. The steam engine had a piston with cylinders on both sides which exerted pressure alternately. Later, in 1801, Richard Trevithick, an Englishman and in 1804, Oliver Evans, an American had built steam engines which were fitted to motor vehicles.

Invention of Tyres

In olden days, all vehicular wheels had been made of wood or metal. These kind of wheels are found even now in trolleys and bullock-carts which are fast disappearing from our country.

When Charles Goodyear refined natural rubber and converted it into practically useful rubber in 1830, the idea that rubber could be used for wheels, emerged.

In 1840, Robert Thomson, a Scotsman, made the first air-filled tyre. During those times, John Dunlop of Ireland attempted making of a rubber tyre for his son's bicycle.

It was Andre Michelin of France who first put forward the idea that rubber tyres filled with air could be used for cars. He made such tyre in 1895; but for want of proper arrangement for keeping the air intact in the tyre, his attempt became a failure. As a result, for the next 16 years, cars had to ply on metallic wheels. During this period, attempts at using rubber tyres filled with hay, wood powder and sand were made, but failed. Later in 1911, rubber tyres filled with air were produced successfully. This tyre was first produced by Phillip Strauss of America. It was Strauss who introduced the arrangement of tubes filled with air to be used with tyres. Thus modern tyres for use in cars had their birth.

The Locomotive

The railway trains are said to be the arteries of the economic system of a country. Earlier, railway tracks were made of bamboo. In 1738, the wooden tracks in England were replaced by iron rails.

In 1825, George Stephenson, a British Engineer, built the first efficient locomotive working on steam. Following this, the first passenger train by name ACTIVE came into being on 27th September, 1825. The locomotive started from Darlington with 450 passengers and arrived at Stockton with 600 passengers.

The Internal Combustion Engine

In 1807, Francois Isaac de Rivaz of Switzerland produced an Internal Combustion Engine working on energy obtained from a mixture of hydrogen and oxygen. This invention invigorated the field of motor vehicles. Using this engine, Rivaz himself built cars. Such a car built in 1813 had a length of six metres and weight of one tonne.

By the middle of the 19th century, internal combustion engines with more efficiency began to be produced. Gas engines began to be used instead of steam engines. In 1860, Jean Joseph Etienne Lenoir of Belgium built a two-stroke engine working on gas engine on the basis of the principle of internal combustion engine. Using this engine he built a car in 1862, which had a speed of 3 kmph.

In 1876, Nikolaus Augustus Otto of Germany modified Lenoir's two-stroke engine into a four-stroke engine. Cars made during this period using the internal combustion engine had a major defect. They had worked on gas and hence had to be taken to the workshop often for refuelling. The idea of using fluid fuel, thus, took roots during this time. The petrol engine invented in 1885 was the first major advance made in this direction. It was Karl Benz of Germany who built the petrol engine.

After studying closely the engines built by Lenoir and Otto, Benz developed a four stroke engine which worked on Benzene, a petroleum product.

In 1886, it was Gottleib Daimler, another German, who built a more superior 4-wheeled car using the petrol engine.

In 1891, Emile Levassor and Rene Panhard of France jointly built a car with front engine as of today. Experiments and researches in the field of motor cars had been going on in many parts of the world but none of these became popular. It was the American industrialist Henry Ford who played a major role in popularizing cars. Ford who did not have any academic degree in the field of technology, had an indefatigable desire for machines. He decided to bring down the car to the lower social strata, from its high pedestal in the upper social class. After his research in this field for a few years, he designed the first popular car, MODEL T in 1908. Later on, cars using electricity instead of petrol fuel reached the market. The development of electric cars was based on the idea for a car which did not emit smoke or carbon. But the electric cars, using rechargeable batteries, have not, so far, been able to supersede petrol cars.

Global Automobile Industry Since Liberalization

The world automobile industry has been witnessing an unprecedented scale of change since 1991 when liberalization took place in India for the first time. The wave of globalization has directly affected the international automobile industry and has accelerated the global reorganization of it. First, the impact of globalization emerged in the financial and securities industries, which experienced the Big Bang in the 1980's. Then it spread to the fast growing information and communication's industries. Now the automobile industry is no exception. The automobile industry was, especially in advanced countries, primarily a national industry, no matter how internationalized its business content developed. It has been a representation of a nations manufacturing industry serving the best interests of the nation.

The global automobile sector which has been on a low gear in 2008, on account of the adverse impact of economic slowdown the world over, may not see a revival in 2009 as well. Major players suffered a huge plunge in their sales due to this phenomenon. The year 2008 was worse for the 'Detroit Three' who literally had to beg for a bailout package in front of the government. In fact with doom looming large on the American car trio – General Motors, Ford and Chrysler, the year 2009 can result in a further fall up to 10 to 12 per cent in the sales volume of the automobile sector.[3]

Automobile and component industries worldwide have entered into the global age. By the Daimler-Chrysler alliance and the global alliance between Nissan and Renault have created a common view that suggests that the alliance era for the worldwide automobile industries are aiming to join the four million unit club.

The automobile sector is a vital sector for any developed economy. It drives upstream industries like steel, iron, aluminum, rubber, oil, paint, plastics, glass, castings, forgings and electronics; and downstream industries like advertising, marketing, transport, banking and insurance. What is good for the automobile sector is beneficial for the economy as well. However, in India, the correlation between the automobile industry and economic growth is low, with the automobile industry's contribution to the GNP being only 3%; in the United States it accounts for over 5% of the GNP.[4]

Thus the automobile has become an important ingredient of nearly every aspect of economic and social life. The automobile industry is also significant from the point of view of employment generation. It brings revenues to the government in the form of taxes and duties. Over the last 25 years the share of road transportation has increased from 11% to 32% for goods carriage and 26% to 59% for passenger transportation.[5]

The last two decades witnessed several small countries like Taiwan and Korea emerging as major exporters of automobiles.

Japan, Germany and the United States of America are the major players in the automobile industry. Brazil has moved from the situation of almost complete dependence on imported vehicles to one in which it is the world's ninth largest producer with an annual output of over one million vehicles. It has now become a significant exporter of vehicles. It was the oil crisis of 1973 that brought into focus the need for fuel-efficient vehicles.

The automobile industry is one of the world's biggest manufacturing industries and a powerful engine of economic growth. The passenger car industry is predominant in North America, Europe and Japan. The United States of America has one of the largest car markets in the world with major manufacturers including General Motors Company, Ford Motors Company and Daimler Chrysler Corporation. The European manufacturers include Bayerische Motoren Werke (BMW), The Volkswagen Group, Fiat Auto (Fabrica Italiana Automobile Torrino) and Renault Mobile.

There were several mergers and acquisitions that the automobile industry witnessed. Some of them are the following:

- The United States of America based company viz., General Motors Company has collaborated with the Indian based Hindustan Motors Company to roll out several vehicles like passenger cars, trucks and sedans. The USA based Ford Motors Company has set up a factory in Chennai to manufacture cars like Ford Ikon and Ford Mondeo.
- The General Motors Company has acquired Korean based Daewoo Auto and Technology (DAT) to launch a new car named "Chevrolet Spark" which was named before as "Daewoo Matiz".
- The Japan based Suzuki Motor Corporation has tied up with Maruti Udyog Ltd to produce cars like 'Maruti 800', 'Maruti Zen', 'Maruti Alto', 'Wagon R', 'Sports Utility Vehicles (SUV) like ''Gypsy' and 'OMNI'; 'Maruti Esteem' & 'Baleno ' and Wagons like 'Altura'.

- The Mitsubishi Motors of Japan has collaborated with Hindustan Motors to launch the car called 'Mitsubishi Lancer'.
- The Korea based Hyundai Motor Corporation has set up a factory in Sree Perumbadur (Tamil Nadu) in India to manufacture cars, sports utility vehicles and multipurpose vehicles. The 'Hyundai Santro' is a passenger car made by Hyundai Motors and 'Terracan' is an SUV (Sports Utility Vehicle) made by Hyundai Motors.
- Toyota Motors Corporation of Japan has collaborated with Kirloskar Motors Company of India to bring out the Multi Utility Vehicle (MUV) called 'New Qualis' and now they have rolled out another MUV called 'Toyota Innova'
- The Nissan Motor Company of Japan has entered into a technical collaboration with Premier Automobiles Ltd (PAL) of India to produce petrol engines for its FIAT Model 124 Car.
- Standard Motor Products of India had imported technology from the Austin Rover of United Kingdom to produce "Standard 2000" cars.
- Hindustan Motor Company has entered into a technical collaboration with ISUZU of Japan to manufacture petrol and diesel engines to be fitted into their Contessa Classic Car.
- Escorts limited of India had entered into a technical collaboration with Citreon of France to produce cars.
- The TVS Motors of India collaborated with Suzuki Corporation to produce two-wheeler motor cycles called TVS Suzuki.
- The tractors were manufactured by Mahindra and Mahindra with the collaborated effort of Escorts Limited.
- The Bajaj Auto Ltd collaborated with Kawasaki Corporation of Japan to bring out the Motorcycle called Kawasaki Bajaj.

- Hero Corporation of India collaborated with Honda Corporation of Japan to launch their two-wheeler named "Hero Honda".
- TATA Motors of India has signed a Memorandum of Understanding with FIAT of Italy to manufacture small cars.
- Mahindra and Mahindra Ltd (M&M) has announced a 51:49 joint venture with Renault of France to make the latter's 'Logan' car in India.[6]

Table 1 reveals the installed capacity in different segments of the automobile industry.

Table 1
Installed Capacity in Different Segments of the Automobile Industry

Segment	*Installed Capacity (in numbers)*
Commercial vehicles	6,10,000
Cars and Multi-Utility Vehicles	21,46,000
Two and three wheelers	96,96,000
Grand total	118,52,000

Source: Commercial vehicle survey – Gartner Report, June 2008.

Table 2 reveals the strategic alliances of major automobile players.

Table 2
Strategic Alliances of Major Players

Company	*Collaboration*
Ashok Leyland	IVECO, Italy
Bajaj Tempo	Mercedes Benz, Germany
Eicher	Mitsubishi, Japan
Mahindra & Mahindra	Nissan Motor Co. Japan
Swaraj Mazda	Mazda Motor Co. Japan

Source: Commercial vehicle survey – Gartner Report, June 2008

Reorganization of Global Automobile Industry

The world automobile industry has been witnessing an unprecedented scale of change since 1991 leading to the end of the cold war structure, the rapid spread of the information revolution and an upsurge in international economic globalization. The wave of globalization has directly affected the international automobile industry and has accelerated the global reorganization of it. First, the impact of globalization emerged in the financial and securities industries, which experienced the Big Bang in the 1980's. Then it spread to the fast growing information and communication's industries. Now the automobile industry is no exception. The automobile industry, especially in advanced countries, was primarily a national industry, no matter how internationalized its business content developed. It has been a representation of a nations manufacturing industry serving the best interests of the nation. Take, for instance, trade disputes concerning automobiles. It has been discussed as being related to the arguments of what should be the correct way to handle automobile trade, the balance of trade, and the job security for a countries labour force. The automobile industry also has a wide range of related industries such as the component or material industries, on which it has had a great impact at an entire national level. In this sense, the industry was a national industry. Because of this background, automobile manufacturers in advanced nations constructed their management strategies that centered on their own country. Overseas strategies were tightly connected to the domestic strategies and had a strong tendency to compliment them, no matter how heavily they depended on their overseas business and exports. Therefore, car manufacturers' competitiveness was closely related to how superior their competitiveness is in their domestic markets.[7]

Against this backdrop, especially in the 1980's, and before the 1990's when globalization rapidly developed, the automobile industries competed with each other at a nation-to-nation level. In addition to that, we still remember that the Japanese automobile industry was the one that grew rapidly by the so-called lean production method and which had grave impacts on the European and American automakers. We have to explicitly state that the lean production revolution ignited reforms taking place in the western countries. Under the reforms, automobile manufacturers in those countries executed restructuring several times although their stance and approaches might be different. They carried out drastic reforms that ranged from their product development to production systems in factories and to the systems used for component purchases. This trend led to the globalization in the 1990's.

Needless to say, economic globalization means a free and rapid flow of management resources (people, goods, money and information) beyond national borders. Business activities expand beyond the framework of one nation and dynamically develop everywhere in the world as far as markets exist. The trend in sections of the automobile industry such as; a) product development, b) supply systems including factory locations, c) systems to purchase from the suppliers of parts, components, intermediary material and raw material, d) production systems at factories, e) automobile sales and distribution systems although they may be different region by region. All of these are not contained within the framework of a country, but they have been developed into a global base. It must also be pointed out that they are integrated under a global management strategy. Therefore it is now possible to clarify the direction of global business. This globalization of the automobile industry not only enables the business procedures stated above to take place, but also makes them a mandatory condition for the automobile manufacturers to survive in the international arena whether or not they conduct mergers or amalgamations. It is because the economic globalization has made human and financial resources global as well. Against this background, the recent reorganization of the global automobile industry is developing. Some processes of reorganization are putting major focus on scale economy at the global level and attracting public attention in cases like Daimler – Chrysler and Nissan – Renault.

Other manufacturers like Honda are promoting their own global strategies by themselves. Therefore the directions of globalization are not necessarily monotonous. Regarding this phenomenon, there is often an argument that there will only be about five automobile manufacturers in the world who will survive further development of the global reorganization. The argument points out that manufacturers who are not members of the so called 4 million unit club, (which consists of makers producing 4 million units or more annually) probably will not survive alone. Considering this, there is a fundamental question for a simple argument dealing with scale merit as the only measure that can decide if you are big enough or if you are smart enough, to develop superiority in the automobile industry in the age of globalization.

Before studying the argument, it is clarified why global reorganization took place in the automobile industry in the first place. Then there is an alternative to mergers and amalgamation, which single-mindedly pursue scale merit. The way could be a network style tie-up among manufacturers while they maintain their own corporate identities. Furthermore, there is structural change of the automobile component industry that is directly affected by the automobile industry's global reorganization and environmental strategies of the automobile technology.

Direction of the Global Strategy

In the discussion about the globalization of the automobile industry, it is necessary to focus on two incidents that have had a decisive impact on the direction of the globalization on a corporate level. One is the merger between Daimler and Chrysler that took place in 1999. They are powerful automobile makers representing Germany and the USA respectively. Another is Ford's global strategy, Ford 2000 aiming at the 21st century, which was announced in 1993.

Let us look at the mega-merger between Daimler and Chrysler. The impact of the merger of the automobile industries in the world was huge. We can see how large the impact was when understanding that the mega merger triggered a series of tie-ups beyond national borders. For example, the alliance type tie-up between Nissan and Renault, which was announced in 2005 was directly triggered by the D-C (i.e. Daimler-Chrysler: the abbreviation will be used hereafter) mega-merger. After this merger, Ford snapped up the passenger car department of Volvo. The world also witnessed the start of a tie-up negotiation between Fiat and Mitsubishi. (However, it has only reached partial cooperation for joint production using the partner's factories.) Even among manufacturers that already had joint relationships like Toyota-Nissan, Daihatsu, and GM-Suzuki, they all have increased their stock holding ratios, which is part of their corporate groups' global strategies. The D-C mega merger directly brings about this increasing tendency.

Now, what was the background that caused the D-C mega merger? It was unthinkable about 10 years ago that the major automobile manufacturers would merge beyond national borders. True, there have been buy-ups of automobile makers across national boundaries in the past. For example, Renault in France once bought up the number four U.S. manufacturers; American motors (although it was sold to Chrysler in 1987). Germany's BMW bought Rover, the only nationalistic manufacturer in the U.K. It was in 1989 when Ford bought Jaguar, a manufacturer of luxury cars in the U.K. However, those who were merged were niche makers producing only 300,000 cars per year at the most. The D-C mega merger was the first one in history that involved two huge players producing from 1.2 million to 3 million cars annually.[8]

Then what was it that enabled such a mega merger to take place, the unthinkable 10 years ago? Many research organizations expected from the early stages that automobile manufacturers of the world would take the path of reorganization. In fact, France's ministry of economy and industry stated in 1982 that almost 30 automobile makers in the world at that time would be converged into 6 companies within 10 years (1). It was proven wrong in the past 10 years because of the emergence of some new aspects in the automobile industry's competition, which could not be judged by simple scale merit in the 1980's.

Japanese automobile industry began to push its international competitiveness by using the lean production revolution in the 1980's. Because of the lean production revolution, the reorganization of the existing 11 automobile manufacturers was put off. At the same time, European and American automobile companies learned from the lean, production revolution while they strove to restructure themselves. The situation did not offer any conditions for the companies to begin to think about mergers or amalgamations. Ten years ago, we saw the peak of such a movement. Not only Japanese manufacturers but also western counterparts were making all out efforts to survive independently by reforming their corporate characteristics. They had no intention to embark on any mergers or amalgamations. There were some changing aspects in the competition of the 80's. This does not mean that competition in those days was global, crossing national boundaries as it is now. It was international competition of the automobile industries based on their own nation or region. However, swift progress in the economic globalization provided a decisive condition where globalization strategies were established. Under these strategies, the automobile industry pursued product development and component purchases at a global level. It also aimed at arranging factory locations and supply systems in a global scale. In addition to the movement, several other factors have underlined the necessity of global strategies toward the 21st century. These factors include; a) expansion of middle and eastern European automobile markets due to the end of Cold War, b) Asian population super powers, China and India joining the global market economy, c) emerging automobile markets in such regions as Asia, Central and South Americas. The Asian automobile market is temporarily suffering from a dramatic plunge in demand due to the economic crisis that started recently.

Despite the harsh situation, the dormant market has a large potential, which makes it indispensable for automobile makers to come up with an Asian strategy from a global point of view. In any way, new global strategies to cover emerging markets such as Asia have drastically changed the existing approaches. Those past approaches in the 80's put emphasis on the markets in advanced nations and were more concerned about the regions and the nations where automobile manufacturers were located. Through this process, linkage between advanced nations' markets and emerging markets has shown progress in entering into the international arena. What is important is that the automobile makers of the world don't have a chance to survive in the future if they function only within one country acting as a regional maker. A manufacturer can maintain stable conditions when it grows from a regional maker into a global one. This is possible only when the manufacturer establishes a comprehensive global strategy keeping sight of Asia, Eastern regions, Europe, and other European regions, North America, Central and South America; in short, all the markets on earth. It is because supply and demand trends of automobile markets differ from region to region and offset each other. The companies balance the profits throughout these markets by compensating for losses and fluctuating exchange rates.

The D-C mega merger was the huge phenomenon taking place against the backdrop stated above; where automobile markets and the conditions of competition became global. Amidst this background, both Daimler and Chrysler can be said to have aimed not at a global strategy of making themselves into global automakers, but instead at entering into a mutually beneficial alliance that made the best use of each company's strengths. Both companies realized that being an independent global automaker included a lot of risk. Chrysler, a large-scale regional manufacturer centered in North America, is dominant in the under $23,500 per unit passenger vehicle segment which includes mini vans and SUVs. On the other hand, Daimler is known as a medium scale niche manufacturer with a worldwide reputation for its luxury vehicles. However, in terms of market and production bases, Daimler is a regional manufacturer centered in Europe. Thus, the natural conclusion was that neither of these manufacturers alone would have faced numerous hardships as global competition rapidly heated up. Especially for Chrysler, even as a regional manufacturer in North America, it would have been necessary to strengthen production capacity to 10 million units and to begin to make huge new investments in engines and components.[9] Competing as a global automaker through building the weak European, Asian and South American markets while at the same time shouldering the risk of huge investments that would have been no easy task. At the same time, Daimler could not have become a global automaker in the growing Asian, Central American and South American markets solely on the strength of the worldwide brand image of their luxury vehicles. This is even true for the North American market. It would have been indispensable to add both economical passenger cars and mini vans/SUVs to their line up.

In this way, these two manufacturers with very different values, cultures and characteristics took action to become part of a large-scale cross-border alliance in order to survive in the face of stiff global competition. This was the end of the age of single-country mergers and reform, which had been taking place repeatedly in Europe.

One more aspect, which we should not overlook, is the existence of a global financial system, which makes large-scale global alliances possible. With the big bang proceeding in the financial and stock markets, automakers and other companies, which act globally, do not need to rely on domestic bank investments, bonds and stocks to raise funds. These days, instead they aim to raise funds through global financial institutions and stock markets and systematically boost the public estimation of the company through high cash flow.

Especially prominent are Japanese manufacturers such as Nissan and Mitsubishi. This is mainly due to the combined effect of the domestic recession in Japan and the economic crisis in Asia, with the collapse of the Japanese financial system, especially the stagnation of the main banking system, which is also contributing to the problem. In contrast, cash flow for GM, Ford and Chrysler are all high. However, this amount includes revenues from their respective finance companies, which manages huge amounts of capital and reserve funds for employee health insurance. Differences in accounting systems are also responsible for the wide discrepancies between Japan and the US. Regardless, one important factor here is the symbolism involved with GM, who pride themselves on being the number one automaker in the world, and being surpassed in terms of cash flow by Ford. With the expansion of globalization, shifts in competitive power ranking from the point of cash flow have intensified in comparison to that of car production, sales and even market share, with unexpected changes occurring to the ranking system.[10]

Competitive power in terms of cash flow is undoubtedly affected not only by domestic competitive power but by global competitive power as well. It is easy to see that manufacturers such as Ford and Volkwagen with increased levels of cash flow have discernible global strategies, which have been working effectively. In this way, the importance of global strategies has been highlighted, regardless of participation in alliances or mergers, and survival among automakers in the 21st century will depend even more heavily on effective skills in designing global strategies. However, the economy of scale theory is still often used in discussions concerning cross border alliances and tie-ups.

Here, we would like to consider the background of the quick move toward large-scale international alliances and mergers. Foremost was the introduction of innovations based on digital design, which facilitated the sharing of global platforms as computer assisted engineering (CAE) and digital CAD and CAM came into common use. The number of platforms, traditionally different for each model, could be reduced and the industry unified, thus lowering the barriers between manufacturers. This reduction in the number of platforms and increased common sharing is not new. Some manufacturers in the west had already embarked on this path as early as the first half of the 1980s, with some Japanese manufacturers starting in 1992 or 1993 during the second big strengthening of the yen and restructuring period that followed the collapse of the bubble economy. Today, reduction of the number of platforms has become a common trend worldwide. For example, GM reduced its more than 36 platforms by half and is aiming at 8 platforms for the near future, and Toyota and Nissan plan to reduce their more than 20 platforms to 8 platforms. Honda, which forestalled introducing common platforms, is aiming to unify product development with a flexible world platform. Comparing current production numbers per 13 platforms in North America, small trucks and mini vans manufactured by the Big Three occupy the top 8 positions. Two basic types of small trucks account for the highest production number per platform at more than 1 million, and even the lowest production number is up around 450,000.

As for Japanese cars in North America, the Honda Accord and Toyota Camry rank 9th and 10th respectively. Production is 440,000 and 430,000 per platform. A simple comparison reveals that small trucks, one of the American manufacturers' strong points, hold double the scale merit compared to Japanese passenger vehicles. This is a source of high profits, now at around five or ten thousand dollars per unit. Therefore, unification of platforms brings a rise in production numbers per platform and a reduction in costs as the scale merit goes up. Taking this one step further, big mergers will bring increased scale merit by establishing common platforms between the manufacturers involved. Moreover, there is a movement to unify basic components such as engines and transmissions in addition to the unification and spread of common platforms. For example, Ford is developing a global engine series with annual production of over 2 million. This tendency is also part of the scheme or concept in which mergers or alliances are being promoted.[11]

One more point related to global mergers and cooperation is that global component supplies make possible a reduction in costs for component supplies through narrowing down the number of component manufacturers. Unifying component supplies while advanced system unification also reduces costs by shaving the number of components and the manufacturing processes using module systems. Surely, a quick look tells us that mergers and cooperation bring about lower costs for component supply and promote module systems because of the resulting concentrated purchase of components and increased buying power.

The suppliers are being reduced, goals for reducing costs related to component supply and development, reduction of the number of platform types and separation of intra-company component operations. In this way, a global system of vehicle development and component supply has become possible. This paved the way for later endeavors to establish a global system of production, supply, distribution and sales.

Moreover, further impetus to develop global strategies resulted from the increased importance of forming environmental strategies for handling such issues as CO2 reduction and recycling, which will strongly influence competitive power in the automobile industry during the 21st century. The above-mentioned development of global strategies and conditions which made this possible coincided with the background and timing of the Daimler-Chrysler large-scale alliance. However, full-scale global competition in the form of competitive strategies among automakers was set off by the announcement in 1993 of the Ford Project 2000, Ford's flagship global strategy. More than anything, Fords Project 2000 signalled the start of an era of global strategies in the worldwide automobile industry and has played a leading role in global strategies with an eye on the 21st century.

Under President Trotman, Ford set out a bold global strategy, but the basis for this strategy was the recognition that the globalization of people, things, money and information was rapidly proceeding. The building of corporate culture recognition is ultimately necessary to keep up with the speed of change.[12] Therefore, Ford promoted a strategic unification of the Ford family including Ford Europe, Mazda and Jaguar and infusing a common global vision. Details of this strategy are as follows: Global unification of automobile chassis' and platforms was promoted by carrying out worldwide unification of the development system. Then, related to this, a world car concept was established with the Mondeo and Mystique light vehicle series. This was the springboard for the debut of a basic world car, the recently announced KA series. Also, overlap which had previously taken place in development of similar concepts in North America, Europe and Asia was ceased and five vehicle centers were organized and development functions concentrated as much as possible in Dearborn. A strategy was set forth to organize the division of labor and cooperation among North America, Europe and Asia under a global development system. This was carried out mainly in development centers in North America with the introduction of common platforms, common components and the global engine series. Moreover, under Ford 2000, the global strategy for component supply shown earlier was set forth. Ford promoted the reduction and systematization of suppliers, establishment of module systems, independence of Visteon, the intra company component operations and growth of global suppliers. In the process, benchmarking was thoroughly implemented by setting up a database of supplier capacity (cost competitiveness, price competitiveness, time for delivery and technological/developmental ability). In this way, groundwork was boldly laid for global sourcing, referred to as the best locations and supply world wide.[13]

This global strategy of Ford 2000 was formed with farsighted vision and was very dynamic in nature. As you can recognize from the key words, "Think globally, act locally with agility", in planning their world car, Ford carefully considered the compatibility of products (compatibility to local market) while taking into account complications surrounding local market needs and numerous market changes. At the time, Ford 2000 was considered too radical and bold a concept and specialist in the US criticized the project as being too futuristic and carrying too great a risk. Some people saw the plan as lacking in reality and being some sort of moral boosting tactic to spur on President Trotman's corporate culture reforms. Additionally, various conflicts and confusion occurred within the company organization after the actual implementation of the strategy. The world car concept was reconsidered and the direction of development sharing was slightly altered with Europe. However, it later became clear that this bold global strategy would succeed when looking at increases in Ford's share of the world market, improved cash flow and reduction of costs related to development and component supplies.[14]

In an interview at Ford headquarters, I discovered also that Ford Project 2000 was not aimed solely at strategic global preparations. In order to even out the bureaucratic organization and make Ford even more active, promoting reform of the corporate culture at Ford was aimed not only at reform of the mentality within the company but also at making the best use of information technology. These reforms ranged from full implementation of databases, to simplifying management procedures and organization. The main point of the project was to speed up business procedures and decision making. This type of advanced global strategy together with reform of corporate culture strengthened Ford's presence in the worldwide automobile industry and led to the establishment of global strategies by many other manufacturers such as VW and GM. In a way, this movement became the primer for worldwide reform as represented by the Daimler-Chrysler alliance and the Nissan-Renault merger.

ECONOMIES OF SCALE IN AUTOMOBILE INDUSTRY

The global strategies that received all the attention, was the Ford example, Project 2000 which triggered the attention to global strategies. The global strategies have triggered the global reorganization and have now become the requirements for the survival of the future automakers worldwide. There are theories to follow regarding the global reorganization based on the scale economy. Thus, the word in the international automobile industry and among journalists is that only the few automobile companies with annual production of 4 million cars or more will remain in the future. If this annual production of 4 million cars is the magic number, merger fever is a natural phenomenon among many automobile manufacturers and management. The scale of economy theory can explain the globalization of the worldwide automobile industry. The changing world automobile market can really be explained under the scale of economy theory. If the future international automobile market continues to undergo complicated and diversified changes and movement in demand continues to roller coaster depending on the region and time without synchronizing such changes by region, there are theories other than simple scale of economies. That is to say, other policies include lowering the break-even point for a limited production scale withcut sticking to the ideal of scale supremacy, developing creative products aimed at a specific niche market. The ability of building the power to develop dynamic new products one after another with a short lead-time, and flexible production systems which can be adapted for different types and quantities. Currently, globalization of the automobile industry is proceeding in two directions. One is adopting a strategy based on scale of economies and the other is adopting a strategy of maintaining a flexible production system that can respond to any changes. As seen in the previous chapters, expansion of scale merit through mergers and cooperation surely brings an increase in production number per platform and reduced costs for component supplies. The problem however is that these points are not always accompanied by increased development ability which guarantees improvements in product quality. There is also no guarantee that individual identity, as distinctive product architecture will remain after reducing the number of platforms. It is also possible for individual manufacturers with annual production of around 1 million to reduce the number of platforms and to adopt common platforms in their own way. Narrowing the number of component manufacturers and the move towards modularity can be carried out to meet demand through cooperation among networks of middle-sized automobile manufacturers even without mergers. An excessive move towards modularity, i.e. large-scale subassembly, will weaken the attraction of products and make automobiles standard products like personal computers. The charm of the product will disappear. Another consideration is the current diversification of needs and drastic changes in the automobile market. Competition in product development will heat up and quicker development will be required with the increased use of electronic information in automobile design architecture for environmental, safety and its countermeasures. In actuality, shortening development times is already proceeding, and recently, 12 to 18 months timeframe is in the picture. Thus a simple scale merit theory does not fully explain how this matches diversification and speed of change in the market. Competitiveness with superior quality products cannot be guaranteed by just increasing output.[14] In order to correspond to market diversification and speed of change, new production systems, which make flexible production and suitable quantities possible, will be a key. Scale merit is not the only way. Flexible production can be seen in the just in time (JIT) system traditionally carried out by Japanese automobile manufacturers and shortening of the production line and appropriate use of production processes creates production lines which can correspond to changes of quantity as well as type.[15]

At present, reduction of supply capacity is proceeding and shortening of production lines is being planned. Japanese automobile manufacturers are pursuing flexible production and trying to create flexible production lines to adjust the rate of operations at plants or on production lines. The newest production lines at Toyota Shimoyama engine plant and Honda Suzuka plant are good examples.

Toyota's Shimoyama engine plant was established as the main plant equivalent to the Kamisato Plant in 1975. Since then the plant has manufactured 25 million engines and now they support engine plants overseas in Britain, North America and Thailand. New challenges to manufacture a different line of engines are taking place at this plant by starting a new line to manufacture 30,000 ZZ-type engines per month at the Shimoyama Plant. The new challenge is to add flexibility and shorten the production lead-time for the lightweight fuel efficient engine production system. This engine uses a 4-cylinder, 1800-cc front intake rear exhaust and has an aluminum casting liner. Up to this point, flexibility meant to handle the variation changes within the same type of machine. The main characteristic of this new production aims to apply flexibility to handle design modifications as well as production fluctuations, in other words, flexibility to handle quantity.[16]

Plant side explanations for this new challenge it is difficult to secure a stable amount of production due to the stagnant domestic demand, because engine manufacturing is being transferred overseas. Thus, they aim to organize the process to absorb fluctuations as much as possible even if they cannot "just fit" production fluctuations. They promoted a "no more transfer machine" process and eliminated CIM (Computer Integrated Manufacturing) processes that can handle the mass production but requires more than a certain amount of production to avoid the production being rigid. To handle crank and camshaft processing, they lined up the general use machines and adopted a single shaft NC, and to handle block and cylinder head processing, they used multiple lines, four lines for example. This means that the conventional CIM and production processes with transfer machines put weight on the increased production. Because this additional cost almost doubled the initial investment, they now try to absorb the effects by reducing the production amounts at the production lines to eliminate additional investment cost. In addition, by establishing multiple lines, they can handle the production amount fluctuations. By having multiple lines, they can terminate operations in extreme cases, maybe one or two lines, when they have only 70% of the total processing they can concentrate the operators to the remaining lines. This can shorten the assembly and process lead-time and improve operatability. The production engineering management department at the design development phase investigated establishment of the new lines. The plant side participated in giving suggestions that are reflected in the early design development phase regarding the reliability and assembly relative to the operations and processes. In order to maintain high productivity with this process while still accommodating the production fluctuations and guarantee quality throughout the lines it is crucial to train and mature operators by this process rotation. Because this will enable them to be allocated to different processes and accommodate quantitative fluctuations. However, it is very difficult to rotate them through all the processes, thus they divide the process into three zones and learn different types of processes. These three zones are box related such as blocks and heads, shaft related processing such as cranks and rods, and assembly processing.[17]

By implementing these mentioned methods, they are hoping to handle operatability fluctuations at 70-100% levels by creating flexible lines that can handle design modifications and production quantity fluctuations. Thus, depending on the capacity, they may terminate equipment, such as presses as an example. They are also considering the possibility to establish a module structure of equipment, to use the terminated equipment for another purpose on another line. This type of line structure has also been adopted in other companies in Japan. Now Ford is participating in this challenge, which eventually will determine the direction of flexibility pursuit in the global competition. This movement, to pursue production of various models in different quantities and process flexibility, is linked to the shortening of product development time and preparation time for mass-production as well as front loading (solving problems in advance during the trial process). At the same time, there are some common aspects with limited small-scale production. Equipment investment will be less than that for existing production lines and yearly production limits will be established. This then unavoidably pushes manufacturers to work on plants and production systems which can make a profit even with annual production at 50,000, or even 10,000 when needed. Honda is now carrying out an experimental trial in Turkey.[18]

Large-scale international alliances or entering the 4 million units-per-year clubs are not the only strategies for survival in the automobile industry in this global era. Even with these large-scale alliances, results depend on whether or not there is a true synergistic effect through making the best use of the partners brand value and manufacturing characteristics. Examples of unsuccessful endeavors in the past include the merger between BMW and Rover, and that between Renault and AMC. The conclusion is that the way to survive includes adopting flexible production systems while forming flexible and diversified networks of cooperation, even if the scale is small. Such necessary global strategies are common for global automakers but substance and the methods of operation are not the same. Thus, pursuing scale economy by alliances and ventures just to match up numbers will not be sufficient to accommodate the rapid changes of the automobile technologies. There is a diverse and rapidly changing market to meet consumers needs. The capability to pursue the dynamic product development capability, flexible production systems to accommodate such development and possibly the production systems of various models and quantities is inevitable. Matching numbers of the scale economy does not develop global strategies that are sufficient to survive the global competition. Effective global strategies must include the capability with value contents to handle changes accurately and promptly. The founder of the modern global strategies, Ford, did not pursue only the scale merits to standardize the platform or to supply components globally. They rather progressed with their global strategies with careful considerations of global contents and the value side by focusing on the compatibility of the products in the community and agility of the business operations. It is not smart to pursue the scale for individual purposes. However, it is important to receive the scale merits as a result of the establishment of value contents such as product identity and capability to handle changes.

Structural Change - Automobile Component Industry

The assembler-level manufacturers in the automobile industry pushed forward with restructuring efforts and global strategies, the same wave of globalization and the structural changes that result from it are rolling through the automobile components industry where local business structures and systems differ from country to country. These structural changes are being caused in part by the expanded global outsourcing that automobile manufacturers have marked as a pillar move in their global development strategies. Another driving factor behind the structural changes is the globalization of the automobile components suppliers themselves who are integrating, merging and building network tie-ups on their own accord as well as stepping into the driver's seat with globalization strategies of their own. Then, there is the fact that these two trends are interrelated and fuelling one another's evolution.[19]

Though automobile components industries around the world are restructuring because of the expanded global outsourcing of automobile manufacturers in general, western automakers are leading the trend in reducing their herd of suppliers. The sales ranking of the world's top component suppliers are ranked and recorded but what should be noticed here is how much the rankings have changed from 1995 to 1997. Attention should also be given to the brisk activity in mergers and acquisitions amongst automobile component manufacturers for the links they have to the sales ranking. This outsourcing squeeze appeared first in the west particularly because of moves from the Big 3, but the targets of the automobile manufacturers and the processes they used to achieve those targets have promoted mergers and acquisitions amongst components manufacturers and led to the emergence of global suppliers.

But, what exactly are automobile manufacturers targeting by reducing their number of suppliers and what kind of process are they using? It is well known that there were distinct differences between the components procurement systems historically practised in the west and that of Japan. In America, most of the components were made in-house in what is referred to as one kind of internal vertical system. Europe, on the other hand, used few in-house components choosing instead a horizontal relationship in supply and business with suppliers. Though American and European automobile makers differed on the point of internal manufacturing ratios. They were similar in the fact that they both used numerous component suppliers and numerous miscellaneous components. Even American companies, which used a high percentage of internally manufactured components, far-outdistanced Japanese automobile manufacturers in the number of suppliers they retained. Take for example GM with 6,000 suppliers or Ford with 2,000 and compare that with the rough 200 primary suppliers of a Japanese company. The same goes for European manufacturers: they used many suppliers.

The components business of western automobile manufacturers emphasized more than anything else the cost evaluation on a short-term tender base. Because of the competitive bidding, component suppliers were changing constantly. Also, with exception to fuel pumps made by Bosch or transmissions made by Borg-Warner, functional components and system components were completely designed, developed, tested and assembled by the automobile manufacturer himself, with no information being released outside the company whatsoever. More than anything else, these practices have influenced the ongoing structural changes in the component supplies industry, meaning that the current outsourcing squeeze is the result of changes in traditional components business practices used in the west. In other words, western automobile manufacturers are changing their component procurement practices and are now asking suppliers to deliver components as systems and units. Moreover, manufacturers are evaluating suppliers for the design strength; development strength and engineering solutions needed to supply these systems and units, and additionally shifting their focus from inspected delivery to quality assurances from the supplier's end. From our position, it looks to some degree like the west is copying Japan in hopes of infusing the stability of Japan's vertical pyramid and doing business through affiliations. However, it has cost conventional automobile manufacturers time and money to reorganize their purchasing departments and form cooperative groups. In any case, an information revolution has emerged on the tailwind of these structural changes. That is to say, because manufacturers are building a database of suppliers and a system for benchmarking quality, cost, delivery and engineering, they can at a glance know the capabilities and hidden potential of suppliers, a task that had left them groping around in the dark before. Hence, supplier integration and reduction have progressed a clear policy. The database of suppliers and the benchmarking system are not just being built for a single country but on a global base.

These structural changes have naturally invited dynamic mergers between component suppliers around the world. But, what should be noted is that these mergers do not merely target expansion, but restructuring that can boost the suppliers' design and development strength and system-building capabilities. In essence, the restructuring we are seeing amongst components suppliers is not led by the automobile manufacturers but is the suppliers' own attempt at global integration.

When the term "global outsourcing" was coined, manufacturers were trying to solve the falsehood that volume components of a car such as electronic components had to be procured and supplied on a country base. Whatever the conclusion, it came to be a core element of global outsourcing which everyone identifies with today that suppliers also (since development and engineering strengths were being stressed) have to be capable of exchanging CAD and CAM data on a global scale. They have to incorporate their potential as the best location and best supplier in their own global strategy. What this means, as Ryoichi Hara has pointed out, is that suppliers not only require the design ability that allows them to participate in development under the approved country system. The ones the automobile manufacturers have laid down as their basic policies on development, but also the ability to propose basic development concepts. Things have turned out this way because automobile manufacturers need to focus development resources on advanced and basic technology in areas such as the environment. As restructuring continues along these lines in the global component industry, modularization is becoming a keyword in global components. Modularization was originally introduced in Europe, especially by German automobile manufacturers as a means for overcoming the high cost of labour and procurement that their own horizontal supply business created with the numerous number of components they had to deal with. The actual beginning came with model plants that these manufacturers built in developing countries of Eastern Europe and Latin America, where modularization was first adopted.

Watching this, global suppliers like Boost, Delphi and Visteon, who had their targets set on global business expansion, jumped on the design and development bandwagon and came up with a proposal to strategically use modular components. This constituted a completely different perspective of the assembler leadership that existed to date. One after one, western manufacturers constructively adopted this approach, and this marked the start of a link between so-called "global outsourcing" and components modularization.

Japanese automobile manufacturers were generally circumspect of the trend. This was because the procurement system they had with domestic component suppliers was viewed as the most efficient in the entire world. They decided that there was no urgent need to promote modularization because primary suppliers were taking part in simultaneous engineering, modularization was progressing with procured competence and sideline delivery was becoming a custom with system components. They additionally pointed out that modular components would place restrictions on individual designs, for which they found it hard to put modularization before the vehicle. Nonetheless, in the past few years, they have given modularization a second look and a trend can be seen in those actually trying to introduce it. One reason for this is that the growing need to introduce modular components came at an opportune time when manufacturers had to deal with recycling and low fuel-consuming vehicles for the sake of the environment, and develop a next generation vehicle based on ITS. Another reason why Japanese manufacturers are changing their stance is that effective results are starting to show from western manufacturers who constructively introduced modularization. Design restrictions are being lifted somewhat on the design work for modularization thanks to improvements in the digital design techniques and advances in architectural design. Modularization is making it possible not only to reduce the number of component suppliers but also to greatly reduce costs, using inventions that divide and link suppliers and assemblers by their specialties.

Japanese manufacturers are today promoting modularization by helping suppliers design doors, internal panels and other components, while providing them with technical guidance along the production line. At the same time, they are promoting modularization in the design stage. As topics, what they need to do more than anything else is to improve their design capabilities and strength. On this point, Masataka Ikeda feels that Japanese automobile manufacturers are greatly interested in modularization on the development level "as a wider range of development outsourcing". He cites the following reasons: [1] large cost reductions and the creation of added-value from business that is done on a modular base, [2] reduced development burden for the assembler, [3] the possibility of coming up with something innovative despite the fact that Japan is behind the west in modularization, and [4] the necessity to prepare for the eventuality that Japanese components manufacturers will be unable to participate as suppliers as western automobile manufacturers shift from ordering components to ordering modules. Ikeda adds that, now European component suppliers outperform their Japanese cohorts in their ability to propose modular products. This should come as a warning to Japanese component manufacturers. It will determine both whether they need to form strategic alliances and whether they can. The Japanese suppliers, who have enjoyed the advantages of traditional subsidiary business, are affected by this structural change in the global automobile industry. The global sourcing development has brought the same type strategies to the automakers. Two trends can be seen among the automakers. One is to strengthen the relationship with their subsidiary suppliers. The other is to evaluate suppliers based on the systems integration and the ability for a modular structure to go beyond subsidiary relationships and their ability to aggressively propose technologies. These two movements are not necessarily one or the other; but rather the suppliers are expected to be global suppliers with high technological abilities. As an overall trend, global subsidiary businesses are becoming networked businesses and the business structure is changing to be more dynamic, actually free from nationalities. Among these movements, Japanese suppliers are in the middle of deciding to be primary global suppliers or secondary global suppliers utilizing the own technologies. This suggests that the future changes of the initiative taking be in the subsidiary businesses, such as global module trends, assembler-initiating reorganization or global supplier-initiated reorganization.

Automobile Industry and its Challenges from Oil Prices

Research and Markets have announced the addition of the "Automobile Industry in Europe - Regional Sector Profile - 2008" report to their offering. The global automobile industry is going through a phase of change, which is creating a number of opportunities for the IT vendors. For example - led by strong economic growth in countries such as Brazil, Russia, India and China, the automobile industry is shifting its focus from the traditionally strong markets such as the Western Europe towards these emerging markets. This trend is seen in both production and sales of automobiles. This trend has led to a demand for operations & manufacturing applications, supply chain management applications, collaboration tools etc.

The industry is also affected by strict environment norms and is investing heavily in research and development (R&D) to make vehicles more fuel efficient or run on alternate fuels like biogas. Even this is an opportunity for IT vendors in the area of information/data management, server hardware, engineering applications etc.

The report is meant for IT vendors and intends to help them identify selling opportunities within the company. Furthermore, the identified sales drivers can be used to penetrate these accounts or increase current share of the customer's wallet.

TechNavio Insights is a set of reports based on TechNavio - a market intelligence platform for the IT industry. It builds on the intelligence available within TechNavio, and leverages on the custom research experience of the Technology Navigators. TechNavio is built on years of experience of the authors in deep dive custom research and consulting for over

30 Fortune 500 companies and numerous large and mid-sized companies.

Automobiles in the Fast Lane

The automobile is a little more than a century old but the last 50 years have gone into refining the basic engineering and fine tuning the technology. Within the first 15 - 20 years of the creation of the automobile the basic parameters had already been drawn. Before the automobile concept could stand, it had already started running. The first race took place in 1908 when seven cars started from America to reach the continent over Alaska after driving for more than 60 days but only 3 finished. This was only the beginning. Track and road racing also started in and around 1915 and near perfection of technology of producing a sports car with a compatible engine was reached during the mid twenties (a sports engine for a 1927 Mercedes 680-K has just been rebuilt). A handful of them were made, but it is surprising to see the kind of technology using hollow con-rods and light alloy aluminium engine blocks with wet cast iron cylinder liners to enhance engine performance.

J.D. Power Asia Pacific

The *J.D. Power Asia Pacific* is an international organization that does a complete research on car industry and various other industries including the information technology, utilities, airlines, healthcare, telecommunications, hotels, home building, and finance across the globe. The aim behind the research and survey is to convey the voice of people to products manufacturers, dealers, and service providers so that they can improve on quality issues, service delivery, and even enhance customer satisfaction.

History

The J.D. Power Asia Pacific is the parent company of J.D. Power and Associates and was established in October 17, 1990 in Tokyo. The parent company J.D. Power and Associates was founded in 1968 by J.D. Power III in California, U.S.A. Since its foundation, the international firm has started marketing and research surveys on the automotive industry. The first syndicated survey was the Customer Satisfaction Index Study in 1981. Later on, the research moved across various industries including hospitality, telecommunications, and finance. The firm has even established new offices in Canada, Asia, Europe, and Australia to serve global clients. In 1997 it expanded its services to other Asian countries including India. The year 1997 introduced a new series of rankings and scorings of various products and services across diverse industries in India.

Role in Automobile Industry

Though the organization does a complete research on various industrial sectors, it plays a vital role in the automobile industry. Infact the first research done by the firm was based on the same industrial sector that delivered the satisfaction level of car consumers to the entire arena. Today, the organization performs various researches and studies based on the experience and expectations of car owners as well as the car consumers. J.D has a strong belief that no *car manufacturer* can grip the market unless and until they understand the needs, aspirations, and behaviours of car consumers. Some of the most common surveys conducted by J.D. Power with respect to car industry are customer satisfaction index, sales satisfaction index, and vehicle dependability study. These surveys or studies provide an insight into the aspirations of customers which further helps car manufacturers across the globe to improve the artistry of designing, quality of production, and the technicality of engineering.

Indian Rankings

The J.D. Power Asia Pacific has a great influence on the Indian car industry. In India, the organization conducts various surveys on cars and related products and services to deliver a ranking system of various car models and other aspects of the car industry. Some of the renowned surveys conducted for Indian car market are as follows:

- Initial Quality Study: This study defines the quality standards of new vehicles across nine vehicle components including vehicle exterior, interior, driving experience, features-controls and displays, audio and entertainment, seats, HVAC (heating, ventilation and cooling), engine, and transmission. These components are categorized under two distinct categories, quality of design and quality of production.
- Customer Satisfaction Index: The study reveals how satisfied car customers are with the services offered by various car manufacturers. It research across seven vehicle components including problems experienced; service quality; user-friendly service; service advisor; service initiation; service delivery; and inservice experience.
- Escaped Shopper Study: The study identifies the possible reasons why *new car* buyers reject a particular car model. For this the firm compares the shopping behaviours of two types of car customers, buyers of newly launched cars and old car models.
- Sales Satisfaction Index: The study is to analyze sales satisfaction of customers across six vehicle components including delivery process, delivery timing, salesperson, dealer facility, paperwork, and deal.
- India Original Tyre Customer Satisfaction Index: The study analyzes new-vehicle buyer perceptions regarding the car tyres based on five critical factors comprising appearance of tyres, durability, ride quality, traction, and handling.

Automotive Performance, Execution and Layout (APEAL) Study: The study analyzes the factors and reasons that excite and delight car owners based on 11 vehicle factors including vehicle's exterior; interior; storage and space; audio/entertainment/navigation; seats; heating, ventilation and air conditioning (HVAC); driving dynamics; engine/transmission; visibility and driving safety; and fuel economy.

Promotion Strategies

A successful product or service means nothing, unless the benefit of such a service can be communicated clearly to the target market. An organisations promotional strategy can consist of:

Advertising

Advertising is any non personal paid form of communication using any form of mass media.

Public Relations

Public relations involves developing positive relationships with the organisation's media public. The art of good public relations is not only to obtain favorable publicity within the media, but it also involves being able to handle successfully negative attention.

Sales Promotion

Sales promotion is commonly used to obtain an increase in sales short term. It could involve using money off coupons or special offers.

Personal Selling

Personal selling is selling a product or service by one to one interaction.

Direct Mail

Direct Mail is the sending of publicity material to a named person within an organisation. There has been a massive growth in direct mail campaigns over the last 5 years. Spending on direct mail now amounts to £18 bn a year representing 11.8% of advertising expenditure. Organisations can pay thousands of pounds for databases, which contain names and addresses of potential customers.

Direct mail allows an organisation to use their resources more effectively by allowing them to send publicity material to a named person within their target segment. By personalising advertising, response rates increase thus increasing the chance of improving sales. Listed below are links to organisation whose business involves direct mail.

Message & Media Strategy

An effective communication campaign should comprise a well thought out message strategy. What message are you trying to put across to your target audience? How will you deliver that message? Will it be through the appropriate use of branding? Logos or slogan design? The message should reinforce the benefit of the product and should help the company in developing the positioning strategy of the product. Companies with effective message strategies include:

Nike: "Just do it".

Toyota: "The car in front is a Toyota".

Media strategy refers to how the organisation is going to deliver their message. What aspects of the promotional mix will the company use to deliver their message strategy. Where will they promote? Clearly the company must take into account the readership and general behaviour of their target audience before they select their media strategy. What newspapers do their target market read? What TV programmes do they watch? Effective targeting of their media campaign could save the company on valuable financial resources.

Push & Pull Strategies

Communication by the manufacturer is not only directed towards consumers to create demand. A push strategy is where the manufacturer concentrates some of their marketing effort on promoting their product to retailers to convince them to stock the product. A combination of promotional mix strategies are used at this stage aimed at the retailer including personal selling, and direct mail. The product is pushed onto the retailer, hence the name. A pull strategy is based around the manufacturer promoting their product amongst the target market to create demand. Consumers pull the product through the distribution channel forcing the wholesaler and retailer to stock it, hence the name pull strategy. Organisations tend to use both push and pull strategies to create demand from retailers and consumers.

Communication Model - AIDA

AIDA is a communication model which can be used by firms to aid them in selling their product or services. AIDA is an Acronym for Attention, Interest, Desire, Action. When a product is launched the first goal is to grab attention. Think, how can an organisation use its skills to do this? Use well-known personalities to sell products? Once you grab attention how can you hold Interest, through promoting features, clearly stating the benefit the product has to offer. The third stage is desire, how can you make the product desirable to the consumer? Is it by demonstration ? The final stage is the purchase action; if the company has been successful with its strategy then the target customer should purchase the product.

Promotion through the Product Life Cycle

As products move through the four stages of the product lifecycle different promotional strategies should be employed at these stages to ensure the healthy success and life of the product. Following are the stages and promotion strategies employed:-

Introduction

A product when it is new, the organizations objective will be to inform the target audience of its entry. Television, radio, magazine, coupons etc may be used to push the product through the introduction stage of the lifecycle. Push and Pull Strategies will be used at this crucial stage.

Growth

As the product becomes accepted by the target market the organisation at this stage of the lifecycle the organisation works on the strategy of further increasing brand awareness to encourage loyalty.

Maturity

At this stage with increased competition the organisation take persuasive tactics to encourage the consumers to purchase their product over their rivals. Any differential advantage will be clearly communicated to the target audience to inform of their benefit over their competitors.

Decline

As the product reaches the decline stage the organisation will use the strategy of reminding people of the product to slow the inevitable

Internet Promotion

The development of the world wide web has changed the business environment forever. Dot com fever has taken the industry and stock markets by storm. The e-commerce revolution promises to deliver a more efficient way of conducting business. Shoppers can now purchase from the comfort of their home 24 hours a day and 7 days a week. However, particularly in the UK the e-commerce revolution is hindered by two factors. Firstly the cost of logging on to the net. Consumers are still weary of the time-spent surfing, the high cost is slowing down the take-up. The number of homes that are linked to the web in the UK is only 25% of all house owner. If e-commerce businesses are to succeed the home penetration rate of internet access must also increase. Secondly, most homes are linked to modems of 56 Kbps. As the growth of people signing on-line grows, the access speed slows down. In America most consumers only spend 10 seconds browsing on a web page, before they change sites; within the UK it is 2 minutes. The future seems to be with ADSL networks, which will speed up access to the Internet dramatically running at 512 KB per second. However, again whether this format is adapted depends much on the cost.

Owning a website is a now a crucial ingredient to the marketing mix strategy of an organisation. Consumers can now obtain instant information on products or services to aid them in their crucial purchase decision. Sony Japan took pre-orders of their popular Playstaion 2 console over the net, which topped a 1 million after a few days, European football stars are now issuing press releases over the web with the sites registered under their own names. Hit rates are phenomenal.

Britain has launched a study to identify measures to tackle the twin challenges of low-cost competition, to be faced by the UK's car industry from India and other countries, and to lower-carbon transport in order to remain competitive in the globalised world.

The UK's car industry is one of the most successful in the world, with a number of manufacturers currently enjoying record levels of production at their UK plants. But the industry, like many others, is facing a number of challenges as it moves into the next decade, particularly in terms of reducing emissions and tackling a continued rise in competition from low cost countries such as China, India and Eastern Europe. We need to ensure our car industry can build on its existing strengths and remain competitive in an increasingly globalised world.

The UK automotive industry is expected to face competition from low cost products such as 'Tata Nano' from India and other economies like China and Eastern Europe.

The committee, led by former Ford vice-president Richard Parry-Jones and other industry experts, is expected to make recommendations to the government by September 2009.

New challenges, such as sustainable mobility solutions, and the emergence of strong auto markets and sectors in the East, provide powerful stimuli for change. The industry is looking forward to work with its employees to define the challenges and suggest ways to enhance our ability to meet them through collaboration.

The investigation will also look at a new departmental survey on the business environment for Japanese automotive supply companies in the UK, aimed at improving the UK's supply chain capabilities.

AUTOMOBILE INDUSTRY: AN INDIAN SCENARIO

Indian automobile industry is instrumental in the growth and consolidation of the Indian economy. It has developed into one of the most modern and vibrant industries in the world. India has occupied a paramount position as being the second highest two-wheeler manufacturer in the world. The four-wheeler market is one of the fastest growing industries in India.

A well developed transport network indicates a well developed economy. For rapid development, a well-developed and well-knit transportation system is essential. As India's transport network is developing at a fast pace, Indian automobile industry is growing too. Also, the automobile industry has strong backward and forward linkages and hence provides employment to a large section of the population. Thus the role of automobile industry cannot be overlooked in Indian Economy. All kinds of vehicles are produced by the automobile industry. India Automobile Industry includes the manufacture of trucks, buses, passenger cars, defence vehicles, two-wheelers, etc. The industry can be broadly divided into the car manufacturing, two-wheeler manufacturing and heavy vehicle manufacturing units. The major car manufacturer are Hindustan Motors, Maruti Udyog, Fiat India Private Ltd., Ford India Ltd ., General Motors India Pvt. Ltd., Honda Siel Cars India Ltd., Hyundai Motors India Ltd., Skoda India Private Ltd., Toyota Kirloskar Motor Ltd., to name a few.

The two-wheeler manufacturing is dominated by companies like TVS, Honda Motorcycle & Scooter India (Pvt.) Ltd., Hero Honda, Yamaha and Bajaj. The heavy motors like buses, trucks, defence vehicles, auto rickshaws and other multi-utility vehicles are manufactured by Tata Motors, Ashok Leyland, Eicher Motors, Bajaj and Mahindra and Mahindra.

Two-Wheeler Segment

This segment comprises the largest segment of the domestic auto industry in terms of absolute numbers.[20] From a semi luxury product for the urban middle class in the eighties and earlier, the two wheeler has now become not only the favourite mode of personal transport but also the most coveted personal (household durable) possession among nearly all consumer classes, except perhaps the most affluent. The leading vehicle in the two-wheeler segment is the stylish, fuel-efficient and sturdy 4-stroke motorcycle.

The two-wheeler segment is divided into five major product classifications: (1) Scooters; (2) Motor cycles; (3); Mopeds; (4) Step thrus and (5) Ungeared scooters.

Scooters

Scooter is a vehicle with an engine and two small wheels that looks like a small motorcycle.

Scooters are perceived as more of a utility vehicle or a family vehicle than an entertained vehicle in India. It has more safety features than a motorcycle e.g. the front metallic cover that prevents the rider's legs from an injury on collision or some accident. The major players are Bajaj Auto Ltd, LML and TVS Ltd.

Motor Cycles

The major players in the motorcycle market are: (1) Bajaj Auto Ltd., (2) TVS (Tiru Venkata Sundaram Iyengar), (3) Suzuki, (4) Hero Honda, (5) Escorts Yamaha, (6) Honda and (7) Royal Enfield.

Motorcycles are mainly of two types: (1) 2-stroke motorcycle; (2) 4-stroke motorcycle: In a 2-stroke motorcycle, the engine works on a two stroke cycle viz., 1) compression cum suction and (2) expansion cum exhaust. In a 4-stroke motorcycle, the engine works on a four-stroke cycle viz., (1) suction stroke, (2) compression stroke (3) expansion stroke and (4) exhaust stroke.

Mopeds

The market for mopeds has not been witnessing much activity in the last few years i.e. from 2000 to 2004. This is mainly on account of the gradual shift in the demand pattern which has seen consumers buying the other categories of two wheelers, motorcycles segment gaining the most. This shift is mainly due to relatively stable prices of scooters and motorcycles and rising incomes at the rural level with increasing number of households.

Profile of Two-Wheeler Manufacturers

The major players in the two-wheeler industry are Bajaj Auto Limited, TVS Suzuki, Hero Honda, Yamaha, Kinetic Engineering, LML, Royal Enfield, Honda Motor Cycles and Monto Motors.

Bajaj Auto Limited

It is one of the largest and oldest automobile companies in India. Bajaj Auto has come into existence on November 29th 1945. Jamlalal Bajaj, founder of the Bajaj group, was confident and disciple of Mahatma Gandhi. The integrity, dedication, resourcefulness and determination to succeed which are characteristics of the company today are often traced back during those long days of relentless devotion to a common cause. Bajaj is India's largest two and three wheeler manufacturing company and is the biggest in the world. The company has left behind the annual turnover of Rs. 70 million in the year 1968 and reached an impressive figure of Rs. 40 billion during 2005. Sales commenced in India by importing two and three wheelers in the year 1948. Bajaj Auto Limited has 3 manufacturing units namely Akundai plant at Pune, Waluj Plant at Aurangabad and Challu plant. The product range of Bajaj company are mopeds, scooters and motor cycles in two- wheeler category and also manufactured goods and passenger carriers in three-wheeler categories. The major achievements of the company are; 1) it became a public limited company in 1960, 2) rolled out its 100,000 vehicle in 1970, 3) three-wheeler goods vehicle was launched in 1971, Bajaj Chetak was launched in 1972, Bajaj Super was introduced in 1976, Bajaj M-80 motor cycles were introduced and 500,000 produced and sold in a single financial year in 1986, Bajaj Sunny was introduced in 1990, Kawasaki Bajaj 4 S Champion was introduced in 1991. Bajaj classic was launched in 1994.

TVS Suzuki

TVS Suzuki, a leading two- wheeler company, began with vision of the future of the Sundaram Clayton Group, the late T.S. Sreenivasan to design, develop and produce an affordable moped for the Indian family. The vision was realized in 1980 when TVS 50, India's first two-seater moped rolled out of the factory of Hosur in Tamilnadu. It proved to be a promising success and paved way for many successors for TVS Suzuki ever since.

Alongside the economy two-wheeler range, it has constantly worked for innovation of the motor cycle segment as well. The Suzuki Samurai was launched for the time conscious urban commuter. The Max 100 R was engineered for those who demanded strength and ruggedness. The Suzuki Shogan was for those who wanted raw power and today TVS Suzuki continues to keep one step ahead of its time by creating India's first 5 speed, 140 cc motor cycle, the Suzuki Shaolin. The TVS Scooty, a 60 cc scooter is yet another example of the company pioneering a new category and emerging as market leaders in it. TVS was the first to introduce computerization, achieve high productivity, low cost and consistent high quality in the two-wheeler segment. The major products of the company are Suzuki Samurari, Suzuki Shogun, Suzuki Shaolin, Centura, Fiero, Scooty, Scooty Pep, Spectra, Star and Suzuki Fiero.

Hero Honda Motors

Hero, a name synonymous with two-wheelers in India, began its journey around four decades ago. It started as a manufacture of bicycle component, Hero has today grown into a multi-unit, multi-product, geographically diversified group of companies. Like every success story, Hero's saga contains an element of spirit and enterprise of achievement through grit and determination, coupled with vision and meticulous planning. The Hero group began with a simple philosophy: to provide excellent transportation to the common man, at a price he could easily afford. A thorough understanding of fast changing consumer behaviour, new market segments, product opportunities and a marketing mix sensitive to changing customer needs form the core of Hero's marketing strategy and philosophy. Hero is the largest manufacturer of 100 cc motor cycles in India and has a substantial presence in mopeds and auto ancillaries. The two-wheeler division of the Hero group has a network of 3500 dealer outlets each with its complement of trained mechanics and workers. The products of Hero Honda are: Achiever, Ambition, CBZ, CD 100, CD Dawn, Passion, Splendour and Street.

Yamaha Motors

Yamaha Motor India (YMI) is the fully owned subsidiary of Yamaha Motor Company of Japan.YMI was initially known as Yamaha Motor Escorts Limited.Its mission is 'Kando'-a unique Japanese word which means 'Touching people's hearts'. YMI's motto is 'Speed, Quality and Yamaha's original design'. The objectives of the company are: 1) to achieve customer satisfaction, 2) strengthening R&D constantly, 3) to optimize the internal working system. The products of YMI are: Crux, Enticer, Fazer, Libero and YD 125.

Kinetic Engineering Limited

Kinetic Engineering Limited is the flagship company of the Kinetic group of companies. Kinetic Engineering Limited is also associated with Bajaj Tempo Limited, which is a part of the Firodia Enterprises, which manufactures light commercial vehicles, jeeps and tractors. Kinetic is synonymous with innovative and pioneering capabilities. It is the company, which brought the first moped, the Luna, to India in 1972. Luna is now generic to mopeds. Kinetic has also been the pioneer in bringing modern scooters to India in the form of Kinetic Marvel .The other products of Kinetic are: Nova, Aquila, Boss and Velocity.

LML India Limited

LML, which is Delhi based, first put up an enviable show in scooters and carved out a 30 percent market share in volume terms with its popular scooter brand 'Supreme'. It is working towards setting up five training schools, one each in Mumbai, Kanpur, Bangalore, Calcutta and Noida to train mechanics and service personnel. It began with 120 people in 1999 and now hopes to build up a base of 20,000 trained mechanics over time.

Its dealer strength will shoot up from 300 dealers to 500 dealers in 2010. The product ranges of the company are Adreno, Energy, Freedom, Select, Star, Supremo and Trendy.

Royal Enfield Motors

Royal Enfield Motors was established in 1955 and now is a part of the Eicher group of companies, which is a Rs. 40 billioin conglomerate. The Eicher group has a range of intensity in the automotive industry, including tractors, automotive gears, small trucks, exports, management consultancy and cartography. Royal Enfield's corporate Philosophy is built around quality and unflinching loyalty to the customer. This is the reason why the legendary Bullet is not just bike but a motorcycling icon. The ruggedness and reliability of the bike is endorsed by the Army, Police, Parliamentary forces and over 100 institutions which form part of the die-hard customer base of the Bullet. Royal Enfield Motors has its Head Quarters at Thiruvottiyur, Chennai. The company operates from 13 area offices, 19 depots, over 250 dealers and 150 authorised service centers in India. Royal Enfield also exports to over 20 countries including Japan, USA, Canda, France, Germany and UK. The models of the company are: Bullet 350, Bullet 500, Bullet Electra, Lightning 535, Machismo, Taurus and Thunder Bird.

Honda Motorcycle and Scooters

Honda is the world's largest manufacturer of two wheelers. Its symbol, the wings, represent the company's unwavering dedication, the achieving goals that are unique and above international norms. The Honda Motorcycle Scooter India Private Limited is a wholly owned subsidiary of Honda Motor Company Limited, Japan. Its products are Activa, Dio, Eterno and Unicorn.

Monto Motors

Monto motors limited, a newly formed company, has been promoted by SPACCO grant of companies, which has been in the automotive components business for the last 36 years. The products of the company are Avanthi Kobra and Avanthi Top Tank.

The Three-Wheeler Segment

Bajaj Auto has a near monopoly in this segment. The other players are Piaggio, Mahindra, Force Motors, Greaves Limited and Scooters India Ltd. Greaves has managed to eat into the market share of Bajaj Auto. This was made possible by the launch of its rickshaw "Garuda", the response for which was fantastic since the maintenance cost worked out cheaper.[21]

Commercial Vehicles Segment

Commercial vehicles sector can be classified into light commercial vehicles whose gross vehicle weight is up to six tonnes and medium commercial vehicles whose gross vehicle weight is between six tonnes and ten tonnes and heavy commercial vehicles whose gross vehicle weight is more than ten tones. The major manufacturing companies of LCV are Ashok Leyland, Bajaj Tempo, Eicher, Hindustan Motors, Mahindra and Mahindra, Swaraj Mazda and Tata. Out of the 98,831 vehicles marketed in the year 2003 – 04 maximum number of 48, 476 were market by Tata followed by Mahindra and Mahindra. In respect of growth, the vehicles marketed by Bajaj Tempo have increased from 6961 to 8310. Vehicles marketed by Ashok Leyland had declined from 1628 to 791 in the year 2003 – 04[21].

Table 3 reveals main export destination for commercial vehicles from India.

Table 3
Main Export Destination for Commercial Vehicles from India

Source	*Destination*
India	Egypt
	African countries
	Nepal
	Sri Lanka
	Hungary
	Russia
	France
	Brazil
	Hungary

Source: Commercial vehicle survey – Gartner Report, June 2008.

Table 4 exhibits the market structure for light commercial vehicles.

Table 4
Market Structure for Light Commercial Vehicles

Segment	*Share (%)*
North	18
East	9
West	33
South	40

Source: Commercial vehicle survey – Gartner Report, June 2008.

Table 5
Major Players in the Market

Company	*Share (%)*
TATA Motors	52
Eicher Motors	17
Swaraj Mazda	12
Mahindra & Mahindra	12
Bajaj Tempo	6
Ashok Leyland	1

Source: Commercial vehicle survey – Gartner Report, June 2008.

Tractors

India is the world's largest tractor market followed by USA and China. The fortunes of the tractor industry are linked with agricultural growth. Consecutive droughts can hit the industry hard. However, tractors are becoming more of a Multi Utility Vehicle (MUV). The Indian tractor industry performed better than the automobile sector as a whole. Competition exists in all segments of the automobile industry and tractor segment is no exception. Hence, a company's success mainly depends up on planning, management and marketing strategies, quality, low cost, durability, technology, model designing and fuel efficiency of the vehicles. The level of the utilization of tractors is growing rapidly in the rural areas. Moreover, the people's mobility has enormously increased in existing and future scenario. All these conditions are significantly increasing the use of tractors, as well as to shift vehicles use from two-wheelers to four-wheelers.

Projections of India's Automobile Industry

The Indian Automobile industry is witnessing a significant growth in the three major segments viz., cars, MUVs and LCVs. The projection of Cars, MUV's and LCV's during the period from 2001 to 2012 is shown in Table 6 below.

Table 6
Projections of India's Automobile Industry, 2001-2012

Year	*Cars*	*MUVs*	*LCVs*
2001-2002	5,45,026	1,31,227	66,679
2002-2003	5,88,628	1,36,476	69,346
2003-2004	6,35,718	1,41,935	72,120
2004-2005	6,86,575	1,47,613	75,005
2005-2006	7,41,501	1,53,517	78,005
2006-2007	8,00,821	1,59,658	81,225
2007-2008	8,64,887	1,66,040	84,370
2008-2009	9,34,078	1,72,686	87,745
2009-2010	10,08,804	1,79,593	91,255
2010-2011	10,89,508	1,86,977	94,905
2011-2012	11,76,669	1,94,248	98,701

Source: Commercial vehicle survey–Gartner Report, 2008.

The number of cars in the year 2001–2002 was 5,45,026 and the number of cars to be available in the year 2011–2012 was projected as 11,76,669. In the case of MUV's the projected number in the year 2011 – 2012 was 1,94,248 and in the case of LCV's the projected number in the year 2011- 2012 was 98, 701.

Market Growth Rates

The commercial vehicle survey conducted by Gartner in the year 2008, revealed the following facts shown in Table 7 below.

Table 7
Market Growth Rates

Year	*Percentage (%)*
1990-91 to 1996-97	8.4
1996-97 to 2001-02	- 4.3
2001-02 to 2006-07	4.3
2006-07 to 2011-12	5.0

Source: Commercial vehicle survey – Gartner Report, June 2008.

Measure of Roads

The roads running along the country across its length and breadth bears a weight of more than 40 million vehicles. The quadrilateral project is a great boon for the nation because its connects the important metros viz., Delhi, Mumbai, Chennai and Kolkata. Table 8 discloses the commercial vehicle survey conducted by Gartner in 2008.

Table 8
Measure of Roads in the Country

Category of Roads	*(in kms)*
Expressways	200
National Highways	70,548
State Highways	1,31,899
Major district roads	4,67,763
Village and other roads	26,50,000
Total length	33,20,410

Source: Commercial vehicle survey–Gartner Report, June 2008.

National highways are less than 3% of network but carry 40% of total traffic.

Status of Freight and Passenger Movement in India

The Indian Railway budget stipulates and apportions a significant amount of money for the transport of passenger and freight in the country. The number of trains that carry passenger freight has also significantly increased and has made traveling by train a great paradise and the freight movement has also become economical. Roads also enjoy an equivalent market acceptance as the Railway in terms of transport of passenger and freight from one destination to another. As shown in Table 9 the passenger movement on road is 80% and on rail it is 20%.

Table 9
Current Status of Freight and Passenger Movement in India

	Road	*Railways*
Passenger	80%	20%
Freight	70%	30%

Source: Commercial vehicle survey – Gartner Report, June 2008.

Challenges Faced by Indian Automobile Industry

Indian auto industry is one of the most promising and growing auto industries across the world. But at this juncture the Indian auto industry is facing various challenges catering to the growing domestic market.

Recently, SIAM (Society of Indian Automobile Manufacturers) organized an Annual Convention in association with the Ministry of Heavy Industries and Public Enterprises to discuss the current scenario of the auto industry as well as to define the key challenges faced by the industry. The meeting focused to pave a way to transform challenges into business opportunities and boost the status of automotive industry in India. Some of the key challenges discussed faced by auto industry are fuel technology and nurturing talented manpower.

Fuel Technology

Technology is significant and needed to ignite the growth of auto industry. Whether it's a two-wheeler or a car, technology drives the growth.

The challenge of alternative fuel technology ensures a brighter vision of the auto industry in the country. The increasing environmental pollution has become a concern for manufacturers and all associated with the industry. All of them are struggling hard to come up with a holistic and integrated approach to reduce carbon dioxide emission.

Some of the initiatives to reduce the level of automotive emission include introduction of fuel-efficient cars, obligatory periodic maintenance, and inspection of automotives, designing automotives with recyclable materials, use of alternative fuels like CNG, LPG, biodiesel, and introduction of electric and hybrid cars. Car manufacturer like Maruti Suzuki has already introduced the new concept of using recyclable substance for car production in its dazzling car Maruti Suzuki A-Star. After the production of Maruti Suzuki A-Star, the company thrives to apply the same concept in all its future car models.

In addition, it is believed that the Bharat IV Emission Norms are stringent and are to become mandatory in the next couple of years. The growing industry is hunting for more advanced ways and measures to meet the stringent norms. Some of the cars and other automotives may even be phased out during that period.

Nurturing Talented Manpower

Manpower and human resources has always been a key growth driver in any industry including the automobile industry. Though India has a vast pool of talented and skilled professionals, the country needs initiatives and support to treasure these resources to excel in all arenas of the industries.

Automobile industry is no exception and highly skilled manpower will further become the most reliable source of competitive advantage across the global as well as Indian automobile industry. More than even before, creativity, innovative ideas, and expertise in different areas have become an asset these days. Talking about cars, car designers infuse their creativity in their designed car models and that's something which attracts car customers. The renowned Indian car designer, Dilip Chhabria has designed many impressive cars for the global car industry that is continuously luring the consumers.

Further to that, the industry has to foster the talent for servicing and maintenance as well. India has personnel to create better and reliable automotives but still lack the expertise in servicing and maintenance of the automotives through their life span. Some professionals, who feel they are over-talented move across the boundaries. According to SIAM, India is expected to have shortage of well qualified manpower.

Therefore, SIAM introduces new strategies to optimize the skills and support proposals to train youth across the country including the rural areas. Today, SIAM, Ministry of Rural Development, National Skills Development Corporation, Indian Government, and the Indian Automotive Industry, are working in synergy to generate a vast pool of skilled manpower for the Indian Auto Industry.

Strategies for Automobile Industry in India

- Special economic zones and automobile parks, exclusively suitable for automobile industries, should be developed. Special economic zones can be developed in every state, which in turn can develop many ancillary and downstream industries and significantly contribute to industrial development.
- Provision of infrastructural facilities should be accorded priority, comprehensive labour law reforms should be formulated, tax structures should be rationalized, investor friendly policies should be introduced. Encouragement of research and development to improve quality, cost effective mass production, reduction in production cost, development of logistics network systems for the supply of goods at cheaper transport cost etc. should be implemented.
- The Central and State governments should formulate a policy considering various aspects like land allocation, investment, provision of water and power, environmental constraints and approvals.
- Fixed time frame should be indicated for all the approvals by way of a single window system.
- Existing industrial policy should be reviewed and the deficiencies in the policies should be traced out. Foreign investments should be attracted for meeting future demand in automobile sector.
- Areas, which have more employment potential such as mechanical, electrical, electronics, software skills required in the automobile industry and in downstream industries should be identified.
- Technology should be upgraded to improve safety, driving comfort, energy efficiency and higher load on steering axle.
- Government should provide all the requisite facilities like fund allocation, technology transfer, exemption of customs duty and tax.
- Outsourcing at all levels should be explored.

- Separate organization in the ministry of industries should be there to look after the developmental activities of the automobile industry.

Automobile Associations in India

FADA

The Federation of Automobile Dealers Associations (FADA) is an apex national body representing automobile dealers of India. It was founded in 1964 by four regional Auto Trade associations to protect and promote the Indian retail automobile market. It is now a registered body under the Companies Act 1956.

The four founder members of FADA are:

- The Automobile Dealers Association of Maharashtra, Mumbai
- The Motor Industries Association, Kolkata.
- The Automobile Traders Association, Delhi.
- Motor Vehicles & Allied Industries Association, Chennai.

FADA has as its members - dealers of passenger cars, commercial vehicles and two/three wheelers. These members deal in sales, servicing of vehicles and sale of spare parts as well. They also arrange finance and trade-ins. In some cases they also sell used cars.

Other than automobile dealers, FADA has representatives of vehicle manufacturers, tyre manufacturers, insurance and finance sectors and other allied industries and trade, as supporting members. Morning Edition, July 8, 2008· It is billed as the world's cheapest car - and the world is eager for it to hit the streets of India.

SIAM

Society of Indian Automobile Manufacturers (SIAM) is the apex Industry body representing 44 leading vehicle and vehicular engine manufacturers in India.

SIAM is an important channel of communication for the Automobile Industry with the Government, National and International organisations. The Society works closely withy all the concerned stake holders and actively participates in formulation of rules, regulations and policies related to the Automobile Industry.

SIAM provides a window to the Indian Automobile industry and aims to enhance exchanges and communication, expand economics, trade and technical cooperation between the Automotive Industry and its international counterparts. With its regular and continuous interaction with international bodies and organizations it aims to facilitate up gradation of technical capabilities of the Indian Industry to match the best practice worldwide.

SIAM also interacts with worldwide experts to assess the global trends and developments shaping the Automotive Industry. It has been actively pursuing issues like Frontier Technologies viz. Telematics: Promotion of Alternative Fuels including Hydrogen Energy for automotive use through cell vehicles and Harmonisation of Safety and Emission Standards etc.

Dissemination of information is an integral part of SIAM'S activities, which it does through various publications, reports, seminars and conferences.

SIAM organizes the biennial Auto Expo series of trade fairs in co-operation with Confederation of Indian Industry (CII) and Automotive Component Manufacturers Association of India (ACMA).

SIAM has been striving to keep pace with the socio-economic and technological changes shaping the Automobile Industry and endeavour to be a catalyst in the development of a stronger Automobile Industry in India.

SWOT Analysis of the Automobile Industry

Strengths

- The automobile industry inherently provides higher dealer margins, which indirectly leads to an improved quality of interface between the customer and the manufacturer.

- With most Indian auto companies tying up with foreign majors, quality for the end users will be assured.
- Cheap and skilled labour, and efficient management of overheads definitely is translated into lower costs.
- A widespread dealer network (although not exhaustive) along with an established brand, equity among existing players can be capitalized upon.
- Demand for automobiles is purely dependent on Indian consumer specific factors and is not affected by fluctuation in prices in the international markets, as is the case for most commodities.
- The presence of a large number of car finance companies in the country would definitely contribute to the growth of the industry.

Weaknesses

- Traditionally, the industry has been characterized by a poor after sales service market leading to the mushrooming of a fake spare parts market.
- India's roads are already under the weight of more than 40 million vehicles, 50% of which are in the metros. Hardly there are any projects to improve the efficiency of the roads and highways.
- Overdependence of foreign collaboration without a move towards indigenization may prove to be harmful in the long run. Investment on research and development by Indian car manufacturers is very low compared to the investment made by their foreign counterparts.
- Indian car manufacturers cannot afford to incur such high costs on R&D alone. Hence, there is an excessive dependence on foreign car producers for technology.
- A major percentage of car manufacturing is outsourced. The auto component industry in India is highly fragmented and not yet fully geared to meet the technological advances taking place in the auto industry. Many of the manufacturers operate on a small scale with outdated technology. So many

manufacturers in Indian auto industry have to depend on imports to meet part of their requirements. However, global players are entering this sector.

Opportunities

- Income levels and hence, the purchasing power, of the Indian middle class has definitely increased leading to a broader market. The car has become a necessity rather than being a luxury.
- The rural market is hitherto untapped.
- With cheaper costs of production, export potential certainly exists.
- With car finance offering high returns, innovative finance schemes are being introduced to attract the buyers.
- With effective management, traffic congestion can be reduced.

Threats

- Too many people have been concentrating on the mid size passenger car segment whose potential might have been grossly overestimated.
- There is danger of overcapacity in the industry.
- There is a likely shift in demand from the medium and small segment to luxury car segment. This switch may lead to a growth in the sales of used cars as more cars become available for resale. Hence, the price of used cars might drop.This could result in a decline in demand for new cars in the medium and small segment.
- People may prefer to buy a readily available and cheaper second hand cars rather than new cars which may be priced higher and have longer waiting periods.
- The inevitable hike in petroleum prices including diesel, will naturally dampen the spirits of a prospective automobile purchaser.
- The growing concern for a cleaner environment has put brakes on the proliferation of vehicles. A notification by

the surface transport ministry declared new emission norms for the auto industry. Although the industry is allowed to sell vehicles without catalytic converter in non metro areas due to the non availability of unleaded petrol, quite a few companies will have to re-engineer or scrap their products.

Revolutionising Tyre Purchase

The only tyre brand approved as OEM by all the manufacturers in the country is Goodyear tyres. This tyre manufacturer is unleashing a new retail experience for the Indian consumer.

For the first time, tyre showrooms offer much more than just tyres. These spacious new air conditioned Goodyear showrooms have an international look showcasing the complete range of Goodyear tyres. Customers can access any information on every Goodyear tyre through easy-to-use computerized software.

The stores offer the customers more than just the range of latest Goodyear tyres. Goodyear India Ltd has entered into an exclusive tie-up for car care products like car perfumes, car wash and tyre shine making it very convenient for customers to purchase their car related requirements under one roof. All Goodyear new-format stores also offer wheel- alignment and balancing, expert advice on tyre maintenance, advice on various tyre options for each car model, tyre check-up, alloy wheels and much more. Each store is manned by trained staff in smart uniforms to cater to the customer's every need. The stores have clearly separated display and service areas. The display areas ensure easy access to information on tyres for consumers so that they can make an informed decision on their purchase. Goodyear India Ltd has launched five branded retail outlets in Bangalore, six in Chennai and three in Kerala, which will be extended to other major cities soon. This is part of the company's strategic initiative in organized tyre retailing, aimed at strengthening its presence in the large tyre replacement market in the country. Organized tyre retailing is still a novel concept as most tyre showrooms and most tyre retailer's focus only on the sale and fitment of tyres .With the launch of these new outlets, the company aims to offer an unmatched brand experience within the shop-in-shop format and increase customer delight.

PASSENGER CAR INDUSTRY IN INDIA

The passenger car segment of Indian automotive industry has assumed great importance since post-liberalization. In the 1990s, the Government of India opened the doors for the entry of foreign car makers. The Automotive Mission Plan 2006-16, and Automotive Policy-2002, embodies a mission to make India an automotive hub. According to the Society of Indian Automotive Manufacturers (SIAM) in the year 2007-08, over 1.5 million cars were sold in the domestic market. There are over 15 carmakers operating in India today, and the number of available car models/variants exceeds 100. An innovation par excellence – the unveiling of Nano, the 'people's car' – has made the global car industry sit up and take notice of the mastery over 'frugal engineering' displayed by an Indian car maker. By the same token, the acquisition of Jaguar and Land Rover by Tata Motors speaks volumes for the enterprise and capability of an Indian major. In order to leverage the low cost of R & D and manufacturing in India, several global car makers have already embarked on projects that signal their intention to make India a manufacturing hub to cater to the domestic and export markets. This book provides an up-to-date picture of the growth and dynamics of the passenger car segment in India. It also enables one to gain an insight into the prospects of the passenger car market in India in the context of recent developments.

Penetration of cars is an important indicator of the cars owned by people in a country. The 'penetration of cars' is defined as the number of cars owned per 1000 people. The penetration of cars in India is around nine cars per 1000 people and in China it is six cars per 1000 people.[22]

Profile of Car Manufacturers

There are several car players in the passenger car industry in India, viz., Maruti Udyog Ltd, Tata Motors, Hundai Motors,

Hindustan Motors, Ford Motors, Fiat Motors and General Motors.

Maruti Udyog Ltd

Maruti Udyog Ltd started manufacturing cars in 1982. 'M 800' was the first car that it launched in 1983 in India. Then in 1993 the 'Zen' was launched. In 1996 the 'Esteem' was launched and thereafter several cars like 'Alto', 'Wagon R', 'Baleno', 'Gypsy', 'Omni', 'Maruti 1000', Swift, Dzire, Zen Estilo, SX4, Maruti A-Star were launched and Maruti Ritz (Splash) is in the offing. 'Maruti Altura' is a Wagon launched by Maruti Udyog Ltd. Maruti 'Grand Vitara' is a sports utility vehicle launched by Maruti Udyog Ltd.

In 2001, Maruti Udyog Ltd became one of the first automobile companies anywhere in the world to get an ISO 9001:2000 certification. Recently, to meet the growing demands of four-wheeler automobile, Maruti Udyog Limited, collaborated with Suzuki Motor Corporation of Japan, to manufacture cars. On the 17th September 2007, Maruti Udyog was renamed as Maruti Suzuki India Limited and the company headquarters is in Gurgaon, Delhi. Maruti cars have ruled the roads in the past, in the present, and promises to do so in the future also with its highly efficient cars.

Maruti is India's most saleable car. There are a variety of Maruti car brands that has dominated the Indian roads. Maruti cars are buyable from the car dealerships, used car dealers, car websites and car owners. Maruti car reviews explain the worth of buying Maruti Car. There are Maruti used car dealer and know more about the car prices. One could go for extensive car search to find the best car at best affordable price.

Hindustan Motors Limited

Hindustan Motors Limited (HML), the India's pioneering automobile manufacturing company and flagship of the C.K. Birla group was established before the Indian Independence in 1942 by Sri. B.M. Birla of the industrial Birla family. Commencing operations in a small assembly plant near Okha port in Gujarat, the manufacturing facilities later moved to

Uttar Para, West Bengal in 1948, where it began the production of Ambassador car which has been contributing significantly to the Indian automobile industry for over 5 decades. The vehicles manufactured by Hindustan motors are Ambassador, Lancer, Pajero, Porter, Pushpak, RTV and Trekker. This company sold about 89,294 automobiles during April 2004 to June 2005.

Tata Motors

Tata motors limited is the India's largest automobile company established in 1945. It is the leader in commercial vehicles in each segment and second largest in passenger car vehicles. It acquired Daewoo commercial vehicle company, in 2005, Tata motors developed the first indigenous light commercial vehicle and sports utility vehicle. In the year 1998, the Tata Indica, the India's fully indigenous passenger car was produced.

Hyundai Motor India Limited

Hyundai Motor India Limited (HMIL) is a wholly owned subsidiary of Hyundai Motor Company, South Korea and is the second largest and the fastest growing car manufacturer in India. Hyundai Motor India has a fully integrated, state of the art, manufacturing plant near Chennai which was constructed at a cost of 614 US Million dollars with most advanced production, quality and testing capabilities in the company. HMIL presently markets over 25 varieties of passenger cars in six segments. The Santro in the B segment, Getz in the B+ segment, Accent in the C segment, Elantra and Sonata in the D segment and Terracan in the SUV segment.

India's Nano to Challenge Global Auto Industry

The launch of Tata Nano not only reinforces the country's strengths in IT and engineering, but also highlights the fact that global markets today are led by demand, and not supply. Ratan Tata, chairman of the Mumbai, India-headquartered US $50 billion Tata Group, has realized his biggest dream, Tata Nano, since the company introduced Tata Indica in December 1998. Commercially launched in Mumbai on Monday, the ultra-cheap small car runs on a 624 cc-rear engine and is priced at around US $ 2,000. The Indian middle class, along with the global auto industry, have been awaiting the Nano since it was first announced in January 2008. With the Nano, Tata has challenged the global auto industry and created an absolutely new segment with this car. The Nano is a huge lesson for other, bigger global auto majors.

Bajaj Auto Ltd. is set to launch Bajaj Lite priced at 1.3 lakhs which will hit the roads in 2010 and delivers a mileage of 35 kilometers per litre.

Sales of passenger cars in India jumped 22% in February 2009, while sales of commercial vehicles plunged by more than half. Prompting analysis to warm that it's too early to say India's auto sector has recovered.

After four months of decline, domestic sales of passenger cars rose to 115386 cars in February 2009 from 94757 cars in February 2008. Exports of passenger cars grew 31.3% to 26,063 cars from 19848 a year ago.[23] The spurt was driven by earning bank credit and government tax cut, two factors that may not spell a long term recovery.

Public sector banks, which dominate lending in India, have finally responded to months of aggressive rate cuts by India's central bank (RBI) and reduced the interest rate on auto loans from about 13% to about 10%.

India's top exporter, Maruti Suzuki and Hyundai have been helped by the growing appetite for small, fuel efficient cars in Europe, which is India's major export market.

Maruti Suzuki, India's largest automakers said that the sales in February 2009 and exports were the highest ever.

Domestic sales hit 70625 in February 2009, up 19.1% from a year ago in 2008 and exports surged 89.9% to 8565 vehicles.

Hyundai Motor India: India's largest passenger car exports said domestic sales rose 45.3% in February 2009 to 21215 vehicles, while exports hit 17039 vehicles an 18.3% increase from the same period last year in 2008.

The overall market situation continues to be challenging and not much should be read into the February growth. Hyundai exports a fairly flat sales growth curve for the industry for the first quarter ending March 2009.

Consumed vehicle sales continued their free fall in February with domestic sales down 51.3% to 13003 vehicles and exports off 36.1% at 1083 vehicles as per SIAM.

Commercial vehicle stakes are tightly linked to industrial production and economic growth, both of which have been sliding in India. India's economic growth skidded to 5.3% from January to March 2008 after four years of near 9% growth.

Tata Motors, India's largest commercial vehicle makers, said overall domestic sales were 42493 vehicles, a 15% decline from February 2008 despite the fact that the company sold 35% more commercial vehicles in February 2009 than it did in January 2009.

Tata Nano Competing Against Two-Wheelers

The Nano, which was announced in January 2008, and is expected to debut later this year, is the first in a wave of extremely cheap cars intended to put a multitude of new motorists behind the wheel for the first time. It carries a basic price of 100,000 Indian rupees, or roughly $2,500, about half the current cost of its nearest rival.

The manufacturer, Tata Motors, says a wholly new market is opening up in India. Its claims to have received a "mind-boggling" number of comments and inquires about its new vehicle.

Unveiling the Nano earlier this year amid huge fanfare, company chairman Ratan Tata placed the car alongside some of history's most revolutionizing achievements, including the moon landing and the inventions of the laptop and the airplane.

The Nano is about 10 feet long and 5 feet wide, has four doors and can accommodate four adults. Its two-cylinder engine is expected to get around 47 miles to the U.S. gallon - a crucial statistic in this age of sky-high oil prices. And Tata Motors claims that it will produce lower emissions than two-wheelers.

Nowhere is interest in the new car greater than in the Indian motorcycle and scooter industry. Last year, the industry sold about 7 million two-wheelers - six times the number of cars sold.

But Tata has made clear that his new vehicle is intended as an all-weather and safer alternative. He got his inspiration from seeing a man riding on a scooter with his wife and children, including a baby. This is one of the most disturbing - and common - sights on India's lethal roads. The man wears a helmet. The wife and kids often do not.

Motorcycles and scooters are a key part of India's economic life. In the countryside, where 70 percent of Indians live, the two-wheelers are like horses, carrying goods to the market and delivering supplies. They travel roads impassable by car, connecting remote villages. In cities, two-wheelers deliver a multitude of commuters to work every day. Car Ownership Rise Worries Environmentalists.

Per capita, the number of Indians who own passenger cars is still very low when compared with developed countries - just eight in 1,000. But, to the alarm of environmentalists, that number is growing rapidly.

Tata plans to start out producing 250,000 Nanos a year, eventually rising to 1 million. The car is expected to start rolling out late this year. The Indian government has embarked on a vast national highway building project to try to cater to this new motoring boom. City authorities are building roads and flyovers, but they are struggling to keep pace with the rocketing number of vehicles. Some of the country's vast and overcrowded cities, including Calcutta and Mumbai, are frequently jammed for hours every day.

Passenger Car Market to grow 51% by 2010

The domestic passenger vehicle market is expected to grow more than 51 per cent by 2010, according to PricewaterhouseCoopers' eighth annual 'Global Automotive Financial Review'. From a volume of 7.5 lakh passenger cars in 2000, the country will witness a market of 19 lakh cars in 2010, the study said.

Among a number of growth drivers, primary would be graduation from two-wheelers to four-wheeled vehicles (at present, two-wheelers constitute 77 per cent of the domestic automotive industry's production), a growing middle-class population with rising income levels and greater disposable incomes, a stable economy, growing urbanisation, rising tendency of owning a second car in urban areas, low vehicle penetration (current ratio: nine cars per 1,000 people), increased availability of financing at relatively low rates of interest and price discounts offered by dealers and manufacturers. The automotive manufacturing sector witnessed a steady growth of 12 per cent CAGR (Compounded Annual Growth Rate) during 2000-2005.

Small cars represent the largest segment accounting for about 70 per cent of the passenger vehicle market. Future growth would mainly hinge on this segment because of the vehicles' fuel efficiency and low operating costs. With almost every major global vehicle manufacturer establishing assembly facilities in the country, investment in the automotive sector was approximately $3.95 billion in 2004-05. Further, while Maruti's market share will decline 15 per cent to 33 per cent in 2010, Hyundai will maintain it at 25 per cent. Again, Tata Motors is likely to fall in market share to 5 per cent from 7 per cent in 2008, while Honda Siel will retain its share of 4 per cent.

Passenger Car Industry in India for Next Generation

Not very long ago, the only cars that were available in India were the Ambassador and the Premier Padmini. The Ambassador is a replica of the Morris Oxford – an old British car, while the Premier Padmini was a Fiat 1100 assembled in India. All that was in pre-liberalization India, which existed before 1991, when the first liberalization measures were announced. Earlier, the production of Maruti Suzuki 800 hatchback car in 1983 – a joint venture between Government of India and Suzuki Motors Japan, paved the way for a renaissance in the Indian automobile sector.

Post liberalization, India is on every car manufacturer's map. The reasons are not hard to notice. Currently, India is the second largest tow-wheeler market and the fourth largest commercial vehicle market in the world. Not only it is the eleventh largest passenger car market globally, but it is also expected to be the seventh largest by 2016.

Post liberalization, many foreign manufactures have lined up and have set up base in India. Other domestic manufacturers have also improved production levels and are in the race for producing better models as well.

Some of the car manufacturers who have set up base in India are Audi, BMW, Chevrolet, Fiat, Ford, Honda, Hyundai, Mahindra, Maruti, Mercedes, Mitsubishi, Skoda, Suzuki, Tata, Toyota, Volkswagen and Volvo. India's economic growth is booming currently. These manufacturers have set up manufacturing facilities in India, or are importing cars and spares to meet the demands of this growing market.

Companies like Ford are planning to make India a regional hub for exports of both small cars as well as engines. Ford India company plans to export the small car and the engine for markets abroad. One of the markets would be chiefly Ford Asia Pacific Region while other markets are under consideration presently.

There are many reasons for the impressive growth of the Indian car industry. Some of these are comparatively easy availability of vehicle finance, attractive rates of interest, and convenient installments.

Competition has forced manufacturers to be innovative and responsive to customer demands and needs. Now that India is not alien to quality and perfection, customer expectations have soared to higher levels. Depending upon customers needs, four segments, viz., small, midsize, premium and sports utility vehicles currently represent the car market in the country.

A niche concept cars segment is also emerging wherein reputed re-modellers like DC Chhabria cater to individuals who wish to remodel their vehicles to create concept cars for their use. Contrarily, a segment is also emerging comprising people who wish to upgrade to cars from two wheelers. Tata already is in the process of launching the small car Nano to suit this segment's needs. Many other car manufacturers such as Bajaj Auto are also following suit and are in the process of coming up with their specific versions to cater to this segment.

Currently, there is high demand for cars across all these segments. With the growing economy, people left with a lot of disposable income, spend it towards meeting their mobility needs such as cars. Banks and other financial institutions have an assortment of vehicle loan schemes with attractive rates of interest and convenient installments.

These schemes encourage people to go in for loans to purchase cars of their choice. Additionally, a convenient union budget in the current financial year (2008-09) has worked in favour of the automobile sector, which has been an uptrend in sales across various segments.

The latest trend of new cars on Indian road has led to the emergence of an entirely new market in second hand cars too. Many entrepreneurial and professional dealerships have sprung up in many cities in India dealing in second hand cars.

The growth of the second had market is not surprising. The new car market has grown at an incredible pace in India. As mentioned, loans are easily available in the country for purchase of new cars. Moreover, many people are now upwardly mobile. Therefore, people who were earlier part of the small car segment now have moved over to the premium car segment, and those in this segment have moved over to the luxury car segment.

Therefore, the trend is to get rid of the cars that defined them as part of the earlier segments and buy cars that identify them with the newer segments. Apparently, the desire for newer cars and models is yet another reason. People get attracted by newer models, which prompt them to acquire them. This makes them sell their current cars for reasonable resale values.

This phenomenon benefits those who want to buy cars, but are not able to afford new ones. Many companies like Maruti Suzuki (Maruti True Value) have also established resale showrooms where people can purchase genuine, good condition, second hand cars at reasonable prices.

With the emergence of favourable trends in the automobile sector in India, what remains to be seen is how these developments will go a long way to transform the mobility needs of the ordinary Indian.

Passenger Car Industry in India Grows Steadily

The passenger car industry in India has grown steadily during the last few years except during the year 2000-01 when there was negative growth due to global economic recession. Passenger car industry in India has 15 manufacturers with an installed capacity of 1,237,000 units. Production of cars during the years 2001-01 and 2002-03 was 564,052 numbers and 606,088 respectively.

Maruti Udyog Ltd

Maruti Udyog Ltd was established in February 1981 through an Act of Parliament to meet the growing demands of a personal code of transport due to lack of an efficient public transport system. This company entered the Indian car market to provide fuel-efficient, low-cost vehicles which were reliable and of high quality with better after sales service leading to customer satisfaction. The manufacturing plant of MUL is located at Gurgaon near Delhi.'M 800' was the first car that MUL launched in 1983 in India. Later in 1993 the 'Zen' was launched. In 1994 the 'Esteem' was launched and thereafter several cars like 'Alto', 'Wagon R', 'Baleno', 'Gypsy', 'Omni', 'Maruti 1000', Swift, Dzire, Zen Estilo, SX4, Maruti A-Star were launched and Maruti Ritz (Splash) is in the offing. 'Maruti Altura' is a Wagon launched by Maruti Udyog Ltd. Maruti 'Grand Vitara' is a sports utility vehicle launched by Maruti Udyog Ltd.

In 2001, Maruti Udyog Ltd became one of the first automobile companies anywhere in the world to get an ISO 9001:2000 certification. Recently, to meet the growing demands of four-wheeler automobile, Maruti Udyog Limited, collaborated with Suzuki Motor Corporation of Japan, to manufacture cars. On the 17th September 2007, Maruti Udyog was renamed as Maruti Suzuki India Limited and the company headquarters is in Gurgaon, Delhi. Maruti cars have ruled the roads in the past, in the present, and promises to do so in the future also with its highly efficient cars.

Maruti is India's most saleable car. There are a variety of Maruti car brands that has dominated the Indian roads. Maruti cars are buyable from the car dealerships, used car dealers, car websites and car owners. Maruti car reviews explain the worth of buying Maruti Car. There are Maruti used car dealer and know more about the car prices. One could go for extensive car search to find the best car at best affordable price.

TATA Motors

Tata Motors started with manufacturing trucks. In 1996, Tata Motors (formerly TELCO–Tata Engineering Locomotive Company Ltd) launched "Tata Indica". Indica Means India's car. It had several complaints in the steering wheel and made unpleasant sounds at high speeds and thus Tata Motors came out with a new version called Tata INDICA V2. V2 means version 2, making corrections in the earlier model. In 2002 December, Tata Motors launched 'Tata Indigo' which had a hatch back in its body. Tata Indica Xeta, Tata Indica Vista and Tata Nano are the new cars launched by Tata Motors.

Tata motors launched Tata Estate, Tata Sumo, Tata Sierra, Tata Safari, Tata Spacio, which fall in the MUV (Multi Utility Vehicle) segment.

Hyundai Motors India Ltd

Hyundai Motors has a factory in Sriperumbadur from which it manufactures Hyundai Santro, Hyundai Getz, Hyundai i10, Hyundai i20, Hyundai Accent, Hyundai Sonata, Hyundai Verna, Hyundai Terracan and Hyundai Tucson (an SUV - Sports Utility Vehicle).

Fiat India Ltd

FIAT has launched Fiat Palio, Fiat Palio Stile, Fiat Uno, Premier Padmini and Premier 118 NE in the Indian market in collaboration with Premier Automobile Ltd.

Ford India Ltd

Ford Motors of United States has entered into a technical collaboration with India to set up Ford India Ltd company in Chennai in the state of Tamil Nadu to manufacture cars. Ford India Ltd Manufactures the cars like Ford Mondeo, Ford Ikon,

Ford Escort, Ford Fusion (Fusion of Technology, Style Comfort etc).

General Motors India Ltd

General Motors of United States has entered into collaboration with India to manufacture cars like 'Opel Corsa', 'Opel Astra', 'Chevrolet Optra', 'Chevrolet Spark', 'Chevrolet Beat' (manufactured in GM's Talegaon plant where 'spark' is manufactured) ,'Chevrolet Aveo' and 'Corsa Sail'.

Hindustan Motors

Hindustan Motors is engaged in manufacturing cars like Ambassador, Contessa, Mitsubishi Lancer, Outlander, Montero, Pajero, Cedia, etc. Hindustan Motors have tied up with its Japanese counterpart 'Mitsubishi' Corporation to launch its car named Mitsubishi Lancer.

Daewoo Motors India Ltd

The Korean based Daewoo corporation has entered into a technical collaboration with India to manufacture cars like Matiz, Cielo etc. Now Daewoo Corporation has been acquired by General Motors to relaunch Matiz in the name of 'Chevrolet Spark' Chevrolet U-VA, Aveo, SRV, Optra Magnum, Tavera and Captiva.

Toyota Kirloskar Ltd

Japanese based Toyota Motors entered into a technical collaboration with Kirloskar Motors Ltd to manufacture cars like Toyota Camry, Toyota Qualis and Toyota Innova. Toyota Qualis was introduced in the year 2000 and due to customer dissatisfaction the company had to withdraw the model in the year 2004. During the period 2000–2004, Toyota had manufactured 1,40,000 units of Toyota Qualis, which was replaced by Toyota Innova.

Daimler Chrysler India Ltd

The US-German based Daimler Chrysler has entered into a technical collaboration with India to manufacture cars like

S-Class Benz, C-Class Benz and New E-class Benz in the Indian market.

Honda Siel Ltd

The History of the Honda Motor company began with the vision of one man – Soichiro Honda. Honda Motor company was founded in 1948. The Honda Siel plant is located at Greater Noida and has an installed capacity of manufacturing 30,000 units in a year. Japan based Honda Siel Ltd has collaborated with India to manufacture cars like 'Honda City' and 'Honda Accord'.

Mahindra Renault Ltd

The Indian company Mahindra merged with the French company Renault to launch the midsize sedan called 'Logan'. M & M was incorporated in 1945 and was originally formed to manufacture utility vehicles for the Indian market, initially by importing and assembling Willy's jeep kits.

Passenger Car Segment in India

The passenger car segment can be divided into three major segments namely.

- Small car segment (A and B segments)
- Mid car segment (B^+ and C segments)
- Premium and large car segment (C^+ and D segments)

Small Car Segment

Cars are classified as small car, medium car and large car on the basis of their size, i.e. their length, width and height (and based on cost and engine capacity).

A car is called a small car if its length is less than 4000 mm, width is less than 1600 mm and height should not be more than 1600 mm.

A small car can have a maximum engine capacity of 1400 cc. The engine capacity of a small car usually ranges from 800 cc to 1400 cc. The pricing of a small car will range from 1 lakh to 4.5 lakhs. A small car is usually priced below 4 lakhs (depending upon its engine capacity).

The following cars come under the small car segments:

- Maruti 800 (Engine capacity : 800 cc*) (cc* = cubic centimeter)
- Maruti Zen (Engine capacity : 1000 cc for petrol version)
- Maruti Alto (Engine capacity : 800 cc, 1000 cc)
- Wagon R (Engine capacity : 1060 cc)
- Fiat Uno (Engine capacity : 1242 cc)
- Fiat Palio (Engine capacity ; 1242 cc) (Fiat Palio 1596 cc is not a small car)
- Maini Reva (Run on Battery power)
- Tata Indica V2* (*Version 2) (Engine capacity : 1405 cc)
- Hyundai Santro Xing (Engine capacity : 1086 cc)
- Corsa Sail (Engine capacity: 1389 cc).
- Hyundai Getz
- Maruti A-Star
- Maruti Swift
- TATA Indica XETA
- Tata Nano
- Bajaj Lite
- Maruti Ritz (Splash)
- Chevrolet Spark

Mid Segment Cars

There are many mid segments cars, which ply on the Indian roads. The mid segment car has a length between 4000 mm and 4500 mm, width between 1550 mm and 1700 mm and height not more than 1600 mm.

A mid segment car will normally have an engine capacity between 1250 cc to 2000 cc. The price of mid segment cars will range from 3.75 lakhs to 6 lakhs.

The following are the mid segment cars in the Indian market.

- Maruti Esteem (Engine capacity : 1298 cc)
- Ford Ikon (Engine capacity : 1300 cc to 1750 cc)
- Ford Fusion
- Ford Fiesta
- Tata Indigo (Engine capacity : 1400 cc)
- FIAT SIENNA (Engine capacity : 1250 cc TO 1600 cc)
- HYUNDAI ACCENT (Engine capacity : 1500 cc)
- HYUNDAI TORNADO (Engine capacity : 1500 cc)
- HYUNDAI VIVA (Engine capacity : 1500 cc)
- AMBASSADOR (Engine capacity : 1800 cc)
- OPEL CORSA (Engine capacity: 1500 cc).
- Maruti Swift Dzire (Engine capacity: 1300 cc)

Premium and Large Car Segment

The premium cars or the large cars are seen on our Indian roads not as many as the small cars or the mid segment cars. The premium or the large cars have: a length varying from 4000 mm to 5200 mm, width varying from 1600 to 1850 mm; height is not more than 1500 mm; large cars will have an engine capacity varying from 1350 to 3200 cc.

The price of large cars varies from 6 lakhs to 30 lakhs, some cars like Bentley and Maybach will cost more than 1 crore.

The following are the premium cars in the Indian market:

- Contessa is a car manufactured by Hindustan Motors whose engine capacity is 1850 cc.
- Ford Mondeo has an engine capacity of 1800 cc.
- Toyota Corolla has an of engine capacity of 1800 cc.
- Maturi Baleno has an engine capacity of 1600 cc.
- Lancer, which is manufactured by Hindustan Motors has an engine capacity of 2000 cc.
- Chevrolet Optra which is manufactured by General Motors India Ltd. Has an engine capacity of 1799 cc.
- Open Astra which is manufactured by General Motors India Ltd has an engine capacity of 1700 cc.

- Honda City which is manufactured by Honda Siel Ltd. has an engine capacity of 1500 cc.
- Maruti SX4 (Engine capacity; 1600 cc)
- Honda Accord which is manufactured by Honda Siel Ltd has an engine capacity of 2400 cc.
- Hyundai Verna
- Ford Fiesta (Engine capacity; 1600 cc)
- Skoda Octavia which is manufactured by Czech Republic based SKODA Ltd. has an engine capacity of 2000 cc.
- Toyota Camry which is manufactured by Toyota Kirloskar has an engine capacity of 2500 cc.
- Opel Vectra which is manufactured by General Motors India Ltd has an engine capacity of 2000 cc).
- New E-class Benz which is manufactured by Daimler Chrysler India Ltd has an engine capacity of 2500 cc.
- S-class Benz which is manufactured by Daimler Chrysler India Ltd has an engine capacity of 3200.
- C-class Benz which is manufactured by Daimler Chrysler India Ltd has an engine capacity of 2000 cc.

Among the passenger cars, 'Wagons' also occupy an important place. The following cars come under the category of 'Wagons'

- Maruti Altura which is manufactured by Maruti Udyog Ltd.
- Fiat Palio Weekend, which is manufactured by FIAT India Ltd.
- Fiat Palio Adventure which is manufactured by FIAT India Ltd.
- Opel Swing which is manufactured by General Motors India Ltd.

Utility Vehicles

Utility vehicles are of several types. We can classify utility vehicles into mainly two types:-

- SUV (Sports Utility Vehicle)
- MUV (Multi Utility Vehicle)

A utility vehicle can be defined as a van or a pickup or a sedan that has a passenger capacity varying from 7 to 12 persons (excluding the driver).

The utility vehicles are also called multi purpose vehicles which are meant to transport not only passengers from one point to another but also meant to transport goods, materials, supplies from one point to another. The utility vehicles are more commonly used by factory owners, company partners etc who utilize their vehicle not only for passenger transport but also for goods, material and supply transport.

Considering the quantity and type of traffic on the Indian roads an SUV is an ideal vehicle. Now the Indian car makers are focusing on the utility vehicles especially the SUV's.

The different SUV's and MUV's are the following: Scorpio, Bolero, Armada, Voyager and Xylo manufactured by M/s. Mahindra & Mahindra, Qualis and Innova manufactured by Toyota, Pajero manufactured by Hindustan Motors, Tata Sumo, Tata Safari, Tata Ace and Tata Spacio manufactured by Tata Motors Ltd; Tempo Trax, Tempo Traveller, manufactured by M/s. Bajaj Tempo Ltd; Forester, Tavera and Captiva manufactured by General Motors India Ltd; RTV manufactured by Hindustan Motors, CR-V manufactured by Honda Motors Ltd; Grand Vitara, Omni, Gypsy King and Maruti Versa manufactured by Maruti Udyog Ltd.

Events and Milestones

A behind-the-scene look of one of India's most vibrant industries. The landmarks along the way:

1928	:	The first imported car was seen on Indian roads
1942	:	Hindustan Motors, a car manufacturing company, was incorporated.
1944	:	Premier Automobiles Ltd, a car manufacturing company, was incorporated.
1948	:	First car, Hindustan Ambassador, was manufactured in India.

1953	:	The Government of India decreed that only those firms which a manufacturing programme should be allowed to operate in India.
1955	:	Only seven firms viz., Hindustan Motors, API, ALL, Standard Motors, SMPIL, PAL, M&M and TELCO (Now TATA Motors) received approval.
1960-70	:	The two-wheeler and three wheeler industry established a foothold in the Indian scenario.
1970-80	:	Not much change was witnessed during this period. The major factors affecting the industry were the implementation of the MRTP Act (Monopolies and Restrictive Trade Practices Act), FERA (Foreign Exchange Regulation Act) and the oil shock of 1973 and 1979.
1980-90	:	The first phase of liberalization was announced by the Government with the liberalization of the Governments' protectionist policies, the advantages hither to enjoyed by the Indian car manufacturers like monopoly, oligopoly, slowly began to disappear.
1990-2000	:	Excise duty reduced from 24 percent to 16 percent
2000-2008	:	New plants of BMW, Volkswagen and Audi started in India due to increase in foreign equity in India.

Development of Car Industry in India

The first motor car on the streets of India was seen in 1898. Mumbai had its first taxicabs in the early 1900. Then for the next fifty years, cars were imported to satisfy domestic demand. Between 1910 and 1920's the automobile industry made a humble beginning by setting up assembly plants in Mumbai, Calcutta and Chennai. In 1946, Premier Automobile Ltd (PAL) manufactured the first car in the country by assembling "Dodge Desoto" and "Plymouth" cars at its Kurla Plant. Hindustan Motors started as a manufacture of auto components and then graduated to manufacture of cars in 1949.

In 1952, the Government of India set up a tariff commission to devise regulations to develop an indigenous automobile industry in the country. After the commission submitted its recommendations, the Government of India asked assembly plants, which did not have plans to set up manufacturing facilities to shut operations. As a result General Motors, Ford and other assemblers closed operations in the country. The year was 1954 and this decision of the Government marked a turning point in the history of the Indian Car Industry.

The Government of India also had a say in what type of vehicle each manufacturer should make, imposed control on the production capacity, distribution and controlled the fixation of prices for cars and dealer commission. Government of India followed restrictive set of policies. This triggered the start of a protracted legal battle in 1969 between some car makers and Government of India. The three decades following the establishment of the passenger car industry in India and leading up to the early 1980s, proved to be the 'dark ages' for the consumer, as his choice throughout this period was limited to two models viz. Ambassador and Padmini. Ambassador was manufactured by Hindustan Motors Ltd. and Padmini was manufactured by Premier Automobile Ltd. It was only in 1985, after the entry of Maruti Udyog, that the carmakers were given a free hand to fix the prices of cars, thus effectively abolishing all controls relating to the pricing of the end product. A series of liberal policy changes were announced marking another turning point for the automobile industry.

The Government of India entered the car business, with a 74% stake in Maruti Udyog Ltd (MUL), the joint venture with Suzuki Motors Ltd of Japan. MUL introduced 'Maruti 800' in 1983 providing a complete facelift to the Indian Car industry. The car was launched as a "people's car". This changed the industry's profile.

Demand and Supply

The demand for cars in the past was supply driven as demand did not match supply. This led to high premium and long waiting periods for the cars. But change in Government policies coupled with aggressive capacity additions and upgradation of models by MUL in the early nineties led to increase in supply and subsequently reduced the waiting periods for cars.

Further, the demand for cars is dependent on a number of factors. The key variables are per capita income i.e. the average annual income of a person, introduction of new models, availability and cost of car financing schemes, price of cars, incidence of duties and taxes, depreciation norms, fuel cost and its subsidization, public transport facilities etc. The first four factors viz., increase in per capita income, introduction of new models; availability and cost of car financing have positive relationship with the demand whereas others have an inverse relationship with demand of cars. The demand for cars in the future is expected to come predominantly from the existing two wheeler owners who will be upgrading to a four wheeler, due to rising income and necessity of car for personal transportation purposes.

Further, the dominance of economy segment will continue in the future as it will provide large volume to Indian car industry. The majority of customers for the economy segment will be two wheelers. Also with the release of new models in the higher end of the economy segment, the supply of second hand economy cars has increased substantially, which costs just about two times the price of premium range two-wheelers. And the demand for mid-sized and premium cars is rising as new models are entering the market, income levels are rising and present car owners in the economy segment are upgrading to higher end cars.

Pre-Owned Car Market in India

Used cars are selling like hotcakes in India. Thanks to their easy availability and lower interest rates, the sale of used cars is only expected to further shoot up the sales ladder in the coming years. It is hard to find accurate data on the sale of used car in India, where the unorganized sector plays a major role. However, if we go through the car dealers and the country's largest vehicle financier list, more second hand cars were bought and sold in 2007 than new ones. According to estimates provided by Maruti Suzuki India Ltd. the True Value used car division and Honda Siel Car India Ltd. Auto Terrace, which sells pre-owned cars, the used car market this fiscal year is about 10 percent more than that of new cars.

Car financers elsewhere have also pointed out this growing trend. They estimate that the used car segment is growing at 25-30 percent compared to the 13 percent for the new car market. In 2007, which ended in March, Indians bought 1.4 million new cars, compared to about 1.3 million used ones in the same period in 2006. Since March, Maruti sold 65,000 used cars, an increase of 45 percent compared to the year in 2006, while Honda sold 2,769 used cars in this period compared with 1765 cars in 2006.

About 80 percent of the transactions in the second-hand car segment still occurred in the unorganized sector, facilitated by an estimated 2000. With advances in technology and a record number of new car models entering the Indian market every year, customers today typically go for an upgrade or exchange within three years of their purchase, compared to the aged ideology of sticking to the same car for 10-15 years.

As many as 50 new and tweaked models have been introduced in India for the past couple of years. This trend is expected to continue and grow till the car makers pump in Rs. 35,000 crore in Asia's third largest automobile market. To think India had barely two models three decades ago – the Fiat Premier and Hindustan Motors Ambassador. The 25-30 per cent growth in the previously owned car market in the last three years from 2003 to 2006. It has happened because interest rates for used and new vehicles are more or less the same.

Organized players like Maruti's True Value and Automart India Ltd have entered this business and contributing to the trend. They offer buyers and sellers the assurance of proper ownership and accident documentation along with quality and add-ons such as warranty and free services previously available only for new car buyers. The general consensus among the industry is that the used car segment may become almost double the new car market in another five years as two-wheeler owners has been opting for four-wheelers.

In markets such as the US and France, the used car segment is 2.5 times larger than the new car one. India may outshoot this record in the year 2010. After all, we do have the second largest population in the world.

Pre-Owned Car Outlets of Maruti Udyog Ltd

The Indian used car market is in a very nascent stage and dominated by the unorganized sector. Quality and reliability of pre-owned cars available through the unorganized sector is often not up to the mark. The pre-owned car outlets of Maruti Udyog Ltd are called as 'True Value' outlets. These True Value outlets are spread across all the cities in India. It exchanges its cars with any other car commensurate with the prevailing market rates. It is also takes into consideration the depreciation of the car for assessing the true value of the car.

Used Cars of Tata Motors - 'Tata Motors Assured'

Tata Motors has commenced its certified pre-owned car programme, 'Tata Motors Assured'.

'Tata Motors Assured' pre-owned car operations have been launched on a pilot basis through 15 dealers in 10 major cities across India. The cities are Mumbai, Delhi, Bangalore, Hyderabad, Chennai, Pune, Ahmedabad, Chandigarh, Ludhiana and Vapi. The programme will be subsequently offered across the country through Tata Motors dealer network in a phased manner.

The Indian used car market is in a very nascent stage and dominated by the unorganized sector. Quality and reliability of pre-owned cars available through the unorganized sector is often not up to the mark. The 'Tata Motors Assured' certified pre-owned car programme will offer a choice of reliable and certified pre-owned Tata cars to the customer. 'Tata Motors Assured' certified pre-owned cars will be refurbished in Tata Motors authorized dealer's workshops using Tata genuine spares by skilled and trained technicians. Each 'Tata Motors Assured' certified pre-owned car will under go stringent inspection by Tata Motors engineers as per a structured quality check list and come with a certification from 'Tata Motors Assured'.

The 'Tata Motors Assured' certified pre-owned cars will be less than 5 years old, non accidental and with not more than two owners. 'Tata Motors Assured' certified pre-owned car will come with a 1 year/20000 km extended warranty. Additionally, three free services will be offered to customers as a part of the certification package. The extended warranty and free service facility will be available in India across the extensive service network of Tata Motors dealerships and select Tata Motors authorized service centres. Customers can now have a very convenient and safe option of buying and selling Tata cars and SUVs at 'Tata Motors Assured' dealerships.

Used Cars of Hyundai Motors – 'Hyundai Advantage'

The pre-owned car outlets of Hyundai Motors are called as 'Hyundai Advantage'. They operate through their dealers in all the cities across India. They accept any car for exchange with their cars at the prevailing market rates.

Used Cars from General Motors

The pre-owned car market in India is getting glamorous by the day. According to reports, General Motors India is aggressively considering entering the pre-owned car business segment in India.

Maruti Udyog, Hyundai Motor India and Ford India have already entered the pre-owned segment. The decision if implemented will make GM India the fourth car manufacturer to enter this area on its own.

GM India's planned foray into the segment is almost reaching the implementation stage. A decision will be taken with in 2010. In all probability, the pre-owned foray will happen this year itself in 2009. While the financial year 2005-2006 saw the pre-owned car market in India touch a figure of 8.8 lakh cars, a year later, during 2006-07, the market grew by 30 per cent, crossing sales of one million. The used cars market is estimated to be of the same size as that of the new cars market. Nearly one million cars change hands annually, according to the Society of Indian Automobile Manufacturers.

Meanwhile, the German luxury car manufacturer Porsche has also entered the used car market and has sold 40 cars in 2009. Bentley has also drawn up plans to enter the pre-owned market.

General Motors India has launched the "Chevrolet-OK Cars program to buy and sell pre-owned cars. The Chevrolet-OK Cars network of outlets is being rolled out nationally in a phased manner and will also buy all popular brands of cars in exchange for the sale of new cars from the Chevrolet stable. The pre-owned program from Chevrolet has since become operational in 9 outlets across 6 cities, with three outlets in Delhi and NCR, two outlets in Mumbai and one each in Pune, Hyderabad, Jalandhar and Ludhiana. The Chevrolet-OK program will expand to 30 country-wide outlets by this year-end.

Commenting on the launch of the Chevrolet-OK Cars program, P. Balendran, Vice President, GM India, said, "With Chevrolet-OK Cars, GM India plans to set up a country-wide network of branded, pre-owned car sales outlets to offer our valued customers an experience very similar to buying a new car. The program will offer our customers mechanically and physically sound pre-owned cars, which will first be certified by highly qualified GM India-trained engineers after passing through a system of stringent checks and refurbishment."

In a sector that is largely unorganized and very often unreliable, the Chevrolet-OK Cars program will assure customers safety and surety of purchase and complete transparency of operations. The vehicles sold through these outlets will ensure very high mechanical and appearance standards set by GM India.

The cars offered through CHEVROLET-OK, outlets will go through a strict, 110-point checklist by GM India trained engineers, a thorough vehicle reconditioning program, besides a detailed history check. Chevrolet-OK Cars will be sold with a 1-year / 15,000 km limited warranty, along with three labour-free services for Chevrolet cars.

The program will also provide an opportunity for additional revenue to GM India's dealers across the nation and ensure the quality of pre-owned cars available to the customer.

It may be recalled that General Motors India, is in the process of appointing more dealers and authorized service outlets in urban and semi-urban cities to widen its network and reach out to its valued customers across the nation. GM India's rapidly growing network of Chevrolet dealerships and service centres include 170 authorized sales points and 177 service outlets, while more are in the pipeline to support the increasing market demand for its products

General Motors India has two car manufacturing facilities at Halol in Gujarat and Talegaon in Maharashtra and it rolls out the Chevrolet Tavera, Chevrolet Optra, Chevrolet Aveo, Chevrolet Aveo U-VA, Chevrolet SRV, Chevrolet Spark and Chevrolet Captiva for the Indian market from its plants. GM India also has its Engineering, R & D and Design Centres in Bangalore.

ROAD TRANSPORT SECTOR IN KERALA

Transportation is an integral part of the development of Kerala viz. road transport, rail transport and inland water transport. The total length of road in Kerala during 2006-07 increased to 162149 km from 160944 km than the previous year. Among Indian Railways, the world's second largest rail network, the Thiruvananthapuram Division has operated 20655 Express/ Mail trains, 18250 passenger trains and 675 special trains during 2006-2007. Also Kerala has one major port at Cochin and 17 non major ports.

ROADS

In Kerala, traffic has been growing at a rate of about 11 percent every year resulting in excessive pressure on the roads in the state. Road density in the state is 417 km/ 100 sq. km and higher than the national average of 100.39 km/ 100 sq. km. 162149 km of road length in the state is maintained by different agencies like Panchayats, PWD (R&B), Municipalities, Corporations, Forests, Irrigation, PWD (NH) and others like Railway, KSEB etc.

Out of the total road length, 109105 Kms were maintained by Panchayats (67.29%) followed by 28203 Kms (17.39%) by

State PWD (R&B). Corporations and Municipalities together maintain road length of 15776 Kms (9.7%) and National Highways cover 1524 Kms (0.94%). While Irrigation Department maintains 2898 Km (1.79%), Forest Department maintains 4215 Km (2.60%) and that of KSEB, 364km.

Of the 14 districts in the State, Ernakulam district accounted for the maximum road length of 2172 Kms (9.99%) followed by Kottayam district with 2117 Kms. (9.74%) Wayanad district had the lowest PWD road length of 555 Kms (2.55%).

NATIONAL HIGHWAYS IN THE STATE

There are eight National Highways in Kerala. The National Highway network in the state is of length 1523.954 km. this is only 2.3% of total National Highways in the country.

National Highways in Kerala

NH 47 - Valayar - Kaliyikkavila	416.80 km.
NH 17 - Thalappadi - Edappally	420.777 km.
NH 49 - Bodimettu - Kundannoor (Cochin-Madhurai)	167.593 km.
NH 47 - A - Kundanoor-Willington Island	5.90 km.
NH 208 - Kollam - Aryankavu	81.28 km.
NH 212 - Kozhikode - Muthanga	117.00 km.
NH 213 - Palakkad - Kozhikode	125.304 km.
NH 220 - Kollam - Theni	189.30 km.
Total Length	1523.954 km.

ROAD TRANSPORT

Motor Vehicles Department, Kerala State Road Transport Corporation and Kerala Transport Development Finance Corporation are the three agencies to regulate road transport development activities in the State.

MOTOR VEHICLES DEPARTMENT (MVD)

Motor Vehicles Department is one of the major revenue earning departments of the State. The main functions of the MVD are registration of motor vehicles, collection of tax on motor vehicles, issuance of permits and licenses for plying the vehicles on roads, regulation and enforcement of Motor Vehicles Rules and Act etc. The number of Motor Vehiles having valid registration as on 31.3.2007 is 4025350 as against 3559504 in the previous year. The newly registered vehicles come to 465846(13.08%) during 2006-07.

Highest vehicle populated district in Kerala is Ernakulam 59451 (12.76%), followed by Thiruvananthapuram 50565 (10.85%) and Waynad has the lowest number of motor vehicles 3701 (0.79%).

KERALA STATE ROAD TRANSPORT CORPORATION (KSRTC)

KSRTC, the largest public sector transport organization in the State, acts as the feeder service to the rail, air and inland water transport. The vehicle density of the state is very high compared to many other states in India. About 12045 passengers travelled in KSRTC buses during 2006-07. KSRTC is the only SRTC in India paying pension and pensionary benefits from its own resources. During 2006-07 92 new buses (one A/c Air bus, 19 super fast, five fast passenger, 25 mini buses and 42 Venad) were commissioned to make it public friendly. But, the fleet strength of KSRTC is decreased from 4668 in 2006 to 4559 in 2007. About 24.89% are aged above ten years i.e. 1135.

PASSENGER CAR MARKET IN KERALA

"Small is Beautiful", said E.F. Schumacher. Time has come to think small! All car manufacturers are racing with the concept of their distinctive small cars. India's largest automobile manufacturing company, Tata Motors, opened its fourth car dealership in Kerala and the second in Kochi, Kerala, under R F Motors, thus raising its passenger Car dealership in the country to 131. Kerala accounted for 25 per cent of the estimated 10,000 Tata Indica cars being sold per month in the four southern states - Kerala, Karnataka, Tamil Nadu and Andhra Pradesh.[24]

The global recession has disturbed the domestic car sales in the recent months. It's true that every black cloud have a

Number of Motor Vehicles Having Valid Registration as on 31.03.2007 (Provisional) in Kerala

District	Goods Vehicles		Buses						
	Four Wheelers & Above	*Three Wheelers including Tempos*	*Stage Carriages*	*Contract Carriages/ Omni Buses*	*Cars and Station Wagons*	*Three Wheelers*	*Two Wheelers*	*Tractors*	*Total*
Thiruvananthapuram	17424	9206	7991	13706	86012	36128	368417	3183	556109
Kollam	14202	5057	1008	5547	63795	29769	183767	1504	304649
Pathanamthitta	6368	3317	953	3877	45100	14299	91757	496	168167
Alappuzha	10032	8745	1050	5283	45566	15803	190592	842	277913
Kottayam	16114	5124	2452	10320	81470	31179	166054	848	313561
Idukki	4189	1244	816	1826	17869	8122	27474	730	62270
Ernakulam	43489	11323	4642	17181	121503	41894	422473	7004	669509
Thrissur	20755	9925	4228	15224	66226	33898	275484	2375	428115
Palakkad	16772	3885	2115	8333	31338	23908	164783	6997	258131
Malappuram	21190	10945	3905	9409	65083	55546	144651	2237	312972
Kozhikode	17403	6578	3267	4417	60400	28010	203927	2211	356213
Wayanad	3055	1174	462	1136	11169	6486	22884	1965	48331
Kannur	14021	5331	3329	5000	40023	27597	110827	3942	210070
Kasargode	4161	1462	858	581	19251	16128	46013	886	89340
Total	211175	83316	37076	101840	768847	368767	2419109	35220	4025350

silver lining. The silver lining is brought by the export sales amid the gloomy cloud canopying the car industry in Kerala. Whereas, the domestic sales has been affected in a big way forcing many car manufacturers to cut down their production capacity. Most of the car dealers in Kerala have announced discounts and schemes with their car models with a hope to boost the car sales. Though these strategies have helped them to some limit but then they are still not able to revive the sales figure. Now, they are banking on the coming New Year to bring some fortune along with a fresh new dawn. Some Indian states including Kerala have increased their local taxes, which has increased the price of all car models in Kerala and other states. With this, the car market in Kerala is placed on a toss with an imbalance in the expected market performance. Car dealers in Kerala have to hunt for a fresh approach and innovative strategies to bring back the lost status and position of the Indian car market.

Car Dealers in Kerala

Car dealers play an important intermediary role in the promotion of brand equity and sale of a particular brand of cars. In the process, they build up the reputation and contribute towards the growth of the company's market share. In India, the role of car dealers was limited to a mere selling of cars that has undergone a substantial change in the recent times with dealers emerging as an important point of connect between the company and the customers for the cars. Car dealers of today are expected to act as a catalyst to promote the sales of a car. At the first instance, car dealers are to have a good collection of cars. Car dealership depends on availability of the brand new cars and the location of the showroom.

Depending upon the brand and type of cars, dealer location ensures that the potential customers get the best of strategic advantages. The ambiance and the customer service are equally important. The customer should feel welcome at the car dealers place and the more a car dealer is able to generate that sort of feelings among his potential customers, the likelihood of car sales is to increase.

Promotional Tools Used by Car Dealers

The promotional tools used by the car dealers in Kerala are advertising, sales promotion, personal selling, direct marketing, word of mouth, public relations, publicity, events and experiences. Table 10 reveals the ranks assigned by nine car dealers interviewed across the northern, central and southern regions in Kerala.

Table 10
Promotional Tools Used by Car Dealers in Kerala

	Rank						
Promotional Tools	*I*	*II*	*III*	*IV*	*V*	*VI*	*Total*
Advertisement	5	3	1	0	0	0	9
Sales Promotion	3	4	1	1	0	0	9
Personal Selling	1	2	3	2	1	0	9
Direct Marketing	0	0	1	4	3	1	9
Public relations & Publicity	0	0	0	1	5	3	9
Events & Experiences	0	0	3	1	0	5	9

Source: Survey Data

Out of the nine car dealers interviewed across the northern, central and southern regions in Kerala, five car dealers assigned first rank to advertisement, three car dealers assigned first rank to sales promotion and one car dealer assigned first rank for personal selling. Out of the nine car dealers across the northern, central and southern regions in Kerala, three car dealers assigned second rank to advertisement, four car dealers assigned second rank to sales promotion and two car dealer assigned second rank for personal selling.

Importance of Factors Considered by Car Dealers

There are several factors that the car dealers considered as important. Table 11 exhibits the importance of various factors considered by car dealers in the small car market in Kerala.

Out of the nine car dealers interviewed across the northern, central and southern regions in Kerala the following observations were made:-

Table 11

Importance of Various Factors Considered by Car Dealers across the Three Regions in Kerala

	Extremely Important	*Very Important*	*Important*	*Less Important*	*Not Important*
Providing car loans to customer	0	5	3	1	0
Allowing long test drives	0	0	6	3	0
Training the sales executives to understand customer behaviour	0	6	3	0	0
Making sales calls by the sales force	0	6	3	0	0
Dealing with branded accessories inside the showroom	0	5	3	1	0
Having an in-house spare parts center	0	5	3	1	0
Having an in-house service center	6	2	1	0	0
Having a stockyard near the showroom premises	0	0	3	5	1
Having a toll-free number for the customers	0	0	0	1	8
Having a prompt customer care service	0	5	4	0	0
Making charitable donations	0	0	0	5	4
Building community relations	0	0	5	4	0
Demonstration of the working of the car	0	5	4	0	0
Entertainment	0	5	4	0	0
Conducting contests	0	0	6	3	0
Conducting fairs and trade shows	0	6	3	0	0
Conducting sales meetings	0	6	3	0	0
Sponsoring events	0	0	6	3	0

Source: Survey Data

- Five car dealers opined that providing car loans to customers was very important, three opined that it was important and one said that it was less important.
- Six opined that allowing long test drives was important and three said it was less important.
- Six opined that training the sales executives to understand customer behaviour was very important and three said that it was important.
- Six opined that making sales calls by the sales force was very important and three said that it was important.
- Five opined that dealing with branded accessories inside the showroom was very important. Three said that it was important and one said that it was less important.
- Five opined that having an in-house spare parts center was very important. Three said that it was important and one said that it was less important.
- Six opined that having an in-house service center was extremely important. Two said very important and one said important.
- Three opined that having a stockyard near the showroom premises was important, five said less important and one said not important.
- One said having a toll-free number for the customers was less important and eight said it was not important.
- Five opined that having a prompt customer care service was very important and four said it important.
- Five opined that making charitable donations was less important and four said that it was not important.
- Five opined that building community relations was important and four said it less important.
- Five opined that demonstration of the working of the car was very important and four said that it was important.

- Five said that entertainment was very important and four said important.
- Six opined that conducting contests was important and three said less important.
- Six opined that conducting fairs and trade shows was very important and three said that it was important.
- Six opined that conducting sales meetings was very important and three said that it was important.
- Six opined that sponsoring events was important and three said that it was less important.

Maruti Car Dealers in Kerala

Maruti Car Dealers in Kerala help to protect the company's monopoly among the middle class Indians in the automobile sector.

The following are the Maruti Car Dealers in Kerala.

- Hercules automobiles International (P) Ltd
- Indus Motor Co Pvt. Ltd
- Popular Vehicles And Services Ltd
- Sai Service Station Ltd
- Har cars
- AVG Motors Pvt. Ltd
- A M Motors
- Sitaram Motors
- Sarathy Auto cars

Hyundai Car Dealers in Kerala

The following are the Hyundai car Dealers in Kerala.

- Hilton Hyundai
- KTC Hyundai
- MGF Hyundai
- Popular Hyundai
- TBG Hyundai
- APCO Hyundai

Tata Car Dealers in Kerala

- Koyenco Autos Pvt. Ltd
- Hyson Motors (P) Ltd
- Kulathungal Motors
- Focuz Motors
- R.F. Motors

Amana Toyota of Toyota Motors, Geeyem Motors (P) Ltd. and German Motors of General Motors, Marikkar Motors, ACC, PVS Ford and TVS Motors are the other car dealers in Kerala.

Car Manufacturers in Kerala

The three manufactures of cars (operating at the regional level) in Kerala namely, Maruti Udyog Limited, Hyundai Motors Limited, Tata Motors Limited were interviewed to know the importance of various factors that influenced the car purchase decision in the small car market in Kerala.

Importance of Factors Considered by Car Manufacturers

There are several factors that the car manufacturers considered as important. Table 12 exhibits the importance of various factors considered by car manufacturers in the small car market in Kerala. Among the various factors like car loans, in-house service centre, charitable contribution, test drives, sponsoring events, sales meet, entertainment, in-house stockyard and in-house spare parts centre, there are factors that car manufacturers consider as important and unimportant. The opinions of the three car manufacturers in Kerala have been different for the factors.

Out of the three car manufacturers interviewed across the northern, central and southern regions in Kerala the following observations were made:-

- Three of them opined that providing car loans to customers was very important.
- Three of the them opined that allowing long test drives was important.

Table 12
Importance of Various Factors Considered by Car Manufacturers in Kerala

	Extremely Important	*Very Important*	*Important*	*Less Important*	*Not Important*
Providing car loans to customer	0	3	0	0	0
Allowing long test drives	0	0	3	0	0
Training the sales executives to understand customer behaviour	0	3	0	0	0
Making sales calls by the sales force	0	0	3	0	0
Dealing with branded accessories inside the showroom	0	0	1	2	0
Having an in-house spare parts center	0	2	1	0	0
Having an in-house service center	2	1	0	0	0
Having a stockyard near the showroom premises	0	0	0	3	0
Having a toll-free number for the customers	0	0	0	0	3
Having a prompt customer care service	2	1	0	0	0
Making charitable donations	0	0	2	1	0
Building community relations	0	0	2	1	0
Demonstration of the working of the car	0	2	1	0	0
Entertainment	0	0	2	1	0
Conducting contests	0	0	3	0	0
Conducting fairs and trade shows	0	2	1	0	0
Conducting sales meetings	0	2	1	0	0
Sponsoring events	0	2	1	0	0

Source: Survey Data

- Three of them opined that training the sales executives to understand the customer behaviour was very important.
- Three of them opined that making sales calls by the sales force was important.
- One of them opined that dealing with branded accessories inside the showroom was important and two of them opined that it was less important,
- Two of them opined that having an in-house spare parts centre was very important and one of them said it as important.
- Two of them opined that having an in-house service center was extremely important and one of them said it was very important.
- Three of them said that having a stockyard near the showroom premises was less important,
- Three of them said that having a toll free number for the customers was not important.
- Two of them said that having a prompt customer care service was extremely important and one said that it was very important.
- Two of them said that making charitable donations was important and one said that it was less important.
- Two said that building community relations was important and one said it less important.
- Two of them said demonstration of the working of the car was very important and one said it important.
- Two of them said that entertainment was important and one said it was less important.
- All the three manufactures said that conducting context was important.
- Two of them said that conducting fairs and trade shows was very important and one said it important.
- Two of them said that conducting sales meetings was very important and one said it as important.

- Two of the manufactures opined that sponsoring events was very important and one said that it was important.

Boom Time for Car Buyers

Owning an automobile is no longer a matter of luxury; it has rather become a necessity of today's fast paced life. The burgeoning economy that has opened up new vistas of employment that promise attractive pay packets coupled with convenient loan products have contributed to this increasing demand for automobiles. The automobile manufacturers see India as fast growing market place with immense untapped potential and they are seen vying with one other to catch their share of the pie by introducing new models with improved features in quick succession.

A car, for many, is a prized possession. Ardent lovers of cars are found lavishing their time and money to maintain them in perfect condition. From technologically improved parts that promise a smooth drive to a whole range of accessories for the car's interiors, the market is flooded with multitude options for the buyer to choose from. To cater to the different categories of buyers, car manufacturers come out with different models in the small/entry, medium and large cars segment. The price of cars is largely based on the features enshrined in the car and varies from company to company. There are also options available in the fuel used in the car, ranging from petrol and diesel to even LPG.

If one goes by the different models that are seen plying on the roads, Kerala market appears to be a welcome recipient. Among the different cars, the most moving cars are those in entry level. "The availability of easy loans has increased the number of potential car buyers". Maruti 800 and Alto figure in small segment with a price range of Rs. 1.90 to Rs.3 lakhs.

Indica model of Tata Motors finds great favour among their customers. Indica is bracketed among the medium range cars (priced between Rs. 2.59 and 5.5 lakhs) of this company. Customers include NRIs, business people, Government officials and IT employees. Among Hyundai cars, it is the Santro that is the most movıng. This medium range car with four variants is priced between Rs. 2.69 and 3.77 lakhs (ex-showroom price). On preferred car colours, the metallic colours are more popular.

It has now become very easy to get an auto loan that comes with more than standard accessories. State Bank of India has come out with State Bank car loans at on road prices and with free accident insurance. Low interest rates, interest charged only on loan outstanding, no hidden costs and zero down payment are the features of SBI car loans. India is going to witness a plethora of small cars viz., Jazz from Honda, Yaris from Toyota and Nano from Tata motors.

It is the top-end variant that figures high in the sales of the Scorpio of Mahindra & Mahindra. This vehicle, priced over 8 lakhs, has special features like voice message, tiltable steering, de-fogger, fire resistant seats and wooden panelled dashboard. Speaking on the new variants of Scorpio cars, the new variants have 43 changes compared to the previous ones.

Coming to car loans, a quick scan reveals that the percentage of takers is high. Nearly 90 per cent of customers use loans for purchasing a car. Only 5 to 10% of customers pay cash for buying a car, the rest avail loans. While it is around 80% of Kulathungal's customers, Hilton Hyundai has 90% of its customers going in for car loans.

There is also available for purchase a whole range of vehicles in the used car segment. With different models of cars to fulfil varying requirements and multiple loan schemes, it appears that car buyers have never had it so easy.

REFERENCES

1. Datta, Yogyatta (1997), "Automobile Industry Analysis", *IIM Bangalore*, p. 59.
2. Datta, Yogyatta (1997), "Automobile Industry Analysis", *IIM Bangalore*, p. 69.
3. Jacob, Safra E. (2004), "The History of Transportation", *The New Encyclopaedia Britannica*, Vol. 28, 15th ed., April, pp. 781-785.
4. Madikonda, Kishore Babu and Raghunatha Reddy D. (2004), "A Study on Passenger Car Industry in India", *Indian Journal of Marketing*, Vol. 34, No. 10, October, p. 10.

5. Jacob, Safra E. (2004), "The History of Transportation", *The New Encyclopaedia Britannica,* Vol. 28, 15th ed., April, pp. 531-535.

6. Survey of Indian Industry (2008), *Four Wheeler Industry,* The Hindu, p. 300.

7. Shimokawa, Koichi (1985), "Automobile Industry-Out of Maturity Age", *Japanese,* Yuhikaku Publisher, Tokyo, pp. 131-132.

8. Fujimoto, Takahiro (1999), "Automotive Industry Handbook", *Japanese Automotive News,* June, pp. 12-25.

9. Minami, Ryochi (1999), "Globalization and Issues of the Automobile Components Industry in Japan", *Japan Automobile Manufacturers Association,* Tokyo, August, pp. 5-15.

10. Ikeda, Masataka (1999), "Japanese Automobiles and Automobile Component Industry", *Japan Automobile Industry Association,* August, pp.7-8.

11. Abunathy, W.J. (1978), "The Productive Dilemma: Road Blocks to Innovation in the Automobile Industry", *The John Hawkins University Press,* Baltimore, pp. 32-49.

12. Bloomfield, G. (1999), "The World Automotive Industry", *David Scharles Report,* London, pp. 8-19.

13. Car Survey (2009), *Car India,* Vol. 4, Issue 8, March, p. 70.

14. Menon, Sudha (2007), "Automotive Component Supplies", *Business Line,* Internet ed., The Hindu, Wednesday 18.

15. Agarwal, R.N. (2000), "Corporate Investment and Financing Behaviour: An Econometric Analysis", *Dissertation Published,* Delhi School of Economics, Delhi University, April, p. 1.

16. Datta, Yogyata (1997), "Automobile Industry Analysis", *Unpublished Dissertation,* IIM, Bangalore, April, p. 5.

17. Thomas, Biju (2008), "Automotive Component Parts", *Business Line,* Internet ed., The Hindu, Monday 27.

18. Gupta, Praveen (2008), "Passenger Car Industry", *Society of Automobile Manufacturers Association,* Vol. 2, August, pp. 12-15.

19. Menon, Shyam G. (2005), "Our Tie-up with Renault to Make Logan", *Business Line,* March, p.12.

20. Mishra, Rahul (2008), "Survey of Indian Industry", *Two Wheeler Industry,* The Hindu, p. 279.

21. Kumar, Raja K. and Pandu Ranga Rao (2008), "Indian Automobile Industry", *Excel books,* 1st ed., New Delhi.

22. Power Asia J.D. and Association (1998), "Customer Satisfaction Index", *Auto India*, November, pp. 54-61.

23. Kumar, Raja K. and Rao Pandu Ranga (2008), "Indian Automobile Industry", *Excel books*, 1st ed., New Delhi.

24. Mathew, Biju Thomas (2008), "A study on the Marketing of Passenger Cars", *Unpublished Thesis*, November .

4 Consumer Behaviour and Promotional Strategies in the Small Car Market

INTRODUCTION

A survey was conducted among 602 car owners across northern, central and southern regions of Kerala to study the influence of social and economic factors in the car purchase decision in the small car market. It was also enquired among the sample units to know the influence of promotional strategies adopted by the car manufacturers and car dealers in the small car market in Kerala. The various promotional tools used by car dealers are sales promotion, personal selling, advertisement, publicity and public relation, word of mouth and direct marketing. After the data collection from the sample units, it was subject to different statistical tools like Percentage Analysis, Chi-square Test, ANOVA and Factor Analysis to analyze the data and interpret them in order to summarize the findings and draw appropriate conclusions.

PERCENTAGE ANALYSIS

The Spread of Car Owners across Regions in Kerala

The sample units which are the car owners in the small car market in Kerala is spread across the three regions of Kerala viz., northern region, central region and the southern region. The region wise distribution of the car owners in Kerala is shown in Table 1.

Table 1
Region-wise Distribution of Car Owners in Kerala

Region	*Number of Respondents*	*Percentage*
Northern	203	33.7
Central	199	33.1
Southern	200	33.2
Total	602	100.0

Source: Survey Data

Table 1 shows that out of the 602 car owners surveyed in the small car market in Kerala, 33.7 per cent of the sample units were from the northern region, 33.1 percent were from the central region and 33.2 percent were from the southern region.

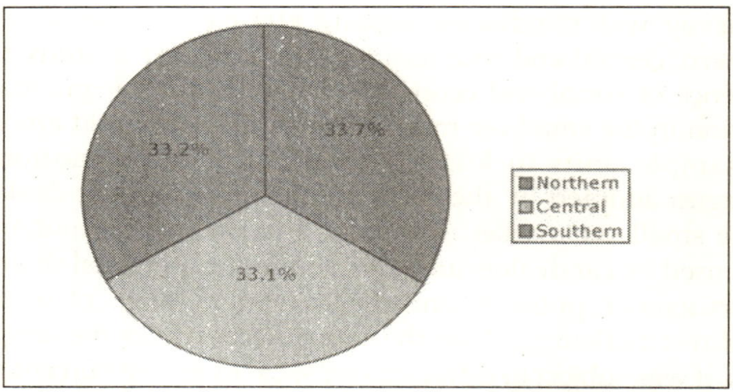

Figure 1: Car Owners Scores the Three Regions of Kerala

From the above figure, it can be seen that the sample units in all the regions are almost equally distributed depicting a uniform geographical representation of the population of the small car market in Kerala.

Spread of Car Owners across Urban and Rural Areas

The sample units which are the car owners in the small car market in Kerala are spread across the urban and rural areas of Kerala. The area wise distribution of the car owners in Kerala is shown in Table 2.

Table 2
Car Owners Spread across the Urban and Rural Areas of Kerala

Area	*Number of Respondents*	*Percentage*
Rural	298	49.5
Urban	304	50.5
Total	602	100.0

Source: Survey Data

As it can be seen from the above Table 2, 49.5% of the sample units represent rural area and 50.5% of the sample units represent urban area in Kerala.

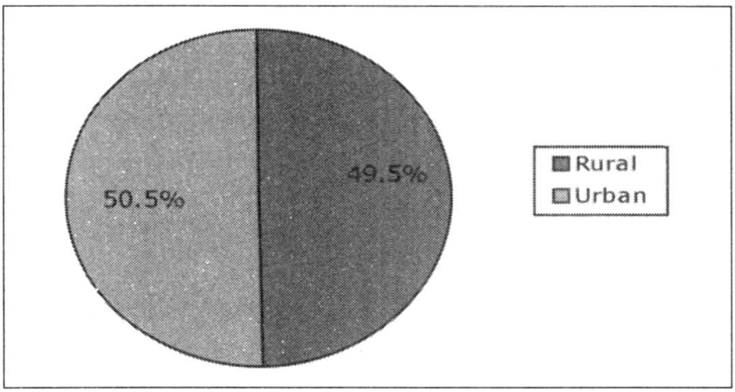

Figure 2: Car Owners Across the Urban and Rural Areas of Kerala

From the above Figure 2, it can be seen that the sample units representing the rural and urban areas in Kerala are almost equally distributed.

Brand of the Cars Owned by the Car Owners in Kerala

There are several brands in the small car market in Kerala viz., Maruti 800, Maruti Alto, Maruti Zen, Tata Indica, Hyundai Santro and WagonR. The small car market in Kerala is abundant in small cars with a wide variety of models and attractive features catering to the tastes and preferences of consumers in Kerala. These cars are sold through dealer outlets at various places convenient to the public at large.

As it could be seen from Table 3 below, 31.4% of the car owners own Maruti 800, 18.1% own Maruti Alto, 8.8% own Maruti Zen, 16.6% own Tata Indica, 14.1% own Santro, 8.5% own WagonR and 2.5% own other small cars.

Table 3
Brand of Cars Owned by the Car Owners in Kerala

Brand	*Number of Respondents*	*Percentage*
Maruti 800	189	31.4
Maruti Alto	109	18.1
Maruti Zen	53	8.8
Tata Indica	100	16.6
Santro	85	14.1
Wagon R	51	8.5
Others	15	2.5
Total	602	100.0

Source: Survey Data

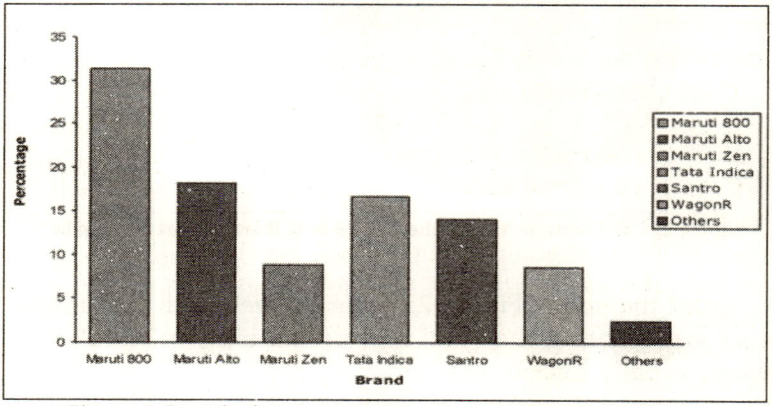

Figure 3: Brand of Cars Owned by the Car Owners in Kerala

As it could be seen from the above Figure 3, 31.4% of the sample units own Maruti 800, 18.1% own Maruti Alto, 8.8% own Maruti Zen, 16.6% own Tata Indica, 14.1% own Hyundai Santro, 8.5 % own Wagon R and 2.5% own other cars like Maruti swift, Daewoo Matiz and Fiat Padmini. From this we infer that Maruti 800 car is used by majority of the car owners in Kerala.

Influence of Social Factors

A car purchase decision could be influenced by many social factors like friends, relatives, neighbours and own family members. These social factors exercise their influence differently across the regions, areas, income groups, age, gender and occupation. Table 4 exhibits the general influence of social factors in the car purchase decision in Kerala.

Table 4
Influence of Social Factors

Social Factors	*Number of Respondents*	*Percentage*
Friends	148	24.6
Relatives	65	10.8
Own Family Members	247	41.0
Neighbours	21	3.5
Own Decision	118	19.6
Others	3	0.5
Total	602	100.0

Source: Survey Data

Table 4 discloses that 24.6% of the car owners are influenced by friends, 10.8 % by relatives, 41% by own family members 3.5% by neighbours, 19.6% by one's own decision, 0.5% by others.

Influence of Family Members

A car purchase decision is influenced by family members like wife/husband, children, father, mother and siblings. The social cultural factors, which pivot around the fulcrum of decision making in families, play a vital role in influencing not only the purchase decision of the husband or the wife but also other family members like father, mother and children. Cognitive theorists are concerned with how information is processed by human mind. It is also interesting to know how information is stored, retained and retrieved in the human mind. Similarly, car manufacturers and dealers are evincing keen interest in unearthing these inner Psychological traits of consumers to market their products profitably.

Table 5
Influence of Family Members

Family Members	*Number of Respondents*	*Percentage*
Wife/Husband	395	65.5
Children	29	4.8
Father	75	12.5
Mother	36	6.0
Siblings	66	11.0
Others	1	.2
Total	602	100.0

Source: Survey Data

Table 5 exhibits that 65.5% of the car owners are influenced by wife/husband, 4.8% by children, 12.5% by father, 6% by mother, 11% by siblings and 0.2% by others.

Average Ranking of Promotional Tools

A car purchase decision could be influenced by promotional tools like newspaper, television, radio, internet, magazines, word of mouth, car shows and melas, test drive, exchange melas/loan melas and others. The extent to which promotional tools influence the car purchase decision will depend on the social, cultural and economic environment around which consumers pivot themselves. The consumer decision making depends on the promotional tools targeted on the consumers and channels through which cars are marketed. The average ranking of promotional tools is shown in Table 6.

Table 6
Average Ranking of Promotional Tools

Promotional Tools	*Average Ranking*
Newspaper	4.62
TV	4.05
Radio	7.15
Internet	4.15
Advertisement in magazine	3.97
Word of mouth	1.99
Car shows & other melas	6.03
Test drive	4.96
Exchange melas/loan melas	8.20
Others	9.85

Source: Survey Data

As it could be seen from the Table 6, among the different promotional tools that influence the car purchase decision 'word of mouth' is ranked the highest (1.99) followed by advertisement in magazine (3.97) and the least ranked among them is exchange melas and loan melas ranked as 8.20. The above ranking was calculated by simple average method.

Influence of Price

Price plays an important role in influencing the car purchase decision in the small car market in Kerala. Price is also an important determinant in deciding the model of a car to be purchased by an individual or a family household. A consumer prefers a small car or a large car depending upon his disposable income and repayment capacity.

Table 7
Influence of Price

Opinion	*Number of Respondents*	*Percentage*
Strongly Disagree	7	1.2
Disagree	21	3.5
Undecided	65	10.8
Agree	99	16.4
Strongly Agree	410	68.1
Total	602	100.0

Source: Survey Data

As seen from Table 7, the percentage of people who strongly disagreed to the opinion that price is an important factor in the car purchase decision was 1.2%, who disagreed were 3.5%, who agreed were 16.45% and who strongly agreed were 68.1%.

Influence of Mileage

Influence of mileage plays an important role in influencing the car purchase decision in Kerala.

Table 8 shows that the percentage of people who strongly disagreed to the opinion that mileage is an important factor in the car purchase decision was 0.5%, who disagreed were 2.7%, who agreed were 12.8% and who strongly agreed were 73.4%.

Table 8
Influence of Mileage

Opinion	*Number of Respondents*	*Percentage*
Strongly Disagree	3	0.5
Disagree	16	2.7
Undecided	64	10.6
Agree	77	12.8
Strongly Agree	442	73.4
Total	602	100.0

Source: Survey Data

Influence of Brand

Influence of brand plays an important role in influencing the car purchase decision in Kerala. The positioning of a brand of car in the minds of the consumers is challenging and an arduous task for promotion managers who are involved in building brand equity for the products, especially in the car market in Kerala.

Table 9
Influence of Brand

Opinion	*Number of Respondents*	*Percentage*
Strongly Disagree	63	10.5
Disagree	101	16.8
Undecided	169	28.1
Agree	77	12.8
Strongly Agree	192	31.8
Total	602	100.0

Source: Survey Data

Table 9 reveals that the percentage of people who strongly disagreed to the opinion that brand is an important factor in the car purchase decision was 10.5%, who disagreed were 16.8%, who agreed were 12.8% and who strongly agreed were 31.8%.

Influence of Design and Style

Design and style plays an important role in influencing the car purchase decision in Kerala. A car is determined as efficient and performing depending on the design in which it is made.

Good designers like Chaabria and Richard Wagner have made their mark in the car industry by designing highly appealing and attractive car models suiting to the tastes and preferences of car buyers. Hence, design and style is an important variable contributing to the aesthetic factor of a car, which has to be apportioned sufficient time, money and effort to satisfy the car buyers.

Table 10
Influence of Design and Style

Opinion	*Number of Respondents*	*Percentage*
Strongly Disagree	50	8.3
Disagree	108	17.9
Undecided	158	26.3
Agree	106	17.6
Strongly Agree	180	29.9
Total	602	100.0

Source: Survey Data

Table 10 discloses that the percentage of people who strongly disagreed to the opinion that design and style is an important factor in the car purchase decision was 8.3%, who disagreed were 17.9%, who agreed were 17.6% and who strongly agreed were 29.9%.

Influence of After Sales Service

After sales service plays an important role in influencing the car purchase decision in Kerala. The after sales service rendered by car dealers is determined by several factors like the service staff, number of service centres, delivery of the vehicle in time and expense of car service. The car dealers of Kerala have been vying with each other in rendering prompt and efficient after sales service to the car buyers to satisfy them in all aspects of customer delight.

As it can be observed from Table 11, the percentage of people who strongly disagreed to the opinion that after sales service is an important factor in the car purchase decision was 3.3%, who disagreed were 11.0%, who agreed were 39.5% and who strongly agreed were 8%.

Table 11
Influence of After Sales Service

Opinion	*Number of Respondents*	*Percentage*
Strongly Disagree	20	3.3
Disagree	66	11.0
Undecided	230	38.2
Agree	238	39.5
Strongly Agree	48	8.0
Total	602	100.0

Source: Survey Data

Influence of Impressive Advertisements

Among the different promotional tools, impressive advertisements have influenced the car owners in their purchase decision in Kerala. The advertisement message, advertisement copy and the five M's of advertisement viz., mission, money, message, media and measurement are important in determining the effectiveness of an advertisement. The media through which cars can be advertised are viz., print media and electronic media. The print media comprises newspapers, magazines and periodicals. The electronic media comprises Television, Radio and Internet.

Table 12
Influence of Impressive Advertisements

Opinion	*Number of Respondents*	*Percentage*
Strongly Disagree	72	12.0
Disagree	73	12.1
Undecided	104	17.3
Agree	212	35.2
Strongly Agree	141	23.4
Total	602	100.0

Source: Survey Data

As it can be seen from Table 12, the percentage of people who strongly disagreed to the opinion that impressive advertisement is an important factor in the car purchase decision was 12%, who disagreed were 12.1%, who agreed were 35.2% and who strongly agreed were 23.4%.

Influence of Discounts

Among the sales promotion tools, discounts have influenced the car purchase decision in the small car market. Discounts can be offered as cash discounts, rebates, and coupons for availing the facility of buying a car at cheaper rates. Car buyers are influenced by the most competitive discounts offered by car manufacturers and dealers. Discounts are good enticements in attracting car buyers to make a good choice among the different varieties of car models in the car market.

Table 13
Influence of Discounts

Opinion	*Number of Respondents*	*Percentage*
Strongly Disagree	33	5.5
Disagree	61	10.1
Undecided	82	13.7
Agree	158	26.2
Strongly Agree	268	44.5
Total	602	100.0

Source: Survey Data

As it can be observed from Table 13, the percentage of people who strongly disagreed to the opinion that discount is an important factor in the car purchase decision was 5.5%, who disagreed were 10.1%, who agreed were 26.2% and who strongly agreed were 44.5%.

Source of Fund

There are several sources of funds for the purchase of cars like commercial banks, private financiers, NBFC and one's own fund. The commercial banks in the public sector have been offering loans for the purchase of car at low interest rate when compared to that of private banks. The NBFC's have also entered in to the market of car financing expecting a good chunk of the car market, which has predominantly been a competitor for the private, and public sector banks. Friends and relatives have also been a good source of fund for the purchase of a car. This is because of the fact that friends and relatives can be relied upon as an easily accessible source of money.

Table 14 highlights the following facts. 9% of the car owners preferred NBFC as the source of their car purchase. 58.8% preferred commercial banks, 11.3% preferred private financiers, 5.1% preferred friends and relatives and 15.8% relied on their own fund.

Table 14
Source of Fund

Source	*Number of Respondents*	*Percentage*
NBFC	54	9.0
Commercial Bank	354	58.8
Private Financiers	68	11.3
Friends/Relatives	31	5.1
Self	95	15.8
Total	602	100.0

Source: Survey Data

Pre-owned Car Outlets

The pre owned car outlets or used car outlets in Kerala has influenced the car purchase decision among the people of Kerala. The Indian used car market is in a very nascent stage and dominated by the unorganized sector. Quality and reliability of pre-owned cars available through the unorganized sector is often not up to the mark. The pre-owned car outlets of Maruti Udyog Ltd are called as 'True Value' outlets, the pre owned car outlets of Hyundai motors are called as 'Hyundai Advantage' and 'Tata Assured' for Tata motors.

Table 15
Opinion of Pre-owned Car Outlets

Opinion	*Number of Respondents*	*Percentage*
Very Good	21	3.5
Good	180	29.9
Bad	233	38.7
Very Bad	98	16.3
No opinion	70	11.6
Total	602	100.0

Source: Survey Data

From Table 15 it could be seen that 3.5% opined that the pre-owned car outlets in Kerala are very good, 29.9 % opined it as good, 38.7% opined it as bad, 16.3% opined it as very bad and 11.6% had no opinion about the pre-owned car outlets operating in Kerala.

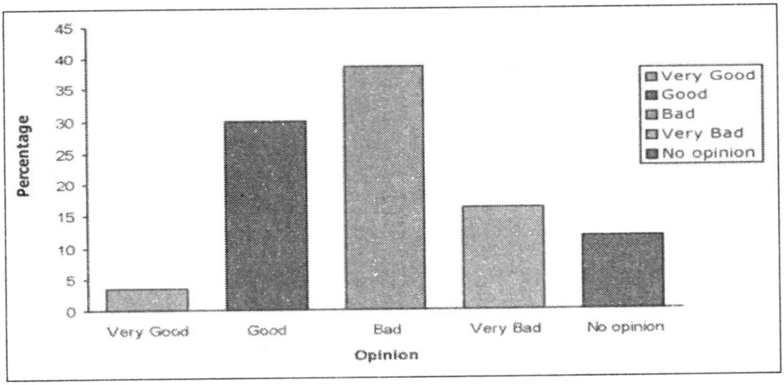

Figure 4: Opinion of Pre-owned Car Outlets

Figure 4 depicts the opinions of the car owners towards the pre-owned car outlets operating in Kerala.

CHI – SQUARE ANALYSIS

Social Factors

A car purchase decision could be influenced by many social factors like friends, relatives, neighbours and own family members. The reference groups namely, contractual groups, disclaimant group and aspirational groups play an important role in the purchase behaviour of a car buyer. Table 16 reveals that out of 203 car owners from northern region, 36 were influenced by friends, 27 were influenced by relatives, 78 were influenced by own family members, 9 were influenced by nieghbours and 53 were influenced by their own decision. Out of the 199 car owners from central region, 47 were influenced by friends, 13 were influenced by relatives, 85 were influenced by own family members, 5 were influenced by neighbours and

49 were influenced by own decision. Out of the 200 car owners from southern region, 65 were influenced by friends, 25 were influenced by relatives, 84 were influenced by own family members, 7 were influenced by neighbours and 19 were influenced by own decision.

Table 16
Influence of Social Factors in the Car Purchase Decision Among the Regions in Kerala

Region	*Social Factors*					*Total*
	Friends	*Relatives*	*Own Family Members*	*Neighbours*	*Own Decision*	
Northern	36	27	78	9	53	203
Central	47	13	85	5	49	199
Southern	65	25	84	7	19	200
Total	148	65	247	21	121	602

Chi-square value = 33.515, degrees of freedom = 10, p value = 0.00
Source: Survey Data

Since the p value (0.00) is less than the 0.05 level of significance, the researcher rejects the null hypothesis that there is no association between the region in which the car owner is situated and the social factors influencing the car purchase decision. Hence it is concluded that there is significant association between the region and the social factors influencing the car purchase decision. Table 16 reveals that the number of people who take a decision on their own regarding a car purchase is more in the northern region than in the central and southern regions. The number of people who depend on their friends for a car purchase decision is more in the southern region than in the northern and central regions.

Family Members as Social Factors

A car purchase decision could be influenced by the members of one's own family like wife, husband, children father, mother, siblings and grand parents. As it can be observed from Table 17 that out of the 203 car owners from the northern region, 107 were influenced by their wives or husbands, 12 were influenced by children, 27 were influenced by father, 23 were influenced by mother and 34 was influenced by siblings. Out of the 199 car owners from the central region, 128 were influenced by their wives or husbands, 14 were influenced by children, 32 were influenced by father, 12 were influenced by mother and 13 was influenced by siblings. Out of the 200 car owners from the southern region, 160 were influenced by their wives or husbands, 3 were influenced by children, 16 were influenced by father, 1 was influenced by mother and 20 were influenced by siblings.

Table 17
Influence of Family Members in the Car Purchase Decision Among the Regions in Kerala

Region	*Family Members*					*Total*
	Wife/ Husband	*Children*	*Father*	*Mother*	*Siblings*	
Northern	107	12	27	23	34	203
Central	128	14	32	12	13	199
Southern	160	3	16	1	20	200
Total	395	29	75	36	67	602

Chi-square value = 55.940, degrees of freedom = 10, p value = 0.00
Source: Survey Data

The p value (0.00) being less than the 0.05 level of significance, the researcher rejects the null hypothesis that there is no association between the region in which the car owner is situated and the family members influencing the car purchase decision. Hence it is concluded that there is significant association between the region and the family members influencing the car purchase decision. As it can be seen from Table 17 that the husband or wife in a family contributes the most in the car purchase decision in the southern region than in the central and northern regions. The role of children in the family decision making in the purchase of a car is more in the central region than in the northern and southern regions.

Advertisement

Advertisement plays a very important role in the car purchase decision in Kerala. Advertisements in the print media and in the electronic media have influenced the decision in purchasing a car in the different regions of Kerala. It was enquired whether advertisement was an important factor in the car purchase decision. Table 18 discloses that out of the 203 car owners in the northern region, 35 of them strongly agreed with this opinion and 86 of them agreed with this opinion and 16 of them strongly disagreed with this opinion and 13 of them disagreed with this opinion. In the central regional, out of 199 car owners 77 of them strongly agreed with the opinion and 28 of them agreed with the opinion and 25 of them strongly disagreed with the opinion and 48 of them disagreed with the opinion. Out of the 200 car owners in the southern region, 29 strongly agreed and 31 strongly disagreed.

Table 18
Importance of Advertisement in the Car Purchase Decision

Region	*Opinion*					*Total*
	Strongly Disagree	*Disagree*	*Undecided*	*Agree*	*Strongly Agree*	
Northern	16	13	53	86	35	203
Central	25	48	21	28	77	199
Southern	31	12	30	98	29	200
Total	72	73	104	212	141	602

Chi-square value = 124.159, degrees of freedom =8, p value = 0.00
Source: Survey Data

As it can be observed that the p value (0.00) being less than the 0.05 level of significance, the researcher rejects the null hypothesis that there is no association between the region in which the car owner is situated and the importance of advertisement in influencing the car purchase decision. Hence it is concluded that there is significant association between the region and the importance of advertisement in influencing the car purchase decision.

Sales Promotion

Sales promotion plays a very important role in the car purchase decision in Kerala. Sales promotion like free offers, free service and other freebies has influenced the decision in purchasing a car in the different regions of Kerala. It was enquired whether the car owners felt that sales promotion was an important factor in the car purchase decision. Table 19 reveals that out of the 203 car owners in the central region 80 of them strongly agreed with this opinion, 50 of them agreed with the opinion, 20 strongly disagreed with the opinion and 27 disagreed with the opinion. In the southern region, out of the 200 car owners, 107 of them strongly agreed with this opinion, 55 agreed with the opinion, 7 strongly disagreed with the opinion and 13 disagreed with the opinion.

Table 19
Importance of Sales Promotion in the Car Purchase Decision

	Opinion					
Region	*Strongly Disagree*	*Disagree*	*Undecided*	*Agree*	*Strongly Agree*	*Total*
Northern	6	21	42	53	81	203
Central	20	27	22	50	80	199
Southern	7	13	18	55	107	200
Total	33	61	82	158	268	602

Chi-square value = 33.493, degrees of freedom =8, p value = 0.00
Source: Survey Data

Since the p value (0.00) is less than the 0.05 level of significance, the researcher rejects the null hypothesis that there is no association between the region in which the car owner is situated and the importance of sales promotion in influencing the car purchase decision. Hence it is concluded that there is significant association between the region and the importance of sales promotion in influencing the car purchase decision. The reason for this association is that the number of respondents in the southern region who opined that the sales promotion is important was due to the fact that the corporate offer given to government employees is much higher than the offers given to the other people. Moreover the car owners in the southern region were more of government employees when compared to the central and northern regions in Kerala.

Sales Promotion Tools

Sales promotion plays a very important role in the car purchase decision in Kerala. Sales promotion tools like discounts, free insurance, exemption from road tax and free accessories has influenced the decision in purchasing a car in the different regions of Kerala. As it can be observed from Table 20 that out of the 325 car owners whom discounts influenced the most, 129 of them were from southern region, 81 from central region and 115 from northern region. Out of the 155 car owners whom free insurance influenced the most, 26 of them were from southern region, 80 and 49 from central and northern region respectively. Out of the 57 car owners whom road tax exemption influenced the most, 14 of them were from the southern region, 21 and 20 from the central and northern region respectively. Out of the 44 car owners whom free accessories influenced the most, 18 of them were from the southern region and 13 each were from the central and northern region respectively.

Table 20
Influence of Sales Promotion in the Car Purchase Decision

Region	*Sales Promotion Tools*					*Total*
	Discount	*Free Insurance*	*Exemption from Road Tax*	*Free Accessories*	*Others*	
Northern	115	49	22	13	2	201
Central	81	80	21	13	4	199
Southern	129	26	14	18	12	199
Total	325	155	57	44	18	599

Chi-square value = 52.267. degrees of freedom =8, p value = 0.00
Source: Survey Data

Since the p value (0.00) is less than the 0.05 level of significance, the researcher rejects the null hypothesis that there is no association between the region in which the car owner is situated and the importance of sales promotion in influencing the car purchase decision. Hence it can be concluded that there is significant association between the region and the importance of sales promotion in influencing the car purchase decision. Thus it can be said that the influence of discounts is more in the northern and southern region than in the central region of the Kerala and the influence of free insurance is more in the central region than in the northern and southern region.

Replacing the Previous Car

It has been observed from the study that there are several factors that are responsible for the sample units to replace their previous cars. The factors responsible for replacing their previous cars are increased income, large family size, availability of car financing schemes, life of the car, attractive models, maintenance cost, service quality and exchange programme. It was enquired as to how many car owners replaced their previous cars due to the above factors.

Income Factor

It was enquired whether car owners thought that increased income led to the purchase of a costlier car. Table 21 reveals that out of 45 car owners interviewed in the northern region, 25 of them strongly agreed to the opinion that cars provide more safety than two-wheelers, 7 of them agreed to the opinion, 11 disagreed to the opinion. Out of the 59 car owners interviewed in the central region, 17 strongly agreed to the opinion, 5 agreed to the opinion, 34 disagreed to the opinion. Out of the 53 car owners interviewed in the southern region, 11 of them strongly agreed to the opinion, 10 agreed to the opinion, 27 disagreed to the opinion.

The p value (0.00) being less than the 0.05 level of significance, the researcher rejects the null hypothesis that there is no association between the region in which the car owner is situated and the increased income in influencing the car purchase decision. Hence it can be concluded that there is significant association between the region and the increased

Table 21
Increased Income Led to the Purchase of a Costlier Car

Region	*Opinion*				*Total*
	Disagree	*Undecided*	*Agree*	*Strongly Agree*	
Northern	11	2	7	25	45
Central	34	3	5	17	59
Southern	27	5	10	11	53
Total	72	10	22	53	157

Chi-square value = 33.160. degrees of freedom = 6, p value = 0.00
Source: Survey Data

income in influencing the car purchase decision. Thus it can be said that the influence of increased income in the purchase of costlier car is more in the northern than in the southern region.

Increase in the Family Size

It was enquired whether car owners thought that increase in the family size was the reason for replacing the previous car. Table 22 exhibits that out of 45 car owners interviewed in the northern region, 17 of them strongly agreed to the opinion that cars provide more safety than two-wheelers, 2 of them agreed to the opinion, 18 disagreed to the opinion. Out of the 59 car owners interviewed in the central region, 13 strongly agreed to the opinion, 4 agreed to the opinion, 32 disagreed to the opinion. Out of the 53 car owners interviewed in the southern region, 7 of them strongly agreed to the opinion, 9 agreed to the opinion, 25 disagreed to the opinion.

At 0.05 level of significance, the p value (0.014) being less, the researcher rejects the null hypothesis that there is no association between the region in which the car owner is situated and the increased family size in influencing the car purchase decision. Hence it can be concluded that there is significant association between the region and the increased family size in influencing the car purchase decision. Thus it can be said that the influence of increased family size in the replacement of the previous car is more in the northern than in the southern region.

Table 22
Increase in the Family Size Led to a Bigger Car

Region	*Opinion*					*Total*
	Strongly Disagree	*Disagree*	*Undecided*	*Agree*	*Strongly Agree*	
Northern	2	18	6	2	17	45
Central	2	32	8	4	13	59
Southern	8	25	4	9	7	53
Total	12	75	18	15	37	157

Chi-square value = 19.104. degrees of freedom = 8, p value = 0.014
Source: Survey Data

Financing Scheme

It was enquired whether car owners thought that increase in the family size was the reason for replacing the previous car. Table 23 highlights that out of 45 car owners interviewed in the northern region, 5 of them strongly agreed to the opinion that cars provide more safety than two wheelers, 7 of them agreed to the opinion, 18 disagreed to the opinion. Out of the 59 car owners interviewed in the central region, 10 strongly agreed to the opinion, 7 agreed to the opinion, 36 disagreed to the opinion. Out of the 53 car owners interviewed in the southern region, 1 of them strongly agreed to the opinion, 3 agreed to the opinion, 27 disagreed to the opinion.

Table 23
Financing Schemes Led to Replacement

Region	*Opinion*					*Total*
	Strongly Disagree	*Disagree*	*Undecided*	*Agree*	*Strongly Agree*	
Northern	2	18	13	7	5	45
Central	3	36	3	7	10	59
Southern	10	27	12	3	1	53
Total	15	81	28	17	16	157

Chi-square value = 27.178. degrees of freedom = 8, p value = 0.001
Source: Survey Data

Since the p value (0.001) is less than the 0.05 level of significance, the researcher rejects the null hypothesis that there is no association between the region in which the car owner is situated and the financing schemes in influencing the car purchase decision. Hence it can be concluded that there is significant association between the region and the financing schemes in influencing the car purchase decision. Thus it can be said that the influence of financing schemes which led to the replacement of the previous car was more in the central region than in the southern region.

Life of the Car

It was enquired whether car owners thought that increase in the family size was the reason for replacing the previous car. Table 24 reveals that out of 45 car owners interviewed in the northern region, 2 of them strongly agreed to the opinion that cars provide more safety than two-wheelers, 12 of them agreed to the opinion, 18 disagreed to the opinion. Out of the 59 car owners interviewed in the central region, 9 strongly agreed to the opinion, 6 agreed to the opinion, 36 disagreed to the opinion. Out of the 53 car owners interviewed in the southern region, 6 of them strongly agreed to the opinion, 8 agreed to the opinion, 20 disagreed to the opinion.

Table 24
Life Period of the Car was Over

	Opinion					
Region	*Strongly Disagree*	*Disagree*	*Undecided*	*Agree*	*Strongly Agree*	*Total*
Northern	5	18	8	12	2	45
Central	1	36	7	6	9	59
Southern	6	20	13	8	6	53
Total	12	74	28	26	17	157

Chi-square value = 17.852. degrees of freedom = 8, p value = 0.022
Source: Survey Data

The p value (0.022) being less than the 0.05 level of significance, the researcher rejects the null hypothesis that there is no association between the region in which the car owner is situated and the life of the car in influencing the car purchase decision. Hence it can be concluded that there is significant association between the region and the life of the car in influencing the car purchase decision. Thus, it can be said that the influence of life of the car, which led to the replacement of the previous car, was more in the central region than in the northern region.

Maintenance Cost

Maintenance cost is an important factor that determines whether a previous car should be replaced by a new car. The performance of a car can be affected by the huge maintenance problems that a car can have. The variables involved in determining the maintenance of a car are the life of spare parts used, driving style, road conditions and the application of brakes. It was enquired whether car owners thought that increase in the maintenance cost was the reason for replacing the previous car. Table 25 exhibits that out of 45 car owners interviewed in the northern region, 3 of them strongly agreed to the opinion that cars provide more safety than two-wheelers, 7 of them agreed to the opinion, 19 disagreed to the opinion. Out of the 59 car owners interviewed in the central region, 9 strongly agreed to the opinion, 8 agreed to the opinion, 34 disagreed to the opinion. Out of the 53 car owners interviewed in the southern region, 2 of them strongly agreed to the opinion, 6 agreed to the opinion, 23 disagreed to the opinion.

Table 25
Increase in the Maintenance Cost

Region	*Opinion*					*Total*
	Strongly Disagree	*Disagree*	*Undecided*	*Agree*	*Strongly Agree*	
Northern	3	19	13	7	3	45
Central	3	34	5	8	9	59
Southern	5	23	17	6	2	53
Total	11	76	35	21	14	157

Chi-square value = 19.296. degrees of freedom = 8, p value = 0.013
Source: Survey Data

Since the p value (0.013) is less than the 0.05 level of significance, the researcher rejects the null hypothesis that there is no association between the region in which the car owner is situated and the increase in the maintenance cost in influencing the car purchase decision. Hence it can be concluded that there is significant association between the region and the increase in the maintenance cost in influencing the car purchase decision. Thus it can be said that the influence of increase in the maintenance cost which led to the replacement of the previous car was more in the central region than in the southern region.

Upgrading from Two-wheelers to Cars

There are several factors that account for the shifting of people from two-wheelers to cars. The various factors responsible for shifting from two-wheelers to cars are safety, convenience for a family to travel, status symbol, neighbour possessing a car, value for money spent on cars, car loan availability, increased disposable income, after sales service and desire for a change. It was enquired as to how many car owners shifted from two-wheelers to cars due to the above factors. Hence there could be more than one factor that is responsible for the shifting from two wheelers to cars.

Safety Factor

It was enquired whether car owners thought that safety was the most important factor in the shifting from two-wheelers to cars. Table 26 discloses that out of 164 car owners interviewed in the northern region, 125 of them strongly agreed to the opinion that cars provide more safety than two-wheelers, 30 of them agreed to the opinion, 5 disagreed to the opinion and one strongly disagreed with the opinion. Out of the 164 car owners interviewed in the central region, 102 strongly agreed to the opinion, 53 agreed to the opinion, 3 disagreed to the opinion and 2 strongly disagreed to the opinion. Out of the 159 car owners interviewed in the southern region, 141 of them strongly agreed to the opinion, 12 agreed to the opinion, 3 disagreed to the opinion and none strongly disagreed to the opinion.

Table 26
Cars Provide More Safety than Two-wheelers

Region	*Opinion*					*Total*
	Strongly Disagree	*Disagree*	*Undecided*	*Agree*	*Strongly Agree*	
Northern	1	5	3	30	125	164
Central	2	3	4	53	102	164
Southern	0	3	3	12	141	159
Total	3	11	10	95	368	487

Chi-square value =35.900, degrees of freedom = 8, p value = 0.00
Source: Survey Data

At 0.05 level of significance, the p value (0.00) is less, the researcher rejects the null hypothesis that there is no association between the region in which the car owner is situated and the opinion of the car owners that cars provide more safety than two-wheelers. Hence it can be concluded that there is significant association between the region and the opinion of the car owners that cars provide more safety than two-wheelers. Thus it can be said that the car owners who opine that cars are safer than two-wheelers are more in the southern region than in the central region.

Convenience Factor

It was enquired whether car owners considered that the convenience for a family to travel was an important factor in the shifting from two-wheelers to cars. Table 27 shows that out of 164 car owners interviewed in the northern region, 121 of them strongly agreed to the opinion that cars are more convenient for a family to travel than two-wheelers, 34 of them agreed to the opinion, 3 disagreed to the opinion and 2 strongly disagreed to the opinion. Out of the 164 car owners interviewed in the central region, 107 of them strongly agreed to the opinion, 49 agreed to the opinion, 2 disagreed to the opinion and none strongly disagreed to the opinion. Out of the 159 car owners interviewed in the southern region, 142 of them strongly agreed to the opinion, 9 of them agreed to the opinion, 4 of them disagreed to the opinion and none strongly disagreed to the opinion. Also, the majority of the people are of the opinion that cars are more convenient for a family to travel and this is the reason why people shift from two-wheelers to cars. Moreover a family comprises more than two people, hence travelling by a car will be more convenient than travelling by a two-wheeler.

Table 27
Convenient for a Family to Travel

Region	*Opinion*					*Total*
	Strongly Disagree	*Disagree*	*Undecided*	*Agree*	*Strongly Agree*	
Northern	2	3	4	34	121	164
Central	0	2	6	49	107	164
Southern	0	4	4	9	142	159
Total	2	9	14	92	370	487

Chi-square value =37.021, degrees of freedom = 8, p value = 0.00
Source: Survey Data

Since the p value (0.00) is less than the 0.05 level of significance, the researcher rejects the null hypothesis that there is no association between the region in which the car owner is situated and the opinion of the car owners that cars are more convenient for a family to travel. Hence it can be concluded that there is significant association between the region and the opinion of the car owners that cars are more convenient for a family to travel. Thus it can be said that the car owners who opine that cars are more convenient for a family to travel are more in the southern region than in the central region.

Status Factor

It was enquired whether car owners considered that possessing a car is a status symbol was an important factor in the shifting from two-wheelers to cars. Table 28 exhibits that out of 164 car owners interviewed in the northern region regarding this opinion, 81 of them strongly agreed to the opinion that cars are a status symbol than two-wheelers, 15 of them agreed to the opinion, 35 disagreed to the opinion and 15 strongly disagreed to the opinion. Out of the 164 car owners interviewed in the central region, 92 of them strongly agreed to the opinion,

14 agreed to the opinion, 20 disagreed to the opinion and 35 strongly disagreed to the opinion. Out of the 159 car owners interviewed in the southern region, 105 of them strongly agreed to the opinion, 17 of them agreed to the opinion, 12 of them disagreed to the opinion and 9 strongly disagreed to the opinion.

Table 28
Owning a Car is a Status Symbol

Region	*Opinion*					*Total*
	Strongly Disagree	*Disagree*	*Undecided*	*Agree*	*Strongly Agree*	
Northern	15	35	18	15	81	164
Central	35	20	3	14	92	164
Southern	9	12	16	17	105	159
Total	59	67	37	46	278	487

Chi-square value = 45.089, degrees of freedom = 8, p value = 0.00
Source: Survey Data

The p value (0.00) being less than the 0.05 level of significance, the researcher rejects the null hypothesis that there is no association between the region in which the car owner is situated and the opinion of the car owners that possessing a car is a status symbol was an important factor in the shifting from two-wheelers to cars. Hence it can be concluded that there is significant association between the region and the opinion of the car owners that possessing a car is a status symbol was an important factor in the shifting from two-wheelers to cars.

Neighbourhood

It was enquired whether car owners considered that neighbour possessing a car was an important factor in the shifting from two-wheelers to cars. Table 29 throws light on the fact that out of 164 car owners interviewed in the northern region regarding the opinion that neighbour possessing a car was an important factor in the shifting from two-wheelers to cars, 7 of them strongly agreed to the opinion that neighbour possessing a car was an important factor in the shifting from two-wheelers to cars, 8 of them agreed to the opinion, 65 disagreed to the opinion and 55 strongly disagreed to the opinion. Out of the 164 car owners interviewed in the central region, 4 of them strongly agreed to the opinion, 2 agreed to the opinion, 58 disagreed to the opinion and 58 strongly disagreed to the opinion. Out of the 158 car owners interviewed in the southern region, 7 of them strongly agreed to the opinion, 13 of them agreed to the opinion, 44 of them disagreed to the opinion and 41 strongly disagreed to the opinion.

Table 29
Neighbour Possessing a Car

Region	*Opinion*					*Total*
	Strongly Disagree	*Disagree*	*Undecided*	*Agree*	*Strongly Agree*	
Northern	55	65	29	8	7	164
Central	58	58	42	2	4	164
Southern	41	44	53	13	7	158
Total	154	167	124	23	18	486

Chi-square value = 23.218, degrees of freedom = 8, p value = 0.003
Source: Survey Data

At the 0.05 level of significance, the p value (0.03) being less, the researcher rejects the null hypothesis that there is no association between the region in which the car owner is situated and the opinion of the car owners that neighbour possessing a car was an important factor in the shifting from two-wheelers to cars. Hence it can be concluded that there is significant association between the region and the opinion of the car owners that neighbour possessing a car was an important factor in the shifting from two-wheelers to cars. Thus it can be said that the car owners who opine that neighbour possessing a car was more in the southern region than in the central region.

Value for Money Factor

It was enquired whether car owners considered that cars provide value for the money spent was an important factor in the shifting from two-wheelers to cars. Table 30 reveals that out of 164 car owners interviewed in the northern region regarding the opinion that cars provide value for the money spent was an important factor in the shifting from two-wheelers to cars, 22 of them strongly agreed to the opinion, 27 of them agreed to the opinion, 40 disagreed to the opinion and 16 strongly disagreed to the opinion. Out of the 164 car owners interviewed in the central region, 3 of them strongly agreed to the opinion, 21 agreed to the opinion, 36 disagreed to the opinion and 43 strongly disagreed to the opinion. Out of the 158 car owners interviewed in the southern region, 7 of them strongly agreed to the opinion, 41 of them agreed to the opinion, 20 of them disagreed to the opinion and 23 strongly disagreed to the opinion.

Table 30
Cars Provide Value for the Money Spent

Region	*Opinion*					*Total*
	Strongly Disagree	*Disagree*	*Undecided*	*Agree*	*Strongly Agree*	
Northern	16	40	59	27	22	164
Central	43	36	61	21	3	164
Southern	23	20	67	41	7	158
Total	82	96	187	89	32	486

Chi-square value = 47.520, degrees of freedom = 8, p value = 0.00
Source: Survey Data

Since the p value (0.00) is less than the 0.05 level of significance, the researcher rejects the null hypothesis that there is no association between the region in which the car owner is situated and the opinion of the car owners that cars provide value for the money spent was an important factor in the shifting from two-wheelers to cars. Hence it can be concluded that there is significant association between the region and the opinion of the car owners that cars provide value for the money spent was an important factor in the shifting from two-wheelers to cars.

Car Loan Availability

It was interviewed to know whether car owners considered that car loan availability was an important factor in the shifting from two-wheelers to cars. As it could be observed from Table 31 that out of 164 car owners interviewed in the northern region regarding the opinion that car loan availability was an important factor in the shifting from two-wheelers to cars, 51 of them strongly agreed to the opinion, 45 of them agreed to the opinion, 24 disagreed to the opinion and 8 strongly disagreed to the opinion. Out of the 164 car owners interviewed in the central region, 55 of them strongly agreed to the opinion, 37 agreed to the opinion, 26 disagreed to the opinion and 19 strongly disagreed to the opinion. Out of the 158 car owners interviewed in the southern region, 56 of them strongly agreed to the opinion, 55 of them agreed to the opinion, 9 of them disagreed to the opinion and 3 strongly disagreed to the opinion.

Table 31
Car Loan Availability

Region	*Opinion*					*Total*
	Strongly Disagree	*Disagree*	*Undecided*	*Agree*	*Strongly Agree*	
Northern	8	24	36	45	51	164
Central	19	26	27	37	55	164
Southern	3	9	35	55	56	158
Total	30	59	98	137	162	486

Chi-square value = 27.487, degrees of freedom = 8, p value = 0.01
Source: Survey Data

On the basis of the fact that, the p value (0.01) is less than the 0.05 level of significance, the researcher rejects the null hypothesis that there is no association between the region in which the car owner is situated and the opinion of the car owners that car loan availability was an important factor in the shifting from two-wheelers to cars. Hence, it can be concluded that there is significant association between the region and the opinion of the car owners that car loan availability was an important factor in the shifting from two-wheelers to cars.

Disposable Income

It was interviewed to know whether car owners considered that increased disposable income was an important factor in the shifting from two-wheelers to cars. As Table 32 highlights that, out of 164 car owners interviewed in the northern region regarding the opinion that increased disposable income was an important factor in the shifting from two-wheelers to cars, 43 of them strongly agreed to the opinion, 75 of them agreed to the opinion, 13 disagreed to the opinion and 1 strongly disagreed to the opinion. Out of the 164 car owners interviewed in the central region, 60 of them strongly agreed to the opinion, 68 agreed to the opinion, 8 disagreed to the opinion and 5 strongly disagreed to the opinion. Out of the 158 car owners interviewed in the southern region, 57 of them strongly agreed to the opinion, 29 of them agreed to the opinion, 27 of them disagreed to the opinion and 14 strongly disagreed to the opinion.

Table 32
Increased Disposable Income

	Opinion					
Region	*Strongly Disagree*	*Disagree*	*Undecided*	*Agree*	*Strongly Agree*	*Total*
Northern	1	13	32	75	43	164
Central	5	8	23	68	60	164
Southern	14	27	31	29	57	158
Total	20	48	86	172	160	486

Chi-square value = 51.989, degrees of freedom = 8, p value = 0.00
Source: Survey Data

As it was examined that at 0.05 level of significance, the p value (0.00) being less, the researcher rejects the null hypothesis that there is no association between the region in which the car owner is situated and the opinion of the car owners that increased disposable income was an important factor in the shifting from two-wheelers to cars. Hence it can be concluded that there is significant association between the region and the opinion of the car owners that increased disposable income was an important factor in the shifting from two-wheelers to cars. Thus it can be said that the car owners who opined about increased disposable income as important was more in the central region than in the southern region.

After Sales Service

It was interviewed to know whether car owners considered that after sales service was an important factor in the shifting from two-wheelers to cars. As it could be observed from Table 33 that out of 164 car owners interviewed in the northern region regarding the opinion that after sales service was an important factor in the shifting from two-wheelers to cars, 30 of them strongly agreed to the opinion, 42 of them agreed to the opinion, 28 disagreed to the opinion and 2 strongly disagreed to the opinion. Out of the 164 car owners interviewed in the central region, 28 of them strongly agreed to the opinion, 55 agreed to the opinion, 25 disagreed to the opinion and 7 strongly disagreed to the opinion. Out of the 158 car owners interviewed in the southern region, 33 of them strongly agreed to the opinion, 56 of them agreed to the opinion, 5 of them disagreed to the opinion and 10 strongly disagreed to the opinion.

Table 33
Availability of Good After Sales Service for Cars

Region	*Opinion*					*Total*
	Strongly Disagree	*Disagree*	*Undecided*	*Agree*	*Strongly Agree*	
Northern	2	28	62	42	30	164
Central	7	25	48	55	28	163
Southern	10	5	54	56	33	158
Total	19	58	164	153	91	485

Chi-square value = 25.970, degrees of freedom = 8, p value = 0.01
Source: Survey Data

At 5 per cent level of significance, the p value (0.01) was found to be less than the significance level. Hence, the researcher rejects the null hypothesis that there is no association between the region in which the car owner is situated and the opinion of the car owners that after sales service was an important factor in the shifting from two-wheelers to cars. Hence it can be concluded that there is significant association between the region and the opinion of the car owners that after sales service was an important factor in the shifting from two-wheelers to cars. Thus it can be said that the car owners who favoured after sales service factor was more in the southern region than in the northern region.

Desire for a Change

It was interviewed to know whether car owners considered that desire for a change was an important factor in the shifting from two-wheelers to cars. As seen from Table 34, out of 164 car owners interviewed in the northern region regarding the opinion that that desire for a change was an important factor in the shifting from two-wheelers to cars, 65 of them strongly agreed to the opinion, 37 of them agreed to the opinion, 20 disagreed to the opinion and 13 strongly disagreed to the opinion. Out of the 164 car owners interviewed in the central region, 62 of them strongly agreed to the opinion, 48 agreed to the opinion, 20 disagreed to the opinion and 7 strongly disagreed to the opinion. Out of the 158 car owners interviewed in the southern region, 75 of them strongly agreed to the opinion, 55 of them agreed to the opinion, 8 of them disagreed to the opinion and 2 strongly disagreed to the opinion.

Table 34
Desire for a Change

	Opinion					
Region	*Strongly Disagree*	*Disagree*	*Undecided*	*Agree*	*Strongly Agree*	*Total*
Northern	13	20	29	37	65	164
Central	7	20	27	48	62	164
Southern	2	8	18	55	75	158
Total	22	48	74	140	202	486

Chi-square value = 21.995, degrees of freedom = 8, p value = 0.005
Source: Survey Data

Since the p value (0.005) is less than the 0.05 level of significance, the researcher rejects the null hypothesis that there is no association between the region in which the car owner is situated and the opinion of the car owners that after sales service was an important factor in the shifting from two-wheelers to cars. Hence it can be concluded that there is significant association between the region and the opinion of the car owners that after sales service was an important factor in the shifting from two-wheelers to cars. Thus it can be said that the car owners who favoured after sales service factor was more in the southern region than in the northern region.

Income of Car Owners

The car owners were interviewed to know their levels of monthly income and to know if there was any significant difference in the income levels across the three regions in Kerala. Table 35 reveals that out of 203 car owners interviewed in the northern region regarding their monthly income was an important factor in the shifting from two-wheelers to cars, 29 of them had a monthly income of more than 20000 rupees and 51 of them had a monthly between 16000 and 20000 rupees, 33 of them had a monthly income between 12000 and 16000 rupees, 78 of them had a monthly income of 8000 and 12000 rupees and 12 of them had monthly income of less than 8000 rupees. Out of 199 car owners interviewed in the northern region regarding their monthly income, 6 of them had a monthly income of more than 20000 rupees and 47 of them had a monthly between 16000 and 20000 rupees, 36 of them had a monthly income between 12000 and 16000 rupees, 89 of them had a monthly income of 8000 and 12000 rupees and 21 of them had monthly income of less than 8000 rupees. Out of 200 car owners interviewed in the northern region regarding their monthly income, 11 of them had a monthly income of more than 20000 rupees and 46 of them had a monthly between 16000 and 20000 rupees, 43 of them had a monthly income between 12000 and 16000 rupees, 92 of them had a monthly income of 8000 and 12000 rupees and 8 of them had monthly income of less than 8000 rupees.

Table 35
Income of Car Owners

Region	*Monthly income Car Owner Group*					Total
	<= 8000	8001 - 12000	12001 - 16000	16001 - 20000	20001+	
Northern	12	78	33	51	29	203
Central	21	89	36	47	6	199
Southern	8	92	43	46	11	200
Total	41	259	112	144	46	602

Chi-square value = 28.431, degrees of freedom = 8, p value = 0.00
Source: Survey Data

At 0.05 level of significance, the p value (0.00) was found to be less and hence, the researcher rejects the null hypothesis that there is no association between the region in which the car owner is situated and the monthly income levels. Hence, it can be concluded that there is significant association between the region and the monthly income levels of the car owners. Thus, it can be said that the car owners whose monthly income level is above 16000 rupees are more in the northern region than in central and southern region. This could be because of the high NRI (Non Resident Indian) remittances in the northern region.

Gender Preferences to Car Brands

An attempt was made to identify the buyer behaviour among the males and females towards different brands of cars in Kerala. The brands of cars under study were Maruti 800, Maruti Alto, Maruti Zen, Tata Indica, Santro and other brands of small cars. Table 36 highlights the fact that out of the 119 female car owners, 69 of them preferred Maruti 800, 26 of them preferred Maruti Alto, 7 of them preferred Maruti Zen, 1 preferred Maruti Swift, 2 of them preferred Tata Indica, 10 of them preferred Hyundai Santro and 4 of them preferred Maruti Wagon R. Out the 483 male car owners, 120 of them preferred Maruti 800, 83 of them preferred Maruti Alto, 46 of them preferred Maruti Zen, 14 preferred Maruti Swift, 98 of them preferred Tata Indica, 75 of them preferred Hyundai Santro and 47 of them preferred Maruti Wagon R.

Table 36
Gender Preferences to Car Brands

Sex	Brands							Total
	Maruti 800	*Maruti Alto*	*Maruti Zen*	*Maruti Swift*	*Tata Indica*	*Santro*	*WagonR*	
Female	69	26	7	1	2	10	4	119
Male	120	83	46	14	98	75	47	483
Total	189	109	53	15	100	85	51	602

Chi-square value = 65.579, degrees of freedom = 6, p value = 0.00
Source: Survey Data

Since the p value (0.00) is less than the 0.05 level of significance, the researcher rejects the null hypcthesis that there is no association between the gender of the car owners and their brand preference of cars. Hence it can be concluded that there is significant association between gender and brand preference. The brand of cars like Tata Indica, Hyundai Santro, Maruti WagonR and Maruti Zen are preferred more by males than by females. Tata Indica being a very sturdy vehicle, it is mostly preferred by males, and Santro and Wagon R being bigger in size than Maruti 800 or Alto, it is less proffered by females in the car market.

Social Factors

A car purchase decision could be influenced by many social factors like friends, relatives, neighbours and own family members. Table 37 reveals that out of 119 female car owners, 27 were influenced by friends, 6 were influenced by relatives, 74 were influenced by own family members, 5 were influenced by neighbours and 7 were influenced by their own decision. Out of the 483 male car owners, 121 were influenced by friends, 59 were influenced by relatives, 173 were influenced by own family members, 16 were influenced by neighbours and 114 were influenced by own decision.

The p value (0.00) being less than the 0.05 level of significance, the researcher rejects the null hypothesis that there is no association between the gender of the car owners and the social factors that influence the car purchase decision.

Table 37
Influence of Social Factors in the Car Purchase Decision Among Gender

Sex	*Social Factors*	*Total*				
	Friends	*RelativesOwn Family MembersNeighboursOwn*				
Decision						
Female	27	6	74	5	7	119
Male	121	59	173	16	114	483
Total	148	65	247	21	121	602

Chi-square value = 36.142, degrees of freedom = 4, p value = 0.00
Source: Survey Data

Hence it can be concluded that there is significant association between gender and influence of social factors. Thus it can be said that males are prone to take individual decisions in the car purchase more than females.

Family Members as Social Factors

A car purchase decision could be influenced by the members of one's own family like wife, husband, children father, mother, siblings and grand parents. Table 38 brings out the fact that, out of the 121 female car owners, 102 were influenced by their husbands, 5 were influenced by children, 10 were influenced by father, 2 were influenced by mother and 2 were influenced by siblings. Out of 481 male car owners, 293 were influenced by their wives, 24 were influenced by children, 65 were influenced by father, 34 were influenced by mother and 65 were influenced by siblings.

Table 38
Influence of Family Members in the Car Purchase Decision Among Gender

	Family Members					
Sex	*Wife/ Husband*	*Children*	*Father*	*Mother*	*Siblings*	*Total*
Female	102	5	10	2	2	121
Male	293	24	65	34	65	481
Total	395	29	75	36	67	602

Chi-square value = 32.298, degrees of freedom = 4, p value = 0.00
Source: Survey Data

Since the p value (0.00) is less than the 0.05 level of significance, the researcher rejects the null hypothesis that there is no association between the gender of the car owners and the influence of family members in the car purchase decision. Hence it can be concluded that there is significant association between gender and influence of family members in the car purchase decision. Thus it can be said that the influence of father, mother and siblings in the car purchase decision is more in the case of males than in females.

Price Factor

A car purchase decision could be influenced by the price of the car. If the price is too high, the demand for it will be low and if the price is too low the demand for the car will be high. As it can be observed from Table 39, out of the 119 female car owners, 97 strongly agreed with the opinion that price is the most important factor while buying a car, 12 agreed with this opinion, 3 disagreed with this opinion and one strongly disagreed with this opinion. Out of the 483 male car owners, 313 of them strongly agreed with this opinion, 87 agreed with the opinion, 18 disagreed with the opinion and 6 strongly disagreed with this opinion.

Table 39
Price is the Most Important Factor

	Opinion					
Gender	*Strongly Disagree*	*Disagree*	*Undecided*	*Agree*	*Strongly Agree*	*Total*
Female	1	3	6	12	97	119
Male	6	18	59	87	313	483
Total	7	21	65	99	410	602

Chi-square value = 12.644, degrees of freedom = 4, p value = 0.013
Source: Survey Data

The p value (0.013) was found to be less than the 0.05 level of significance, the researcher rejects the null hypothesis that there is no association between the gender of the car owners and the opinion that price is the most important factor while buying a car. Hence it can be concluded that there is significant association between gender and the opinion that price is the most important factor while buying a car. Thus it can be said that the proportion of the males to females who strongly agreed in the opinion that price is the most important factor while uying a car is more than in the case they strongly disagreed.

Mileage (Fuel Efficiency)

A car purchase decision could be influenced by the mileage of the car. Table 40 exhibits that, out of the 119 female car owners, 95 strongly agreed with the opinion that price is the most important factor while buying a car, 12 agreed with this opinion, 4 disagreed with this opinion. Out of the 483 male car owners, 347 of them strongly agreed with this opinion, 65 agreed with the opinion, 15 disagreed with the opinion.

Table 40
Mileage (Fuel Efficiency) Matters the Most

Sex	*Opinion*				*Total*
	Disagree	*Undecided*	*Agree*	*Strongly Agree*	
Female	4	8	12	95	119
Male	15	56	65	347	483
Total	19	64	77	442	602

Chi-square value = 4.169, degrees of freedom = 3, p value = 0.384
Source: Survey Data

Since the p value (0.384) is greater than the 0.05 level of significance, the researcher accepts the null hypothesis that there is no association between the gender of the car owners and the opinion that mileage is the most important factor while buying a car. Hence, it can be concluded that there is significant association between gender and the opinion that mileage is not the most important factor while buying a car. Thus it can be said that the proportion of the males to females who strongly agreed in the opinion that mileage is not the most important factor while buying a car is more than those who disagreed.

Brand Image

A car purchase decision could be influenced by the brand image of the car. Table 41 shows that, out of the 119 female car owners, 28 strongly agreed with the opinion that brand image is the most important factor while buying a car, 9 agreed with this opinion, 25 disagreed with this opinion. Out of the 483 male car owners, 164 of them strongly agreed with this opinion, 68 agreed with the opinion, 76 disagreed with the opinion.

Table 41
Brand Image Stands Tall Among all the Factors

	Opinion					
Sex	*Strongly Disagree*	*Disagree*	*Undecided*	*Agree*	*Strongly Agree*	*Total*
Female	17	25	40	9	28	119
Male	46	76	129	68	164	483
Total	63	101	169	77	192	602

Chi-square value = 11.696, degrees of freedom = 4, p value = 0.02
Source: Survey Data

As the p value (0.02) was found to be less than the 0.05 level of significance, the researcher rejects the null hypothesis that there is no association between the gender of the car owners and the opinion that brand image is the most important factor while buying a car. Hence it can be concluded that there is significant association between gender and the opinion that brand image is the most important factor while buying a car. Thus it can be said that the males who strongly agreed in the opinion that brand image is the most important factor was more than the females.

Resale Value of the Car

A car purchase decision could be influenced by the resale value of the car. Table 42 discloses that, out of the 119 female car owners, 7 strongly agreed with the opinion that resale value of the car is the most important factor while buying a car, 24 agreed with this opinion, 39 disagreed with this opinion. Out of the 483 male car owners, 63 of them strongly agreed with this opinion, 132 agreed with the opinion, 94 disagreed with the opinion.

Table 42
Resale Value of the Car

Sex	Opinion					Total
	Strongly Disagree	*Disagree*	*Undecided*	*Agree*	*Strongly Agree*	
Female	19	39	30	24	7	119
Male	54	94	140	132	63	483
Total	73	133	170	156	70	602

Chi-square value = 16.043, degrees of freedom = 4, p value = 0.003
Source: Survey Data

As the p value (0.003) was observed to be less than the 0.05 level of significance, the researcher rejects the null hypothesis that there is no association between the gender of the car owners and the opinion that resale value of the car is the most important factor while buying a car. Hence it can be concluded that there is significant association between gender and the opinion that resale value of the car is the most important factor while buying a car.

Pressure from the Family Members

A car purchase decision could be influenced by the pressure from family members. As it can be seen from Table 43 that, out of the 119 female car owners, 7 strongly agreed with the opinion that pressure from the family is the most important factor while buying a car, 41 agreed with this opinion, 17 disagreed with this opinion. Out of the 483 male car owners, 23 of them strongly agreed with this opinion, 81 agreed with the opinion, 135 disagreed with the opinion.

Since the p value (0.00) is less than the 0.05 level of significance, the researcher rejects the null hypothesis that there is no association between the gender of the car owners and the opinion that pressure from the family members is the most important factor while buying a car. Hence it can be concluded that there is significant association between gender and the

Table 43
Pressure from the Family Members

Sex	*Opinion*					*Total*
	Strongly Disagree	*Disagree*	*Undecided*	*Agree*	*Strongly Agree*	
Female	10	17	44	41	7	119
Male	75	135	169	81	23	483
Total	85	152	213	122	30	602

Chi-square value = 25.572, degrees of freedom = 4, p value = 0.00
Source: Survey Data

opinion that pressure from the family members is the most important factor while buying a car.

Impressive Advertisements

A car purchase decision could be influenced by impressive advertisement. As it can be observed from Table 44 that out of the 119 female car owners, 40 strongly agreed with the opinion that impressive advertisement is the most important factor while buying a car, 45 agreed with this opinion, 6 disagreed with this opinion. Out of the 483 male car owners, 101 of them strongly agreed with this opinion, 167 agreed with the opinion, 67 disagreed with the opinion.

Table 44
Impressive Advertisements

Sex	*Opinion*					*Total*
	Strongly Disagree	*Disagree*	*Undecided*	*Agree*	*Strongly Agree*	
Female	11	6	17	45	40	119
Male	61	67	87	167	101	483
Total	72	73	104	212	141	602

Chi-square value = 14.683, degrees of freedom = 4, p value = 0.005
Source: Survey Data

As the p value (0.005) was observed to be less than the 0.05 level of significance, the researcher rejects the null hypothesis that there is no association between the gender of the car owners and the opinion that impressive advertisement is the most important factor while buying a car. Hence, it can be concluded that there is significant association between gender and the opinion that impressive advertisement is the most important factor while buying a car. Thus, it can be said that the males who agreed to the opinion that impressive advertisement is the most important factor was more than the females.

Discounts

A car purchase decision could be influenced by the discounts offered for a car purchase. Table 45 reveals that, out of the 116 female car owners, 81 of them rated discount offers as first rank, 20 of them rated discounted offers as second rank, 8 of them ranked third and 7 of them ranked fourth. Out of the 483 male car owners, 244 of them rated discount offers as first rank, 135 of them rated discounted offers as second rank, 49 of them ranked third and 55 of them ranked fourth.

Table 45
Influence of Discounts in Car Purchase Decision

	Discounts				
Gender	*1*	*2*	*3*	*4*	*Total*
Female	81	20	8	7	116
Male	244	135	49	55	483
Total	325	155	57	62	599

Chi-square value = 16.270, degrees of freedom = 3, p value = 0.003
Source: Survey Data

The p value (0.003) was noticed to be less than the 0.05 level of significance and thus, the researcher rejects the null hypothesis that there is no association between the gender of the car owners and the discounts offered while buying a car. Hence it can be concluded that there is significant association between gender and the opinion that discounts offered while buying a car. Thus it can be said that the males who preferred discounts was more than the females.

Reasons for Upgrading from Two-wheelers to Cars

It was surveyed to know if the sample units had any reason for upgrading from two wheelers to cars. It was examined that there are several reasons attributed for upgrading from two-wheelers to cars. One among the several reason was the neighbours influence in the car purchase decision. The other reasons attributed to the upgrading from two wheelers to cars are increased disposable income and car loan availability. Based on these reason car promoters can formulate strategies to capture the market share of this particular segment.

Neighbours' Influence

A car purchase decision could be influenced by neighbours. As it can be observed from Table 46 that out of the 67 female car owners, 5 strongly agreed with the opinion that neighbour possessing a car is a reason for the shift from two-wheelers to cars, 10 agreed with this opinion, 16 disagreed with this opinion. Out of the 419 male car owners, 13 of them strongly agreed with this opinion, 13 agreed with the opinion, 151 disagreed with the opinion.

Table 46
Neighbours' Influence

Gender	*Opinion*					*Total*
	Strongly Disagree	*Disagree*	*Undecided*	*Agree*	*Strongly Agree*	
Female	17	16	19	10	5	67
Male	137	151	105	13	13	419
Total	154	167	124	23	18	486

Chi-square value = 23.734, degrees of freedom = 4, p value = 0.00
Source: Survey Data

Since the p value (0.00) is less than the 0.05 level of significance, the researcher rejects the null hypothesis that there is no association between the gender of the car owners and the neighbours' influence while buying a car. Hence it can be concluded that there is significant association between gender and neighbours' influence while buying a car. Thus it can be said that the percentage of females (7%) who agreed to the opinion that neighbour influences the car purchase decision was more than the percentage of males (3%).

Car Loan Availability

A car purchase decision could be influenced by the car loan availability. As it can be learned from Table 47 that, out of the 67 female car owners, 30 strongly agreed with the opinion that car loan availability is a reason for the shift from two-wheelers to cars, 21 agreed with this opinion, 2 disagreed with this opinion. Out of the 419 male car owners, 132 of them strongly agreed with this opinion, 116 agreed with the opinion, 57 disagreed with the opinion.

Table 47
Car Loan Availability

Gender	*Opinion*					*Total*
	Strongly Disagree	*Disagree*	*Undecided*	*Agree*	*Strongly Agree*	
Female	2	2	12	21	30	67
Male	28	57	86	116	132	419
Total	30	59	98	137	162	486

Chi-square value =·10.167, degrees of freedom = 4, p value = 0.038
Source: Survey Data

As the p value (0.038) was learned to be less than the 0.05 level of significance, the researcher rejects the null hypothesis that there is no association between the gender of the car owners and the car loan availability while buying a car. Hence it can be concluded that there is significant association between gender and car loan availability while buying a car. Thus it can be said that the percentage of females (45%) who strongly agreed to the opinion that car loan availability is the reason for shifting from two-wheelers to cars was more than the percentage of males (32%).

Increased Disposable Income

There are several levels of income groups prevailing in our society. The person who has more disposable income can afford to have a car than a person who cannot. A car purchase decision could be influenced by increased disposable income. As it can be observed from Table 48 that, out of the 67 female car owners, 34 strongly agreed with the opinion that increased disposable income is a reason for the shift from two-wheelers to cars, 20 agreed with this opinion, 6 disagreed with this opinion. Out of the 419 male car owners, 126 of them strongly agreed with this opinion, 152 agreed with the opinion, 42 disagreed with the opinion.

Table 48
Increased Disposable Income

Gender	*Opinion*					Total
	Strongly Disagree	*Disagree*	*Undecided*	*Agree*	*Strongly Agree*	
Female	3	6	4	20	34	67
Male	17	42	82	152	126	419
Total	20	48	86	172	160	486

Chi-square value = 14.303, degrees of freedom = 4, p value = 0.006
Source: Survey Data

Since the p value (0.006) is less than the 0.05 level of significance, the researcher rejects the null hypothesis that there is no association between the gender of the car owners and increased disposable income. Hence it can be concluded that there is significant association between gender and increased disposable income while buying a car. Thus it can be said that the percentage of females who strongly agreed to the opinion that increased disposable income is the reason for shifting from two-wheelers to cars was more than the percentage of males.

Relationship between Monthly Income and Brands

A car purchase decision could be influenced by the monthly income of the car owners. An attempt was made to identify the buyer behaviour among of the car owners of different income levels towards different brands of cars in Kerala. The brands of cars under study were Maruti 800, Maruti Alto, Maruti Zen, Tata Indica, Santro, Wagon R and other brands of small cars. Table 49 exhibits that, out of 45 car owners having a monthly income below 8000 rupees, 24 preferred Maruti 800, 8 of them preferred Maruti Alto, 6 of them preferred Maruti Zen, 2 of them preferred Tata Indica, 2 of them preferred Hyundai Santro, 2 of them preferred Maruti Wagon R and 1 of them preferred other small cars. Out the 257 car owners having an income between 8001 and 12000 rupees, 114 of them preferred Maruti 800, 60 of them preferred Maruti Alto, 16 of them preferred Maruti Zen, 36 of them preferred Tata Indica, 14 of them preferred Hyundai Santro, 15 of them preferred Maruti Wagon R and 2 of them preferred other small cars. Out the 110 car owners having an income between 12001 and 16000 rupees, 24 of them preferred Maruti 800, 23 of them preferred Maruti Alto, 11 of them preferred Maruti Zen, 26 of them preferred Tata Indica, 14 of them preferred Hyundai Santro, 9 of them preferred Maruti Wagon R and 3 of them preferred other small cars. Out the 144 car owners having an income between 16001 and 20000 rupees, 23 of them preferred Maruti 800, 15 of them preferred Maruti Alto, 11 of them preferred Maruti Zen, 27 of them preferred Tata Indica, 43 of them preferred Hyundai Santro, 22 of them preferred Maruti Wagon R and 3 of them preferred other small cars. Out the 46 car owners having an income above 20001 rupees, 4 of them preferred Maruti 800, 3 of them preferred Maruti Alto, 7 of them preferred Maruti Zen, 7 of them preferred Tata Indica, 14 of them preferred Hyundai Santro, 5 of them preferred Maruti Wagon R and 3 of them preferred other small cars.

Table 49
Relationship between Monthly Income and Brands

	Brands							
Monthly Income	*Maruti 800*	*Maruti Alto*	*Maruti Zen*	*Tata Indica*	*Hyundai Santro*	*Maruti WagonR*	*Others*	*Total*
<= 8000	24	8	6	2	2	2	1	45
8001 - 12000	114	60	16	36	14	15	2	257
12001 - 16000	24	23	11	26	14	9	3	110
16001 - 20000	23	15	11	27	43	22	3	144
20001+	4	3	7	7	14	5	6	46
Total	189	109	51	98	87	53	15	602

Chi-square value = 165.331, degrees of freedom = 24, p value = 0.00
Source: Survey Data

As the p value (0.00) was found to be less than the 0.05 level of significance, the researcher rejects the null hypothesis that there is no association between the income of the car owners and brands preferred. Hence it can be concluded that there is significant association between income and brands preferred. Thus, it can be said that the sample units having a monthly income below 16000 rupees prefer Maruti 800 and Maruti Alto and sample units having above 16000 rupees prefer Santro, Wagon R and Tata Indica.

Influence of Family Members

A car purchase decision could be influenced by the influence of family members. An attempt was made to identify the buyer behaviour among the car owners of different income levels and the influence of family members. The different family members under study were wife/husband, children, father, mother and siblings. As it can be observed from Table 50, out of 41 car owners having a monthly income below 8000 rupees, 25 have been influenced by either the wife or husband, one by children, 9 by father, 4 by mother and 2 by siblings. Out of 259 car owners having a monthly income between 8001 and 12000 rupees, 175 have been influenced by either the wife or husband, 14 by children, 39 by father, 10 by mother and 21 by siblings. Out of 112 car owners having a monthly income between 12001 and 16000 rupees, 75 have been influenced by either the wife or husband, 4 by children, 5 by father, 14 by mother and 14 by siblings. Out of 144 car owners having a monthly income between 16001 and 20000 rupees, 92 have been influenced by either the wife or husband, 9 by children, 15 by father, 7 by mother and 21 by siblings.

Since the p value (0.00) is less than the 0.05 level of significance, the researcher rejects the null hypothesis that there is no association between the income of the car owners and influence of family members. Hence, it can be concluded that there is significant association between income and influence of family members. Thus it can be said that the sample units having a monthly income between 8000 and 12000 rupees are influenced by their wife or husband more than the other income groups.

Table 50
Relationship between Income and Family Members

Monthly income	*Influence of Family Members* *Wife/ Husband*	*Children*	*Father*	*Mother*	*Siblings*	*Total*
<= 8000	25	1	9	4	2	41
8001 - 12000	175	14	39	10	21	259
12001 - 16000	75	4	5	14	14	112
16001 - 20000	92	9	15	7	21	144
20001+	28	1	7	1	8	45
Total	395	29	75	36	66	601

Chi-square value = 33.046, degrees of freedom = 16, p value = 0.007
Source: Survey Data

Brand Image Stands Tall Among all the Factors

A car purchase decision could be influenced by brand image of the car. A brand is a very important deciding factor in the car purchase decision. There are several premium brands, which influence people with higher income, and other old brands, which do not influence people for many reasons. An attempt was made to identify the buyer behaviour among the car owners of different income levels towards the influence of brand image. As it can be seen from Table 51 that, out of 41 car owners having an income below 8000 rupees, 4 strongly agreed that there is an influence of the brand image of the car purchase decision, 3 agreed to the opinion and 12 disagreed to the opinion. Out of 259 car owners having an income between 8001 and 12000 rupees, 57 strongly agreed that there is an influence of the brand image of the car purchase decision, 22 agreed to the opinion and 56 disagreed to the opinion. Out of 112 car owners having an income between 12001 and 16000 rupees, 35 strongly agreed that there is an influence of the brand image of the car purchase decision, 19 agreed to the opinion and 17 disagreed to the opinion. Out of 144 car owners having an income between 16001 and 20000 rupees, 68 strongly agreed that there is an influence of the brand image of the car purchase decision, 26 agreed to the opinion and 14 disagreed to the opinion. Out of 46 car owners having an income above 20001 rupees, 28 strongly agreed that there is an influence of the brand image of the car purchase decision, 7 agreed to the opinion and 2 disagreed to the opinion.

Table 51
Brand Image Stands Tall Among all the Factors

	Opinion					
Monthly Income	*Strongly Disagree*	*Disagree*	*Undecided*	*Agree*	*Strongly Agree*	*Total*
<= 8000	8	12	14	3	4	41
8001 - 12000	32	56	92	22	57	259
12001 - 16000	9	17	32	19	35	112
16001 - 20000	13	14	23	26	68	144
20001+	1	2	8	7	28	46
Total	63	101	169	77	192	602

Chi-square value = 85.715, degrees of freedom = 16, p value = 0.00
Source: Survey Data

When the p value (0.00) was found to be less than the 0.05 level of significance, the researcher decided to reject the null hypothesis that there is no association between the income of the car owners and brand image. Hence it can be concluded that there is significant association between income and brand image. Thus it can be said that the sample units having a monthly income between 16000 and 20000 rupees have opined that brand image influences most in the car purchase decision which was more than any other income groups.

Design and Style

A car purchase decision could be influenced by design and style of the car. There is a need to distinguish the attributes that contribute to making an outstanding car in different segments. The factors that go into making a grate small car would most definitely be different from the features that make a luxury sedan. Design and style are the features that will make a small car more outstanding than the large cars. An attempt was made to identify the buyer behaviour among the car owners of different income levels towards the influence of design and style of the car. As it can be noticed from Table 52

that, out of 41 car owners having an income below 8000 rupees, 3 strongly agreed that there is an influence of the brand image of the car purchase decision, 4 agreed to the opinion and 17 disagreed to the opinion. Out of 259 car owners having an income between 8001 and 12000 rupees, 54 strongly agreed that there is an influence of the brand image of the car purchase decision, 38 agreed to the opinion and 57 disagreed to the opinion. Out of 112 car owners having an income between 12001 and 16000 rupees, 31 strongly agreed that there is an influence of the brand image of the car purchase decision, 21 agreed to the opinion and 18 disagreed to the opinion. Out of 142 car owners having an income between 16001 and 20000 rupees, 61 strongly agreed that there is an influence of the brand image of the car purchase decision, 34 agreed to the opinion and 14 disagreed to the opinion. Out of 48 car owners having an income above 20001 rupees, 31 strongly agreed that there is an influence of the brand image of the car purchase decision, 9 agreed to the opinion and 2 disagreed to the opinion.

Table 52
Design and Style are the Most Important Parameters

Monthly Income	*Opinion*					*Total*
	Strongly Disagree	*Disagree*	*Undecided*	*Agree*	*Strongly Agree*	
<= 8000	6	17	11	4	3	41
8001 - 12000	24	57	86	38	54	259
12001 - 16000	8	18	34	21	31	112
16001 - 20000	10	14	23	34	61	142
20001+	2	2	4	9	31	48
Total	50	108	158	106	180	602

Chi-square value = 96.789, degrees of freedom = 16, p value = 0.00

Source: Survey Data

Since the p value (0.00) is less than the 0.05 level of significance, the researcher rejects the null hypothesis that there is no association between the income of the car owners and design and style. Hence it can be concluded that there is significant association between income and design and style. Thus, it can be said that the sample units having a monthly income between 16000 and 20000 rupees who opined that design and style influences most in the car purchase decision was more than any other income groups.

Impressive Advertisements are Very Important

A car purchase decision could be influenced by impressive advertisement of the car. An attempt was made to identify the buyer behaviour among the car owners of different income levels towards the influence of impressive advertisement of the car. As it can be observed from Table 53 that, out of 41 car owners having an income below 8000 rupees, 13 strongly agreed, 8 agreed to the opinion and 5 disagreed to the opinion. Out of 259 car owners having an income between 8001 and 12000 rupees, 74 strongly agreed, 93 agreed to the opinion and 21 disagreed to the opinion. Out of 112 car owners having an income between 12001 and 16000 rupees, 14 strongly agreed, 46 agreed to the opinion and 12 disagreed to the opinion. Out of 144 car owners having an income between 16001 and 20000 rupees, 32 strongly agreed, 42 agreed to the opinion and 30 disagreed to the opinion. Out of 46 car owners having an income above 20001 rupees, 8 strongly agreed, 23 agreed to the opinion and 5 disagreed to the opinion.

Table 53
Impressive Advertisements

	Opinion					
Monthly Income	*Strongly Disagree*	*Disagree*	*Undecided*	*Agree*	*Strongly Agree*	*Total*
<= 8000	8	5	7	8	13	41
8001 - 12000	33	21	38	93	74	259
12001 - 16000	15	12	25	46	14	112
16001 - 20000	13	30	27	42	32	144
20001+	3	5	7	23	8	46
Total	72	73	104	212	141	602

Chi-square value = 39.099, degrees of freedom = 16, p value = 0.001
Source: Survey Data

As the p value (0.001) was observed to be less than the 0.05 level of significance, the researcher rejects the null hypothesis that there is no association between the income of the car owners and impressive advertisements. Hence it can be concluded that there is significant association between income and impressive advertisements. Thus it can be said that the sample units having a monthly income between 8000 and 12000 rupees who opined that impressive advertisements influences most in the car purchase decision was more than any other income groups.

Relationship between Discounts and Income Levels

A car purchase decision could be influenced by discounts. An attempt was made to identify the buyer behaviour among the car owners of different income levels towards the influence of discounts. As it can be observed from Table 54 that out of 41 car owners having an income below 8000 rupees, 24 ranked discounts as first preference, 9 as second preference, 6 as third preference and 2 as fourth preference. Out of 257 car owners having an income between 8001 and 12000 rupees, 161 ranked discounts as first preference, 55 as second preference, 20 as third preference and 21 as fourth preference. Out of 111 car owners having an income between 12001 and 16000 rupees, 65 ranked discounts as first preference, 35 as second preference, 3 as third preference and 8 as fourth preference. Out of 144 car owners having an income between 16001 and 20000 rupees, 59 ranked discounts as first preference, 43 as second preference, 22 as third preference and 20 as fourth preference. Out of 46 car owners having an income above 20001 rupees, 16 ranked discounts as first preference, 13 as second preference, 6 as third preference and 11 as fourth preference.

At 0.05 level of significance as the p value (0.00) was found to be less than the significance level, the researcher rejects the null hypothesis that there is no association between the income of the car owners and discounts. Hence, it can be concluded that there is significant association between income and discounts. Thus, it can be said that the sample units having a monthly income between 8000 and 12000 rupees who opined

Table 54
Influence of Discounts

Monthly Income	*Discounts* 1	2	3	4	*Total*
<= 8000	24	9	6	2	41
8001 - 12000	161	55	20	21	257
12001 - 16000	65	35	3	8	111
16001 - 20000	59	43	22	20	144
20001+	16	13	6	11	46
Total	325	155	57	62	599

Chi-square value = 44.106, degrees of freedom = 12, p value = 0.00
Source: Survey Data

that discounts influences most in the car purchase decision was more than any other income groups.

Influence of Factors across Urban and Rural Areas

Factors that influence the car purchase decision in urban and rural areas are galore. Some of them are social factors, price, brand and promotional tools. The influence of social factors in the car purchase decision is as follows.

Social Factors

A car purchase decision could be influenced by many social factors like friends, relatives, neighbours and own family members. Table 55 reveals that, out of 297 car owners from the rural area 81 were influenced by friends, 39 by relatives, 135 by own family members, 8 by neighbours, 34 by their own decision. Out of the 302 car owners from the urban area, 67 were influenced by friends, 26 by relatives, 112 by own family members, 13 by neighbours and 84 by their own decision.

Since the p value (0.00) is less than the 0.05 level of significance, the researcher rejects the null hypothesis that there is no association between the urban or rural area in which the car owner is situated and the social factors influencing the car purchase decision. Hence it is concluded that there is significant association between the area and the social factors influencing

Table 55
Influence of Social Factors in the Car Purchase

Area	*Social Factors*					*Total*
	Friends	*Relatives*	*Own Family Members*	*Neighbours*	*Own Decision*	
Rural	81	39	135	8	34	297
Urban	67	26	112	13	84	302
Total	148	65	247	21	118	599

Chi-square value = 28.403, degrees of freedom = 4, p value = 0.00
Source: Survey Data

the car purchase decision. Table 55 reveals that the number of people who take a decision on their own regarding a car purchase is more in the urban area than in the rural area.

Family Members

A car purchase decision could be influenced by family members like wife or husband, father, mother, children and siblings. Table 56 discloses that, out of 298 car owners from the rural area 203 were influenced by wife or husband, 12 by children, 28 by father, 16 by mother and 39 by siblings. Out of the 303 car owners from the urban area, 192 were influenced by wife or husband, 17 by children, 47 by father, 20 by mother and 27 by siblings.

Table 56
Influence of Family Members in the Car Purchase

Area	*Family Members*					*Total*
	Wife/ Husband	*Children*	*Father*	*Mother*	*Siblings*	
Rural	203	12	28	16	39	298
Urban	192	17	47	20	27	303
Total	395	29	75	36	66	601

Chi-square value = 10.567, degrees of freedom = 4, p value = 0.049
Source: Survey Data

As the p value (0.049) was found to be less than the 0.05 level of significance, the researcher rejects the null hypothesis that there is no association between the urban or rural area in which the car owner is situated and the family members influencing the car purchase decision. Hence it is concluded that there is significant association between the area and the family members influencing the car purchase decision. Table 56 reveals that the number of people who are influenced by their wives or husbands is more in the rural area than in the urban area.

Influence of Promotional Tools

A car purchase decision could be influenced by promotional tools like newspaper, television, radio, internet, magazines, word of mouth, car shows and melas, test drive, exchange melas/loan melas and others. Table 57 divulges that, out of 298 car owners from the rural area 11 of them were influenced most by newspapers, 32 by television, 68 by radio, 65 by internet, 71 by magazines, 29 by word of mouth, 6 by car shows, 11 by test drive and 5 by exchange and loan melas. Out of 304 car owners from the urban area 7 of them were influenced most by newspapers, 11 by television, 38 by radio, 90 by internet, 53 by magazines, 36 by word of mouth, 45 by car shows, 21 by test drive and 3 by exchange and loan melas.

Since the p value (0.00) is less than the 0.05 level of significance, the researcher rejects the null hypothesis that there is no association between the urban or rural area in which the car owner is situated and the promotional tools influencing the car purchase decision. Hence it is concluded that there is significant association between the area and the promotional tools influencing the car purchase decision. Table 57 reveals that the number of people who are influenced most by newspapers, television and radio is more in the rural area than in the urban area.

Influence of Price Factor

A car purchase decision could be influenced by price. Table 58 makes known the fact that, out of 298 car owners from the rural area 213 of them strongly agreed to the opinion that price influenced their car purchase decision, 49 of them agreed,

Table 57
Influence of Promotional Tools in Car Purchase

Area	Promotional Tools									Total
	Newspaper	TV	Radio	Internet	Magazine	Word of Mouth	Car Shows & Other Melas	Test Drive	Exchange Melas/ Loan Melas	
Rural	11	32	68	65	71	29	6	11	5	298
Urban	7	11	38	90	53	36	45	21	3	304
Total	18	43	106	155	124	65	51	32	8	602

Chi-square value = 51.487, degrees of freedom = 8, p value = 0.00
Source: Survey Data

10 disagreed and 3 strongly disagreed to this opinion. Out of 304 car owners from the urban area 197 of them strongly agreed to the opinion that price influenced their car purchase decision, 50 of them agreed, 11 disagreed and 4 strongly disagreed to this opinion.

Table 58
Influence of Price Factor in Car Purchase

Area	*Opinion*					*Total*
	Strongly Disagree	*Disagree*	*Undecided*	*Agree*	*Strongly Agree*	
Rural	3	10	23	49	213	298
Urban	4	11	42	50	197	304
Total	7	21	65	99	410	602

Chi-square value = 6.320, degrees of freedom = 4, p value = 0.177
Source: Survey Data

At 0.05 level of significance, as the p value (0.177) was found to be greater than the significance level, the researcher accepts the null hypothesis that there is no association between the urban or rural area in which the car owner is situated and the price influencing the car purchase decision. Hence, it is concluded that there is no significant association between the urban or rural area and the price influencing the car purchase decision.

Influence of Brand of the Car

A car purchase decision could be influenced by brand of the car. Table 59 exposes that, out of 298 car owners from the rural area 73 of them strongly agreed to the opinion that brand of the car influenced their car purchase decision, 29 of them agreed, 74 disagreed and 21 strongly disagreed to this opinion. Out of 304 car owners from the urban area 119 of them strongly agreed to the opinion that brand of the car influenced their car purchase decision, 48 of them agreed, 27 disagreed and 42 strongly disagreed to this opinion.

As the p value (0.00) is less than the 0.05 level of significance, the researcher rejects the null hypothesis that there

Table 59
Influence of Brand of the Car

Area	*Opinion*					*Total*
	Strongly Disagree	*Disagree*	*Undecided*	*Agree*	*Strongly Agree*	
Rural	21	74	101	29	73	298
Urban	42	27	68	48	119	304
Total	63	101	169	77	192	602

Chi-square value = 50.969, degrees of freedom = 4, p value = 0.00
Source: Survey Data

is no association between the urban or rural area in which the car owner is situated and the brand of the cars influencing the car purchase decision. Hence it is concluded that there is significant association between the area and the brand of the car influencing the car purchase decision.

Influence of Design and Style in the Car Purchase

A car purchase decision could be influenced by design and style of the car. Table 60 discloses that, out of 298 car owners from the rural area 68 of them strongly agreed to the opinion that design and style of the car influenced their car purchase decision, 37 of them agreed, 74 disagreed and 21 strongly disagreed to this opinion. Out of 304 car owners from the urban area 112 of them strongly agreed to the opinion that design and style of the car influenced their car purchase decision, 69 of them agreed, 34 disagreed and 29 strongly disagreed to this opinion.

Table 60
Influence of Design and Style of the Car

Area	*Opinion*					*Total*
	Strongly Disagree	*Disagree*	*Undecided*	*Agree*	*Strongly Agree*	
Rural	21	74	98	37	68	298
Urban	29	34	60	69	112	304
Total	50	108	158	106	180	602

Chi-square value = 45.595, degrees of freedom = 4, p value = 0.00
Source: Survey Data

The p value (0.00) being less than the 0.05 level of significance, the researcher rejects the null hypothesis that there is no association between the urban or rural area in which the car owner is situated and the design and style of the cars influencing the car purchase decision. Hence it is concluded that there is significant association between the area and the design and style of the car influencing the car purchase decision.

Influence of After Sales Service

A car purchase decision could be influenced by after sales service of the car dealers. Table 61 reveals that, out of 298 car owners from the rural area 16 of them strongly agreed to the opinion that after sales service of the car dealer influenced their car purchase decision, 124 of them agreed, 24 disagreed and 3 strongly disagreed to this opinion. Out of 304 car owners from the urban area 32 of them strongly agreed to the opinion that sales service of the car dealer influenced their car purchase decision, 114 of them agreed, 42 disagreed and 17 strongly disagreed to this opinion.

Table 61
Influence of After Sales Service

Area	*Opinion*					*Total*
	Strongly Disagree	*Disagree*	*Undecided*	*Agree*	*Strongly Agree*	
Rural	3	24	131	124	16	298
Urban	17	42	99	114	32	304
Total	20	66	230	238	48	602
Chi-square value = 24.857, degrees of freedom = 4, p value = 0.00						

Source: Survey Data

Since the p value (0.00) is less than the 0.05 level of significance, the researcher rejects the null hypothesis that there is no association between the urban or rural area in which the car owner is situated and the after sales service of the car dealer influencing the car purchase decision. Hence, it is concluded that there is significant association between the area and the after sales service of the car dealer influencing the car purchase decision.

Influence of Impressive Advertisements

A car purchase decision could be influenced by impressive advertisement of the car. Table 62 highlights that, out of 298 car owners from the rural area 88 of them strongly agreed to the opinion that impressive advertisements of the car are important and influenced their car purchase decision, 119 of them agreed, 15 disagreed and 20 strongly disagreed to this opinion. Out of 304 car owners from the urban area 53 of them strongly agreed to the opinion that impressive advertisements of the car are important and influenced their car purchase decision, 93 of them agreed, 58 disagreed and 52 strongly disagreed to this opinion.

Table 62
Influence of Impressive Advertisements

Area	*Opinion*					*Total*
	Strongly Disagree	*Disagree*	*Undecided*	*Agree*	*Strongly Agree*	
Rural	20	15	56	119	88	298
Urban	52	58	48	93	53	304
Total	72	73	104	212	141	602

Chi-square value = 51.988, degrees of freedom = 4, p value = 0.00
Source: Survey Data

The p value (0.00) being less than the 0.05 level of significance, the researcher rejects the null hypothesis that there is no association between the urban or rural area in which the car owner is situated and the impressive advertisements influencing the car purchase decision. Hence, it is concluded that there is significant association between the area and the impressive advertisements influencing the car purchase decision.

Influence of Spare Parts Availability

A car purchase decision could be influenced by spare parts of the car. Table 63 exposes that, out of 298 car owners from the rural area 62 of them strongly agreed to the opinion that spare parts availability of the car are important and influenced their car purchase decision, 177 of them agreed, 8 disagreed and 2 strongly disagreed to this opinion. Out of 304 car owners from the urban area 82 of them strongly agreed to the opinion that spare parts availability of the car are important and influenced their car purchase decision, 113 of them agreed, 36 disagreed and 16 strongly disagreed to this opinion.

Table 63
Opinion of Spare Parts

	Opinion					
Area	*Strongly Disagree*	*Disagree*	*Undecided*	*Agree*	*Strongly Agree*	*Total*
Rural	2	8	49	177	62	298
Urban	16	36	57	113	82	304
Total	18	44	106	290	144	602

Chi-square value = 41.158, degrees of freedom = 4, p value = 0.00
Source: Survey Data

Since the p value (0.00) is less than the 0.05 level of significance, the researcher rejects the null hypothesis that there is no association between the urban or rural area in which the car owner is situated and the spare parts availability influencing the car purchase decision. Hence it is concluded that there is significant association between the area and the spare parts availability influencing the car purchase decision.

Free Sops Available for the Car as Sales Promotion

A car purchase decision could be influenced by free sops for the car. Table 64 divulges that, out of 298 car owners from the rural area 153 of them strongly agreed to the opinion that free sops for the car are important and influenced their car purchase decision, 90 of them agreed, 17 disagreed and 4 strongly disagreed to this opinion. Out of 304 car owners from the urban area 115 of them strongly agreed to the opinion that free sops for the car are important and influenced their car purchase decision, 68 of them agreed, 44 disagreed and 29 strongly disagreed to this opinion.

Table 64
Free Sops Available for the Car as Sales Promotion

Area	*Opinion*					*Total*
	Strongly Disagree	*Disagree*	*Undecided*	*Agree*	*Strongly Agree*	
Rural	4	17	34	90	153	298
Urban	29	44	48	68	115	304
Total	33	61	82	158	268	602

Chi-square value = 41.676, degrees of freedom = 4, p value = 0.00
Source: Survey Data

Since the p value (0.00) is less than the 0.05 level of significance, the researcher rejects the null hypothesis that there is no association between the urban or rural area in which the car owner is situated and the free sops for the car influencing the car purchase decision. Hence, it is concluded that there is significant association between the area and the free sops influencing the car purchase decision. Hence, the number of people who strongly agreed that free sops are important in the car purchase decision is more in the rural area than in the urban area.

Reason for Shifting from Two-Wheelers to Cars

The reasons for shifting from two-wheelers to cars are found to be very common among the urban and rural areas. Some of the factors attributed for the shift are status symbol, increased disposal income and car loan availability. The easy availability of car loans have increased the chances of shifting from two-wheelers to cars.

Status Symbol

There are several reasons for shifting from two-wheelers to cars. The sample units were surveyed to know if status symbol was a reason for their shifting from two-wheelers to cars. Table 65 shows that, out of 225 car owners from the rural area 119 of them strongly agreed to the opinion that status symbol is an important reason for shifting from two-wheelers to cars, 26 agreed, 43 disagreed and 18 strongly disagreed to this opinion. Out of 262 car owners from the urban area 159 of them strongly agreed to the opinion, 20 of them agreed, 24 disagreed and 41 strongly disagreed to this opinion.

Table 65
Influence of Status Symbol

Area	*Opinion*					*Total*
	Strongly Disagree	*Disagree*	*Undecided*	*Agree*	*Strongly Agree*	
Rural	18	43	19	26	119	225
Urban	41	24	18	20	159	262
Total	59	67	37	46	278	487

Chi-square value = 18.213, degrees of freedom = 4, p value = 0.001
Source: Survey Data

The p value (0.001) being less than the 0.05 level of significance, the researcher rejects the null hypothesis that there is no association between the urban or rural area in which the car owner is situated and the status symbol. Hence, it is concluded that there is significant association between the area and status symbol. Hence, the number of people who strongly agreed that status symbol was the reason for shifting from two-wheelers to cars is more in the urban area than in the rural area.

Neighbour Possessing a Car

The sample units were surveyed to know if neighbour possessing a car was a reason for their shifting from two-wheelers to cars. Table 66 exhibits that, out of 224 car owners from the rural area 4 of them strongly agreed to the opinion that neighbour possessing a car is an important reason for shifting from two-wheelers to cars, 8 agreed, 78 disagreed and 61 strongly disagreed. Out of 262 car owners from the urban area 14 of them strongly agreed to the opinion, 15 of them agreed, 89 disagreed and 93 strongly disagreed to this opinion.

Since the p value (0.003) is less than the 0.05 level of significance, the researcher rejects the null hypothesis that there is no association between the urban or rural area in which the car owner is situated and the neighbour possessing a car. Hence

Table 66
Influence of Neighbour Possessing a Car

Area	*Opinion*					*Total*
	Strongly Disagree	*Disagree*	*Undecided*	*Agree*	*Strongly Agree*	
Rural	61	78	73	8	4	224
Urban	93	89	51	15	14	262
Total	154	167	124	23	18	486

Chi-square value = 16.090, degrees of freedom = 4, p value = 0.003
Source: Survey Data

it is concluded that there is significant association between the area and neighbour possessing a car. Hence, the number of people who strongly agreed that neighbour possessing a car was the reason for shifting from two-wheelers to cars is more in the urban area than in the rural area.

Car Loan Availability

The sample units were surveyed to know if car loan availability was a reason for their shifting from two-wheelers to cars. Table 67 makes known that, out of 224 car owners from the rural area 75 of them strongly agreed to the opinion that car loan availability is an important reason for shifting from two-wheelers to cars, 65 agreed, 21 disagreed and 7 strongly disagreed. Out of 262 car owners from the urban area 87 of them strongly agreed to the opinion, 72 of them agreed, 38 disagreed and 23 strongly disagreed to this opinion.

Table 67
Influence of Car Loan Availability

Area	*Opinion*					*Total*
	Strongly Disagree	*Disagree*	*Undecided*	*Agree*	*Strongly Agree*	
Rural	7	21	56	65	75	224
Urban	23	38	42	72	87	262
Total	30	59	98	137	162	486

Chi-square value = 13.791, degrees of freedom = 4, p value = 0.008
Source: Survey Data

At 0.05 level of significance, the p value (0.008) was found to be less than the significance level. Thus, the researcher rejects the null hypothesis that there is no association between the urban or rural area in which the car owner is situated and the car loan availability. Hence it is concluded that there is significant association between the area and car loan availability. Hence the number of people who strongly agreed that car loan availability was the reason for shifting from two-wheelers to cars is more in the urban area than in the rural area.

Increased Disposable Income

The sample units were surveyed to know if increased disposable income was a reason for their shifting from two-wheelers to cars. Table 68 exhibits that, out of 224 car owners from the rural area 58 of them strongly agreed to the opinion that increased d·sposable income is an important reason for shifting from two-wheelers to cars, 81 agreed, 32 disagreed and 8 strongly disagreed. Out of 262 car owners from the urban area 102 of them strongly agreed to the opinion, 91 of them agreed, 16 disagreed and 12 strongly disagreed to this opinion.

Table 68
Influence of Disposable Income

	Opinion					
Area	*Strongly Disagree*	*Disagree*	*Undecided*	*Agree*	*Strongly Agree*	*Total*
Rural	8	32	45	81	58	224
Urban	12	16	41	91	102	262
Total	20	48	86	172	160	486

Chi-square value = 16.128, degrees of freedom = 4, p value = 0.003
Source: Survey Data

Since the p value (0.003) is less than the 0.05 level of significance, the researcher rejects the null hypothesis that there is no association between the urban or rural area in which the car owner is situated and the increased disposable income. Hence it is concluded that there is significant association between the area and increased disposable income. Hence the number of people who strongly agreed that increased disposable income was the reason for shifting from two-wheelers to cars is more in the urban area than in the rural area.

Availability of Good after Sales Service

The sample units were surveyed to know if availability of good after sales service was a reason for their shifting from two-wheelers to cars. Table 69 highlights that, out of 223 car owners from the rural area 37 of them strongly agreed to the opinion that availability of good after sales service is an important reason for shifting from two-wheelers to cars, 85 agreed, 25 disagreed and 3 strongly disagreed. Out of 262 car owners from the urban area 54 of them strongly agreed to the opinion, 68 of them agreed, 33 disagreed and 16 strongly disagreed to this opinion.

Table 69
Influence of Availability of after Sales Service

Area	*Opinion*					*Total*
	Strongly Disagree	*Disagree*	*Undecided*	*Agree*	*Strongly Agree*	
Rural	3	25	73	85	37	223
Urban	16	33	91	68	54	262
Total	19	58	164	153	91	485

Chi-square value = 13.993, degrees of freedom = 4, p value = 0.007
Source: Survey Data

The p value (0.007) was found to be less than the 0.05 level of significance. Thus, the researcher rejects the null hypothesis that there is no association between the urban or rural area in which the car owner is situated and the availability of good after sales service. Hence it is concluded that there is significant association between the area and availability of good after sales service.

Desire for a Change

Change is inevitable. The only constant thing in the world is change. The sample units were surveyed to know if desire for a change was a reason for their shifting from two-wheelers to cars. Table 70 reveals that, out of 224 car owners from the rural area 88 of them strongly agreed to the opinion that desire for a change is an important reason for shifting from two-wheelers to cars, 78 agreed, 24 disagreed and 11 strongly disagreed. Out of 262 car owners from the urban area 114 of them strongly agreed to the opinion, 62 of them agreed, 24 disagreed and 11 strongly disagreed to this opinion.

Table 70
Influence of Desire for a Change

Area	*Opinion*					*Total*
	Strongly Disagree	*Disagree*	*Undecided*	*Agree*	*Strongly Agree*	
Rural	11	24	23	78	88	224
Urban	11	24	51	62	114	262
Total	22	48	74	140	202	486

Chi-square value = 12.877, degrees of freedom = 4, p value = 0.012
Source: Survey Data

As the p value (0.012) was found less than the 0.05 level of significance, the researcher rejects the null hypothesis that there is no association between the urban or rural area in which the car owner is situated and the desire for a change. Hence it is concluded that there is significant association between the area and desire for a change. Hence the number of people who strongly agreed that desire for a change was the reason for shifting from two-wheelers to cars is more in the urban area than in the rural area.

Source of Fund

The sample units were surveyed to know the source of fund for the purchase of their cars. Table 71 shows that out of 298 car owners from the rural area 27 of them preferred NBFC, 176 of them preferred commercial banks, 36 of them preferred private financiers, 20 of them depended on friends and relatives and 39 relied on self. Out of 304 car owners from the rural area 27 of them preferred NBFC, 178 of them preferred commercial banks, 32 of them preferred private financiers, 11 of them depended on friends and relatives and 56 relied on self.

Table 71
Source of Fund in the Purchase of Car

Area	*Sources*					*Total*
	NBFC	*Commercial Bank*	*Private Financiers*	*Friends/ Relatives*	*Self*	
Rural	27	176	36	20	39	298
Urban	27	178	32	11	56	304
Total	54	354	68	31	95	602

Chi-square value = 5.842, degrees of freedom = 4, p value = 0.211
Source: Survey Data

Since the p value (0.211) is greater than the 0.05 level of significance, the researcher accepts the null hypothesis that there is no association between the urban or rural area in which the car owner is situated and the source of fund. Hence it is concluded that there is no significant association between the area and source of fund.

Opinion of Pre-owned Car Outlets

The sample units were surveyed to know their opinion of pre-owned car outlets in Kerala. Table 72 divulges that, out of 298 car owners from the rural area 5 of them opined very good, 91 opined good, 121 opined bad, 50 opined very bad and 31 had no opinion. Out of 304 car owners from the urban area 16 of them opined very good, 89 opined good, 112 opined bad, 48 opined very bad and 39 had no opinion.

Table 72
Opinion about Pre-owned Car Outlets

Area	*Opinion*					*Total*
	Very Good	*Good*	*Bad*	*Very Bad*	*No Opinion*	
Rural	5	91	121	50	31	298
Urban	16	89	112	48	39	304
Total	21	180	233	98	70	602

Chi-square value = 7.028, degrees of freedom = 4, p value = 0.134
Source: Survey Data

At 0.05 level of significance, the p value (0.134) was found greater than the significance level. Thus, the researcher accepts the null hypothesis that there is no association between the urban or rural area in which the car owner is situated and the opinion about pre-owned car outlets in Kerala. Hence it is concluded that the opinion about pre-owned car outlets is the same throughout Kerala.

After Sales Service of Car Dealers

The sample units were surveyed to know their opinion about the after sales service of the car dealers. Table 73 exposes that, out of 298 car owners from the rural area 127 of them opined YES and 171 of them opined NO. Out of 304 car owners from the urban area 153 of them opined yes and 151 of them opined no.

Table 73
Opinion About After Sales Service of the Car Dealers

	Opinion		
Area	*No*	*Yes*	*Total*
Rural	171	127	298
Urban	151	153	304
Total	322	280	602

Chi-square value = 3.597, degrees of freedom = 1, p value = 0.058
Source: Survey Data

Since the p value (0.058) is greater than the 0.05 level of significance, the researcher accepts the null hypothesis that there is no association between the urban or rural area in which the car owner is situated and the opinion about after sales service of car dealers. Hence it is concluded that the opinion about after sales service of car dealers is the same throughout Kerala which means that majority of the car owners both from rural and urban areas of Kerala opined that the car dealers in Kerala do not provide good after service. The reason for this is explained in the next table.

Reasons for Poor after Sales Service

The sample units were surveyed to know their reasons for poor after sales service of the car dealers. Table 74 makes known that, out of 168 car owners from the rural area who said NO to the opinion of the after sales service of the dealers, 26 of them opined that 'inadequate strength of service personnel' was the reason, 10 of them opined that 'incompetent/unskilled service staff' was the reason, 15 opined that 'few number of service centres' was the reason, 12 opined that 'expensive after sales service' was the reason and 105 opined all the above reasons for poor after sales service. Out of 151 car owners from the urban area who said NO to the opinion of the after sales service of the dealers, 21 of them opined that 'inadequate strength of service personnel' was the reason, 4 of them opined that 'incompetent/unskilled service staff' was the reason, 4 opined that 'few number of service centres' was the reason, 32 opined that 'expensive after sales service' was the reason and 90 opined all the above reasons for poor after sales service.

Table 74
Reasons for Poor After Sales Service

Area	*Opinions*					*Total*
	Inadequate strength of service personnel	*Incompetent/ unskilled service staff*	*Few number of service centres*	*Expensive after sales service*	*All the above*	
Rural	26	10	15	12	105	168
Urban	21	4	4	32	90	151
Total	47	14	19	44	195	319

Chi-square value = 18.864, degrees of freedom = 4, p value = 0.001
Source: Survey Data

The p value (0.001) being less than the 0.05 level of significance, the researcher rejects the null hypothesis that there is no association between the urban or rural area in which the car owner is situated and the reasons for poor after sales service. Hence it is concluded that there is significant association between the area and reasons for poor after sales service. Among the number of people who opined that after sales service of car dealer is poor was more in the rural area than in the urban area.

Nature of Employment and Customer Satisfaction

Customer satisfaction is very much related to the nature of employment. Government employees, private employees, self employed, retired and homemaker have different levels of customer satisfaction. The customer satisfaction index is measured by several research firms like A.C. Nielsen indicating the level of satisfaction that the customer enjoys in terms of benefits sought from the product or service purchase from the market. Car dealers promote their cars by announcing several offers for the government employees, doctors, teachers and several other professions. Corporate offer is also available in the car market for the private employees.

After Sales Service of Car Dealers

The sample units were surveyed to know their opinion about the after sales service of the car dealers and to know the level of customer satisfaction. Table 75 exhibits that, out of 174 government employees, 104 opined yes and 70 opined no. Out of 186 private employees, 79 opined yes and 107 opined no. Out of 220 self-employed, 88 opined yes and 132 opined no. Out of 22 retired car owners, 9 opined yes and 13 opined no.

Table 75
Opinion about After Sales Service of the Car Dealers

	Opinion		
Employment	*No*	*Yes*	*Total*
Government Employees	70	104	174
Private Employees	107	79	186
Self-Employed	132	88	220
Retired	13	9	22
Total	322	280	602

Chi-square value = 19.490, degrees of freedom = 6, p value = 0.003
Source: Survey Data

Since the p value (0.003) is less than the 0.05 level of significance, the researcher rejects the null hypothesis that there is no association between the nature of employment and the opinions about the after sales service of the car dealers. Hence it is concluded that there is significant association between the nature of employment and the opinions about the after sales service of the car dealers. Hence the government employees are the only group which opined that the after sales service of the car dealers was good and other groups opined that the after sales service of the car dealers are bad.

ANOVA (ANALYSIS OF VARIANCE)

Influence of Income on the Purchase of Higher End Models of Cars

It was enquired whether increase in the income of the car owners had an influence on the purchase of higher end models of cars in the car market in Kerala. For this six different models of cars were studied namely, Maruti 800, Maruti Alto, Maruti Zen, Tata Indica, Hyundai Santro and other models of cars in which Maruti Wagon R was included. To validate this, a one way ANOVA (Analysis of Variance) test was conducted. The null hypothesis formulated was that there was no significant difference between the average monthly income of the car owner with respect to the purchase of higher end brand of cars.

Table 76
Regions and Brand of Cars

		Value Label	*N*
Region	1	North	203
	2	Central	199
	3	South	200
Brand	1	Maruti 800	189
	2	Maruti Alto	109
	3	Maruti Zen	53
	5	Tata Indica	100
	6	Santro	85
	8	Others	66

Source: Survey data

The Figure 5 showing the error bar for the average monthly income of the car owner with respect to their brands of cars is given below. Thus from the graph it can be observed that higher end models of cars are preferred by those with higher income.

Table 76 highlights the number of respondents owning the different brands of cars in Kerala. Out of the 602 car owners, 189 owned Maruti 800, 109 owned Alto, 53 owned Zen, 100 owned Tata Indica and 85 owned Santro.

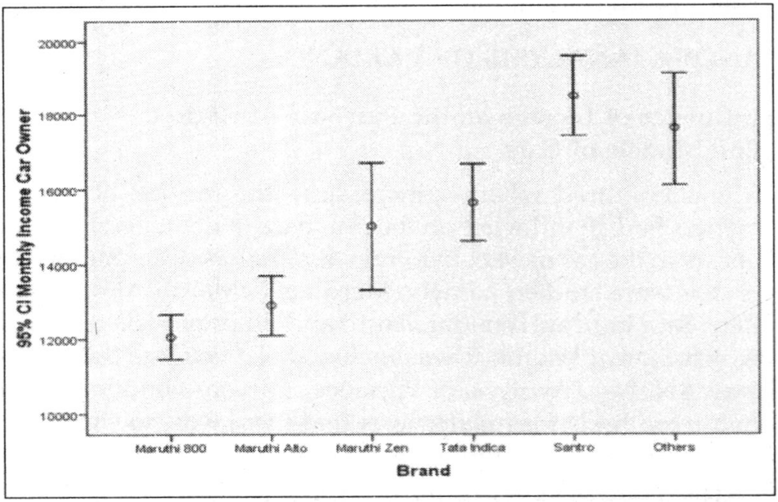

Figure 5: Influence of Income with Respect to the Brands of Cars

Table 77 divulges that there is influence of income in the brands of cars owned by the people in Kerala. The different brands of cars are Maruti 800, Maruti Alto, Santro, Zen and Tata Indica. The mean income of people owning Maruti 800 is 12053 and of Alto is 12895. The standard deviation of Maruti 800 is 4124 and of Alto is 4236.

Since the p value (0.00) is less than the 0.05 level of significance, we reject the null hypothesis that there is no significant difference in the average monthly income of car owners with respect to their brand of cars. Thus it can be concluded that there is significant difference in the average

Table 77
Influence of Income with Respect to the Brands of Cars

					Monthly Income Car Owner			
					95% Confidence Interval for Mean			
Brand of Car	*N*	*Mean*	*Std. Deviation*	*Std. Error*	*Lower Bound*	*Upper Bound*	*Minimum*	*Maximum*
Maruti 800	189	12052.91	4124.054	299.981	11461.15	12644.67	2000	30000
Maruti Alto	109	12894.50	4236.128	405.748	12090.23	13698.76	2500	25000
Maruti Zen	53	15000.00	6136.273	842.882	13308.63	16691.37	6000	30000
Tata Indica	100	15630.00	5198.397	519.840	14598.53	16661.47	8000	40000
Santro	85	18505.88	5077.081	550.687	17410.78	19600.98	9000	30000
Others	66	17621.21	6173.804	759.943	16103.50	19138.92	5000	35000
Total	602	14580.56	5467.852	222.853	14142.90	15018.23	2000	40000

Sum of Squares = 3.557E9, df = 5, Mean Square = 7.113E8, F = 29.418, Sig. = 0.00
Source: Survey Data

monthly income of the car owner with respect to their brand of cars. Hence we can finally conclude that the high income group prefer high end models.

FACTOR ANALYSIS

An attempt was made to identify the underlying factors among the observed variables in the study, which are responsible for the influence of the car purchase decision in the small car market in Kerala. The variables under study have a correlation with the respective factors which can be explained by the factor loadings and the communalities that these factors assume. For this the factorability of the variables is first tested to see if the variables are suitable for undergoing factor analysis. This is tested using Kaiser-Mayer-Olkin measure of sampling adequacy. The factor, which has the highest factor loading is considered to be the most important factor which the sample units consider will influence their car purchase decision. The underlying variables that are subject tc the factor analysis are power steering, colour of the car, power windows, easy entry and exit, upholstery, remote control, air conditioner, body coloured bumpers, easy shift gears, spaciousness, suspension, comfortable seats, leg space, booster assisted brakes, streamlined dash board, audio system, fuel, seat belts and air bags. Since the p value (0.00) is less than the 0.05 level of significance we reject the null hypothesis that the data is not suitable for factor analysis and are not factorable. Hence it can be concluded that the variables are suitable for factor analysis. The eighteen variables here are in eighteen different dimensions. They are not in groups or forming factors. The null hypothesis that the variables are not factorable and are independent variables gets rejected and conclude that the variables are associated and they form factors. Communality is the proportion of a variable's variance explained by a four factor structure. The communalities can be mathematically by squaring the factor loadings of a variable across all factors and then summing the figures. Thus communality may be interpreted as a measure of 'uniqueness'. A low communality figure indicates that the variable if statistically independent and can not be combined with other variables. Factor analysis with principal component extraction under varimax rotation is adopted. Coefficients below 0.3 are not included in the rotated component matrix.

The appropriateness of factor analysis model with given data or whether the data were suitable for conducting factor analysis was tested using Kaiser-Meyer-Olkin Measure of Sampling Adequacy and Bartlett's test of Sphericity.

Table 78
KMO and Bartlett's Test

Kaiser-Meyer-Olkin Measure of Sampling Adequacy		0.875
Bartlett's Test of Sphericity	Approx. Chi-Square	5607.410
	Df	153
	Sig.	0.000

Source: Survey Data

Sampling adequacy measured by the KMO predicts whether the data are likely to factor well, based on correlation and partial correlation. This is used to assess which variables to drop from the model because they are too multi-collinear. There is a KMO statistic for each individual variable, and their sum is the KMO overall statistic. KMO varies from zero to 1.0 and the KMO overall should be 0.6 or higher to proceed with factor analysis.

As it can be seen from Table 78, the KMO value is 0.875, which was sufficiently high to conclude that it was appropriate to use factor analysis with the data to reach meaningful conclusions as 87.5% common variance was explained by the underlying factors.

Bartlett's test of Sphericity is used to test the hypothesis that the correlation matrix of variables is an identity matrix (a matrix where all diagonal terms are 1.0 and all of diagonal terms are zeroes), which would indicate that the variables are unrelated. Here the result was significant (Chi-square value 5607.410, significant at 5%) leading to the conclusion that there were underlying relationships between the variables that might yield a pattern in the factor analysis.

Eighteen variables were forced to refactor. All factors with Eigen values above 1.0 were extracted. The factors that should be retained for analysis should have an Eigen value greater than one. Eigen value is the sum of the square of the factor loadings. Coefficient of correlation less than 0.40 were suppressed and Principle Component with varimax rotation was performed. Four factors emerged clearly in the analysis. In most cases, variables were loading on their appropriate factors. However, some variables were loading on separate factors. At this point, a few variables were removed from different factors to further enhance inter-variable correlation and scale reliability. The remaining variables were included in a factor analysis. The researcher examines the importance of four factors in the study viz., comfort factor, aesthetic factor and technology factor. Table 79 discloses the communalities of the variables used in factor analysis. The extraction of each variable is shown in the table. Principle component analysis was the extraction method use to find out the extraction of each variable in the study.

Table 79
Communalities

Variables	*Extraction*
Power steering	.594
Attractive Colour	.689
Power windows	.691
Easy entry & Exit	.666
Upholstery	.659
Remote Control	.637
Air conditioner	.428
Body coloured bumpers	.511
Easy shift gears	.612
It should be spacious	.709
Good suspension	.687
Comfortable seats	.660
Ample leg space	.686
Booster assisted brakes	.845
Streamlined dash board	.839
Audio system	.592
Diesel/Petrol/LPG/CNG Car(fuel specific)	.665
Sear belts/Air bags	.530

Extraction Method: Principal Component Analysis

Source: Survey Data

Table 80
Total Variance Explained

	Extraction Sums of Squared Loadings			Rotation Sums of Squared Loadings		
Component	*Total*	*% of Variance*	*Cumulative %*	*Total*	*% of Variance*	*Cumulative %*
1	6.575	36.530	36.530	4.037	22.428	22.428
2	2.534	14.075	50.605	2.917	16.206	38.634
3	1.553	8.626	59.231	2.556	14.200	52.834
4	1.039	5.773	65.004	2.191	12.170	65.004

Extraction Method: Principal Component Analysis
Source: Survey Data

Table 80 explains the total variance. The Eigen values of each factor and the contribution of each factor to the total variance is explained in this table. The table reveals the extent of correlation of each underlying variable with each factor. The Eigen value of the first factor is 6.575 and it contributes up to

Table 81
The Rotated Component Matrix

	Component			
	1	*2*	*3*	*4*
It should be spacious	.826			
Ample leg space	.801			
Comfortable seats	.749			
Easy entry & Exit	.694		.427	
Upholstery	.694			
Easy shift gears	.605		.366	
Air conditioner	.465			
Seat belts/Air bags		.701		
Booster assisted brakes		.912		
Good suspension		.759		
Fuel injection			.684	
Audio system			.656	
Power windows			.765	
Power steering		.320	.639	
Body coloured bumpers		.320		.567
Streamlined dash board				.898
Attractive colour	.360			.798

Extraction Method: Principal Component Analysis
Source: Survey Data

36.53 per cent of the total variance. The Eigen value of the second factor is 2.534 and it contributes 14.075 per cent of the total variance. The Eigen value of the third factor is 1.553 and it contributes 8.626 per cent of the total variance. The Eigen value of the fourth factor is 1.039 and it contributes 5.773 per cent of the total variance. The first factor whose Eigen value is 6.575 is called the comfort factor. The second factor whose Eigen value is 2.534 is call the safety factor. The third factor whose Eigen value is 1.553 is called the aesthetic factor and the fourth factor whose Eigen value is 1.039 is termed as technology factor.

Comfort Factor

The first factor is the comfort factor. The underlying variables under this factor are spaciousness, ample leg space, comfortable seats, easy entry and exit, upholstery, easy shift gears and air conditioner. The variable spaciousness is correlated with the first factor called comfort factor to a level of 0.826, ample leg space to a level of 0.801, comfortable seats to a level of 0.749, easy entry and exit to a level of 0.694, upholstery is 0.694, easy shift gears is 0.605 and air conditioner is 0.435. As it can be observed from Table 80, the Eigen value of the first factor (comfort factor) is 6.575 which contributes up to 36.53 per cent of the total variance.

Safety Factor

The second factor is the safety factor. The variables included in this factor are booster assisted brakes which is 0.912 times correlated with the factor, seats and air bags which is 0.701 times correlated with the factor, good suspension which is 0.759 correlated with the factor. As it can be observed from Table 80, the Eigen value is 2.534 with a contribution of 14.075 per cent of the total variance.

Aesthetic Factor

The variables included in this factor are attractive colour which is 0.798 times correlated with the factor called aesthetics, streamlined dash board which is 0.898 times correlated with the factor, body coloured bumpers which is 0.567 times correlated with the factor. As it can be observed from Table 4.80, the Eigen value for this factor is 1.553 with a contribution of 8.626 per cent of the total variance.

Technology Factor

The variables included in this factor are power steering, which is 0.639 times correlated with this factor, power windows which is 0.765 times correlated with this factor, audio system which is 0.656 times correlated to the factor, fuel injection system which is 0.684 times correlated to the factor. As it can be observed from Table 80, the Eigen value for this factor is 1.039 with a contribution of 5.77 per cent of the total variance. All the four factors together explain 65 per cent of the total variance. The remaining 35 per cent variance is explained by the factors, which are not included in the study.

Hence, it can be concluded that out of the four factors namely comfort, safety, aesthetics and technology, the comfort factor has been rated as the most important factor by the sample units in the small car market in Kerala.

5 Findings, Conclusions and Recommendations

This study attempts to throw light on the promotional strategies in the small car market in the State of Kerala in general and its buyer behaviour in particular. In this context, the influence of promotional strategies in the purchase decision of a car has been discussed at length in the preceding chapters. Having done so, it is now proposed to summarise the findings and conclusions in the following pages. This chapter is divided into three sections viz., (i) Findings (ii) Conclusions and (iii) Recommendations.

A survey was conducted among 602 car owners across northern, central and southern regions of Kerala to know the influence of social and economic factors in the car purchase decision in Kerala. It was also enquired among the sample units to know the influence of promotional strategies adopted by the car manufacturers and car dealers in the small car market in Kerala. The researcher has also constructed hypotheses to know if there was any significance in the differences in social factors, economic factors, cultural factors and other buying behaviour among the regions, age groups, income groups, gender and occupation in Kerala. After the data collection from the sample units was conducted, it was subject to different statistical tools like Percentage Analysis, Chi-square Test, ANOVA and Factor Analysis to analyze the data and interpret them in order to summarize the findings and draw appropriate conclusions. The findings of the study were as follows:

FINDINGS

- Majority of the car owners in Kerala use Maruti 800. It is followed by Maruti Alto, Tata Indica and Hyundai Santro.
- The various social factors that influenced the car purchase decision in the small car market in Kerala are friends, relatives, own family members, neighbours and one's own decision. Among these social factors it was found that 'own family members' influenced the car purchase decision the most. It was followed by friends, own decision, relatives and neighbours.
- The family members that influenced the car purchase decision in the small car market in Kerala comprise husband, wife, children, father, mother and siblings. Among them, the husband or the wife or both influenced the car purchase decision the most.
- The various promotional tools that influenced the car purchase decision in the small car market in Kerala are newspaper, television, radio, internet, magazines, word of mouth, car shows, test drives, exchange melas and loan melas. Among them 'word of mouth' was ranked first which influenced the car purchase decision the most, followed by magazine, television, internet, newspaper, test drive, car shows, radio and exchange melas.
- Majority of the people in Kerala strongly agreed that price of the car, mileage, brand of the car, design and style, after sales service, impressive advertisements and discounts are important factors that influence the car purchase decision.
- Majority of the people in Kerala depended on commercial banks as the source of fund for their car purchase. It was followed by self financing, private financiers, NBFC, friends and relatives.
- Majority of the people in Kerala had a bad opinion about the pre-owned car outlets or used car outlets operating in Kerala.
- The various social factors that influenced the car purchase decision in the small car market in Kerala are friends,

relatives, own family members, neighbours and one's own decision.

- The people who take a decision on their own regarding a car purchase were more in the northern region than in the central and southern regions.
- The people who depend on their friends for a car purchase decision were more in the southern region than in the northern and central regions.
- A car purchase decision could be influenced by the members of one's own family like wife, husband, children, father, mother, siblings and grand parents. The husband or wife in a family contributes the most in the car purchase decision in the southern region than in the central and northern regions.
- The role of children in the family decision making in the purchase of a car was more in the central region than in the northern and southern regions.
- Advertisement plays a very important role in the car purchase decision in Kerala. Advertisements in the print media and in the electronic media have influenced the decision in purchasing a car in the different regions of Kerala. Northern and southern regions were more influenced by advertisements than the central region.
- Sales promotion plays a very important role in the car purchase decision in Kerala. Sales promotion like free offers, free service and other freebies have influenced the decision in purchasing a car in the different regions of Kerala. The influence of sales promotion was more in the southern region than in the central and northern regions of Kerala.
- The influence of discounts was more in the northern and southern regions than in the central region of Kerala .
- The influence of free insurance was more in the central region than in the northern and southern regions of Kerala.
- People of Kerala have attributed several factors that are responsible for replacing their previous cars. The factors

responsible for replacing their previous cars are increased income, large family size, availability of car financing schemes, expiry of car life, attractive models, increasing maintenance cost, poor service quality of the present car, and availability of car exchange programme.

- The people who attributed 'increased family size' as the reason for the replacement of their previous car were more in the northern region than in the southern region.
- The people who attributed 'availability of financing schemes' as the reason for the replacement of their previous car were more in the central region than in the southern region.
- The people who attributed 'life of the car' as the reason for the replacement of their previous car were more in the central region than in the northern region.
- The people who attributed 'increase in the maintenance cost' as the reason for the replacement of their previous car were more in the central region than in the southern region.
- The people who opined that cars provide more safety than two-wheelers as the reason for shifting from two-wheelers to cars were more in the central region than in the southern region.
- The people who opined that cars are more convenient for a family to travel is an important factor for shifting from two-wheelers to cars were more in the southern region than in the central region.
- The people who opined that neighbour possessing a car was an important factor for shifting from two-wheelers to cars were more in the southern region than in the central region.
- The people who opined that possessing a car is a status symbol and was an important factor for shifting from two-wheelers to cars was found more in the southern region than in the northern region.

- The people who opined that cars provide value for the money spent was an important factor for shifting from two-wheelers to cars were more in the northern region than in the central region.
- The people who opined that car loan availability was an important factor for shifting from two-wheelers to cars were more in the southern region than in the central region.
- The people who opined that increased disposable income was an important factor for shifting from two-wheelers to cars were more in the central region than in the southern region.
- The people who opined that after sales service factor was an important factor for shifting from two-wheelers to cars were more in the southern region than in the northern region
- The brand of cars like Tata Indica, Hyundai Santro, Maruti Wagon R and Maruti Zen are preferred more by males than by females in Kerala.
- Males are more prone to take individual decisions in the purchase of a car than females.
- The influence of father, mother and siblings in the car purchase decision was more in the case of males than in females in Kerala.
- Males and females strongly agreed to the opinion that price is the most important factor while buying a car.
- Males who strongly agreed to the opinion that brand image, resale value of the car, impressive advertisements and preference of discounts are important factors were more than the females.
- The males who disagreed to the opinion that pressure from the family members was the most important factor were more than the females.
- The females who agreed to the opinion that neighbour influences the car purchase decision were more than the males.

- The females who strongly agreed to the opinion that car loan availability was the reason for shifting from two-wheelers to cars were more than the males.
- The females who strongly agreed to the opinion that increased disposable income was the reason for shifting from two-wheelers to cars were more than the males.
- The people having a monthly income between 8000 and 12000 rupees who were influenced by their wives or husbands, discounts, impressive advertisements, design and style were more than any other income groups.
- The people having a monthly income between 16000 and 20000 rupees who opined that brand image, design and style, influenced most in the car purchase decision were more than any other income groups.
- The people who take a decision on their own, regarding a car purchase were more in the urban area than in the rural area.
- The people who are influenced by their wives or husbands were more in the rural area than in the urban area.
- The people who are influenced most by newspapers, television and radio were more in the rural area than in the urban area.
- There is no significant association between the urban or rural area and the price influencing the car purchase decision. Thus, price influences the car purchase decision in urban and rural areas equally.
- The people who are influenced by brand of the car, design and style, were more in the urban area than in the rural area.
- The people who strongly agreed that impressive advertisements and spare parts availability are important in the car purchase decision were more in the rural area than in the urban area.
- The people who strongly agreed that free sops are important in the car purchase decision were more in the rural area than in the urban area.

- The number of people who strongly agreed that status symbol, neighbour possessing a car, car loan availability, increased disposable income, availability of after sales service, desire for a change were the reasons for shifting from two-wheelers to cars were more in the urban area than in the rural area.
- There is no significant association between the area and source of fund. The source of fund chosen by car owners is the same across urban and rural areas.
- Majority of the people of Kerala, both from rural and urban areas, opined that the car dealers in Kerala do not provide good after sales service.
- Among the number of people who opined that after sales service of car dealer is poor were more in the rural area than in the urban area.
- The government employees are the only group, which opined that the after sales service of the car dealers was good, and other groups opined that the after sales service of the car dealers was bad.
- There is significant difference in the average monthly income of the car owner with respect to their brand of cars. Hence, it was found that, in Kerala, the high income groups prefer high end models.
- Out of the four factors namely comfort, safety, aesthetics and technology, the comfort factor has been rated as the most important factor in the small car market in Kerala.

CONCLUSIONS

1. Among the various small cars in Kerala viz., Maruti 800, Maruti Alto, Tata Indica, Hyundai Santro, Wagon R, Zen Estilo and Swift, Maruti 800 and Maruti Alto are the most preferred brands by the majority of the population in Kerala.
2. Tata Nano has hit the roads on 23rd March 2009. It is going to pose a great challenge to other small cars in India especially the bread and butter models of Maruti Udyog Ltd viz., Maruti 800 and Maruti Alto.

3. Among the various social factors like friends, relatives, own family members, neighbours and one's own decision that influenced the car purchase decision in the small car market in Kerala, it was one's own family members that influenced the car purchase decision the most. Hence, family members are very crucial in the decision making of a car purchase.
4. Among the family members like husband, wife, children, father, mother and siblings that influenced the car purchase decision in the small car market in Kerala, the husband or the wife or both influenced the car purchase decision the most. Hence, husband or wife is the ultimate decision maker in a car purchase.
5. The various promotional tools that influenced the car purchase decision in the small car market in Kerala are newspaper, television, radio, internet, magazines, word of mouth, car shows, test drives, exchange melas and loan melas. Among them 'word of mouth' is ranked first which influenced the car purchase decision the most. Word of mouth is an important and least expensive promotional tool in influencing one's car purchase decision. Hence car dealers and manufacturers should promote their cars primarily through 'word of mouth' promotion.
6. Price of the car, mileage, brand of the car, design and style, after sales service, impressive advertisements and discounts offered are important factors that influence the car purchase decision across all the regions, urban and rural areas, gender, age and income levels.
7. Maruti 800 and Maruti Alto are most preferred brands in Kerala because its price is competitive and affordable by majority of the people, These cars have good mileage, good design and style and also good after sales service. Hence the people of Kerala are very price conscious and brand conscious too.
8. Commercial banks in the public sector have lower interest rates and less documentation procedures compared to other sources of fund. That is the reason why majority of the people in Kerala depend on commercial banks in the

public sector as the source of fund for their car purchase when compared to private financiers and NBFC.

9. The pre-owned car outlets in Kerala sell used cars or second hand cars at a rate, which is not acceptable by many buyers. There is poor market acceptance for this segment because the warranty period is less and it does not deliver the expected performance (mileage). Moreover, its maintenance cost is also high. This is the reason why people have a bad opinion about the pre-owned car outlets in Kerala.

10. The social factors exercise its influence on northern, central and southern regions differently. A few social factors like family members influence northern region more than other two regions and friends influence the southern region more than the other two regions. The reason for this is that there are socio-cultural differences across the regions and age groups in Kerala.

11. The influence of promotional tools in the car purchase decision have been different among urban and rural areas, regions, gender and income groups. The influence of newspapers is more in the rural areas and the influence of televisions and internet are more in urban areas. The reason is that the number of internet connections in households and the number of internet cafes are less in the rural areas than in the urban areas.

12. The people of Kerala replaced their previous cars for the following reasons:-
    - Increased income
    - Increase in the family size
    - Easy availability of financing schemes
    - Life of the car,
    - Attractive models and increasing maintenance cost
    - Poor service quality and the car exchange programme

The above reasons have been seen varying across the different regions, urban and rural areas, gender, age, and income levels in Kerala.

13. Keralites attributed several reasons for shifting from two-wheelers to cars. They are:-
    - Cars provide more safety than two-wheelers
    - Convenient for a family to travel,
    - Status symbol,
    - Neighbour possesses a car,
    - Cars provide value for the money spent,
    - Car loan availability,
    - Increased disposable income,
    - Availability of good after sales service and Desire for a change.

    The above reasons have been seen varying across the different regions, urban and rural areas, gender, age, and income levels in Kerala.
14. Out of the four factors namely comfort, safety, aesthetics and technology, the comfort factor has been rated as the most important factor in the small car market in Kerala. This is because people of Kerala look for more comfort features in a car, than aesthetics and technology.
15. The customer satisfaction of the people in Kerala is very poor with regard to the after sales service of the car dealers. The reasons attributed to the poor after sales service are a) inadequate strength of service personnel, b) incompetent and unskilled service staff, c) few number of service centres d) expensive after sales service and e) service centres do not deliver the serviced vehicle on time.

RECOMMENDATIONS

The following recommendations are offered based on the findings and conclusions drawn from the study.

1. The car manufacturers and dealers may conduct causal marketing like a 'wellness programme' or a 'literacy campaign' for the people of a particular rural or urban area. This will not only improve the sales of the marketer but will also create a brand image of the company and will

benefit the society at large. The marketing efforts should be for the cause of the potential customers and the existing customers.

2. The car dealers should strengthen their direct marketing efforts like house calls, email messages, SMS and telephonic talks so as to generate enquiries for cars in their dealer showrooms.

3. To improve customer satisfaction among potential customers and existing customers, car dealers and car manufacturers should render good after sales service. This can be achieved by:-
   - Providing adequate strength of service personnel in the service centres and showrooms
   - Employing competent and skilled service staff,
   - By increasing the number of service centres especially of Tata motors and Hyundai motors,
   - By providing less expensive after sales service and
   - By providing quick delivery of the serviced vehicle.

4. Presently, the existing customers have rated comfort factor as the most important one. The performance factor should also be given equal importance in marketing a car. Good mileage, sound BHP, efficient torque and superior brake technology should be incorporated so that the buyer of cars should get the advantage of better performance especially when foreign car players are entering the Indian car market.

5. As the reasons for shifting from two-wheelers to cars have been stated by the customers (discussed in the earlier chapter) it is urgent that car manufacturers and dealers should concentrate more on delivering value for the money expended by the car buyers, providing them with car loans of reasonable interest rates and repayment in easy monthly installments.

6. In spite of the political impediments in starting an industry in Kerala, manufacturing plants of Maruti Udyog Ltd, Tata Motors and Hyundai Motors should be started so that it

can provide employment opportunities to many people of Kerala (sons of the soil) and could pass on the benefits of locational advantage to the car buyers in Kerala.

7. Newspapers, televisions and radios being an important promotional tool in the influence of a car purchase decision in the rural areas in Kerala, car dealers and car manufacturers should advertise their cars profusely in these media and also can show clippings of their cars in cinema theatres, have attractive hoardings by way of sponsorship, conduct loan melas and exchange melas frequently, conduct contests, quiz programmes and organize a virtual driving school (simulation) in the area. There should be a free service camp in both rural and urban areas in Kerala for one week in which car wash, car polish and car maintenance can be rendered free of cost.
8. A CRM (Complaint Redressal Machinery) department should be created in every dealer showroom so that a customer or a potential buyer can walk in to this department exclusively for seeking redressal and help for redressing their problems without much difficulty.
9. CSR (Corporate Social Responsibility) should be made mandatory at the manufacturing level. Man is a social animal. He cannot exist on his own. He has to depend on the society for its growth and development. Similarly, car manufacturers should have a social obligation and commitment to the society. The car manufacturer should be able to meet the urgent needs of the society through mutual exchange or a 'give and take' policy.
10. Every car dealer should conduct atleast one customer meet in a month. Conducting customer meets will foster good rapport between the car dealer and the customer. This will improve word of mouth promotion and thus improve sales. The feedback of customers must be taken for analyzing the pitfalls of the car dealers in delivering service to the customer. As Gandhiji has rightly said, "*Customer is the King* - You are not serving the customer but the customer is giving you an opportunity to serve him."

11. Among the various social factors like friends, relatives, own family members, neighbours and one's own decision that influenced the car purchase decision in the small car market in Kerala, it was one's own family members that influenced the car purchase decision the most. Hence family members are very crucial in the decision making of a car purchase.
12. Among the family members like husband, wife, children, father, mother and siblings, the husband or the wife or both influenced the car purchase decision the most. Hence husband or wife is the ultimate decision maker in a car purchase. Keeping this in view car manufacturers and car dealers should target the family members, especially the husband and the wife, for triggering a car purchase. This can be done by providing discount cards or rebate coupons to these family members. These discount cards and rebate coupons will help them purchase a car at discounted rates. These family members should also be given free entry passes to the entertainment programmes, recreation clubs and customer meets organized by the car dealers.
13. 'Buyer Behaviour in the Car Market' or 'Automobile Management' may be offered as a subject for the management courses conducted by the business schools in Kerala.
14. Finally, as one of the major problems cited by one of the dealers is lack of margin given by the car manufacturers. Special arrangements are necessary for ensuring unhindered financial support to the car dealers in Kerala.

SUGGESTIONS FOR FURTHER RESEARCH

The following suggestions are offered for further research in the area connected with the topic of the present study.

1. The distribution channels of car manufacturers be strengthened to ascertain their contribution to the society. It is necessary to find out the social benefits and measure the impact of these distribution activities. A study of this type, if undertaken, would reveal the true results and the benefits thereof by the different sections of the society.

2. A further study on the role played by different promotional agencies is necessary to determine their contribution in serving the purpose of promotion, their problems and suggest measures for further improvement.
3. Yet another area which needs investigation is the causes and the gravity of behavioural patterns, so that, appropriate strategies could be devised for checking the incidence of errand or distorted behavioural pattern in the car purchase decision.

Bibliography

BOOKS

Alba, J.W., Hutchinson J.W. and Lynch J.G., "Memory and Decision Making", Prentice-Hall Englewood Cliffs, NJ, 1991.

Allport, W.G., "Attitudes in C.A. Murchison", *A Handbook of Social Psychology,* Clark University Press, Manchester, 1935.

Amarchand, D. and Vardharajan B., "An Introduction to Marketing", Vikas Publishing House Pvt. Ltd., New Delhi, 1979.

Assael, H., "Consumer Behaviour and Marketing Action", South-Eastern, New York, 1995.

Aswathappa, K., "Organisational Behaviour", Himalaya Publishing House, Mumbai, 1988.

Baker, J., "Marketing–An Introductory Text", 4th ed., MacMillan Publishers Ltd., London, 1985.

Bellur, V.V., "Marketing Research: Theory and Practice", Himalaya Publishing House, Bombay, 1987.

Bellur, V.V., Berkiman and Lau H.F., "Reading in Marketing Management", Himalaya Publishing House, Bombay, 1988.

Bennet, Peter D. and Harold H. Kassarjian, "Consumer Behaviour", Prentice-Hall of India, New Delhi, 1987.

Berlson, B. and Steiner A.G., "Human Behaviour – An Invention of Scientific Findings", New York, 1964.

Bliss and Perry, "Marketing Management and Behavioural Environment", Prentice-Hall of India, New Delhi, 1976.

Bose, B.S., "Handbook of Marketing Management", Himalaya Publishing House, Mumbai, 1998.

Burnett, John J., "Promotion Management", 1st ed., McGraw Hill, 1998.

Chisnall and Peter M., "Marketing: a Behavioural Analysis", McGraw Hill Book Co., UK, 1975.

Chunawala, S.A. and Sethia K.C., "Foundations of Advertising Theory and Practice", Himalaya Publishing House, New Delhi, 1985.

Cohen, A., "Attitude Change and Social Influence", Basic Books, New York, 1964.

Cooper, R.D. and Schindler S.P., "Business Research Methods", Tata McGraw Hill Publishing Co. Ltd., New Delhi, 1999.

Cox, F.D., "The Sorting Role Model of the Consumer Product Evaluation Process", *Harvard Business Review*, Cambridge, March, 1967.

Cundiff, Edward W. and Still R.R., "Basic Marketing Concept, Decisions and Strategies", Prentice-Hall of India, 2nd ed., New Delhi, 1972.

Cundiff, W.E., Still R.R. and Lovoni A.D.N., "Fundamentals of Modern Marketing", Prentice-Hall of India, New Delhi, 1985.

Deret, Abell, "Defining the Business: The Starting Point of Strategic Planning", Prentice-Hall of India, NJ, 1980.

Dickinson, R.A., "Buyer Decision Making", Institute of Business and Economic Research, California, 1967.

East, R., "Changing Consumer Behaviour", *Cassel*, London, 1990.

Eiser, J.R. and Van Der Pligt J., "Attitudes and Decision", Routledge, London, 1988.

Engel, J.F., Blackwell R.D. and Miniard P.W., "Consumer Behaviour", 8th ed., Fort Worth, Dryden, 1995.

Evans, T. and Berman, "Marketing", MacMillan Publishing Co., New York, 1987.

Festinger, L.A., "A Theory of Cognitive Dissonance", Stanford University Press, Stanford, 1957.

Fishbien, M., "The Search for Attitudinal-Behavioural Consisting", Free Press, New York, 1972.

Foxal, G.R. and Goldsmith R.E., "Consumer Psychology for Marketing", Routledge, London, 1994.

Foxal, G.R., "Consumer Psychology in Behavioural Perspective", Routledge, London, 1990.

Ghatak, A., "Consumer Behaviour", Tata McGraw Hill Publishing Co. Ltd., New Delhi, 1991.

Graedel, T.E. and B.R. Allenby, "Industrial Ecology and the Automobile", Prentice-Hall, NJ, 1998.

Howard, J.A. and Sheth N.J., "The Theory of Buyer Behaviour", John Wiley and Sons Inc, New York, 1969.

Howard, J.A., "Consumer Behaviour in Marketing Strategy", Prentice-Hall Englewood Cliff, NJ, 1989.

Howard, John A., "Consumer Behaviour: Application of Theory", McGraw Hill, New York, 1977.

Hughes, G.D., "Attitude Measurement for Marketing Strategy", Foresman, Scotland, 1971.

Jetkins, F., "Modern Marketing", Pitman Publishing, London, 1993.

Jha, S.M. and Singh L.P., "Marketing Management in Indian Perspective, Himalaya Publishing House, Mumbai, 1988.

Jim Blythe, "The Essence of Consumer Behaviour", Prentice-Hall of India, Britain, 1997.

Kothari, C.R., "Research Methodology: Methods and Techniques", Wiley Eastern Ltd., New Delhi, 1988.

Kotler, P. and Armstrong G., "Principles of Marketing", Prentice-Hall of India Pvt. Ltd., New Delhi, 1997.

Kotler, P., "Marketing Management – Analysis, Planning, Implementation and Control", Prentice-Hall of India Pvt. Ltd., New Delhi, 1983.

Kotler, Philip et al., "Marketing Management – An Asian Perspective", Prentice-Hall, Singapore, 1996.

Kotler, Philip, "Principles of Marketing", Prentice-Hall of India, New Delhi, 1989.

Loudon, D. and Bitta A.J.D., "Consumer Behaviour: Concepts and Applications", McGraw Hill Book Co., Singapore, 1988.

Mandella, I.M. and Rosenberg J.L., "Consumer Behaviour", Prentice-Hall of India, New Delhi, 1976.

Maslow, A.H., "Motivation and Personality", Harper and Row, New York, 1954.

Mehta, C.S., "Indian Consumers", Tata McGraw Hill Book Co. Ltd., New Delhi, 1979.

Neal, N.J.V., "An Introduction to Consumer Behaviour", John Wiley and Sons, USA, 1973.

Nicosia, F.M., "Consumer Decision Processes: Marketing and Advertising Implication", Prentice-Hall Inc, Englewood Cliffs, NJ, 1966.

Nieuwenhuis, P. and Peter Wells, "The Automotive Industry and the Environment: A Technical, Business and Social Future", Woodhouse Press, Cambridge, 2003.

Ramaswami, S.V. and Namakumari S., "Marketing Management: Planning, Implementation and Control", MacMillan India Ltd., Madras, 1990.

Raut, K.C. and Nabi M.K., "Buying Behaviour of Consumer Problems In India", Indian Publishers Distributors, Delhi, 1989.

Robin, D.P., "Marketing: Basic Concepts of Decision Making", Harper and Row Publishers Inc, New York, 1978.

Schiffman, Leon G. and Leslie Lazar kanuk, 'Consumer Behaviour', 8th ed., Prentice-Hall of India, New Delhi, 2004.

Schiffman, Leon G. and Leslie Lazer Kanuk, "Consumer Behaviour" Prentice- Hall India Pvt. Ltd., New Delhi, 1997.

Sherlekar, S.A. and Appannaiah H.R., "Essentials of Marketing Management", Himalaya Publishing House, Mumbai, 1995.

Sherlekar, S.A., "Marketing Management", Himalaya Publishing House, Mumbai, 1998.

Singh, A., "Law of Consumer Protection: Principles and Practice", Eastern Book Co., New Delhi, 1994.

Stanton, J.W. and Futrell C., "Fundamentals of Marketing", McGraw Hill Book Co., Singapore, 1987.

Tull, S.D. and Kahle R.L., "Marketing Management", MacMillan Publishing Co., Singapore, 1990.

Walters, C.G. and Paul G.W., "Consumer Behaviour – An Integrated Framework", Homewood, Illinois, 1970.

Wilson, Richard M.S. and Collin Gilligan, "Strategic Marketing Management", Butterworth Heinemann, 2nd ed., Oxford, 2005.

Zikmund, W. and D'Amico M., "Marketing", John Wiley and Sons Inc, New York, 1984.

Theses, Journals and Periodicals

Aaker, D.A. and Day G.S., "Corporate Response to Consumerism Pressures", *Harvard Business Review,* Vol. 50, No. 6, November 1972, pp. 114-124.

Aurangazeb, "Impact of Colour on Consumer Buying Behaviour Among the Car Buyers in India", *Indian Journal of Marketing,* Vol. 27, No. 3, June 2007, pp. 12-22.

Balachandran, V. and J. Venkatesh, "Recent Issues in Changes of Global Brands into Domestic Brands", *Indian Journal of Marketing,* Vol. 36, February 2006, pp. 33-37.

Car Survey, *Car India,* Vol. 4, Issue 8, March 2009, p. 70.

Childers, Terry L. and Akshay R. Rao, "The Influence of Familial and Peer Based Reference Groups on Consumer Decisions", *Journal of Consumer Research,* September 1992, pp. 198-211.

Cotton, B.C. and Emerson M. Bable, "Consumer Response to Promotional Deals", *Journal of Marketing Research,* July 1978, pp. 109-113.

Coutler, Robin A., Gerald Zaltman and Keith S. Coutler, "Interpreting Consumer Perceptions of Advertising", *Journal of Advertising,* Winter 2001, pp. 1-21.

Crispell, Diane, "Women in Charge", *American Demographics,* September 1988, pp. 27-29.

Davis, G., "Materials for Automotive Bodies", *Society of Motor Manufacturers and Traders,* Elsevier, Amsterdam, 2003.

Duncan, C. and Olshavsky R., "External Search – The Role of Consumer Beliefs", *Journal of marketing Research,* April 1982, pp. 32-43.

Dyer, Bhaskar S., "Is the Consumer Really Involved", *Indian Management,* February 1990, pp. 17-19.

Ehrenberg, Hammond and Good Hardt, "The After Effects of Price Related Consumer Promotion", *Journal of Advertising Research,* July 1994, pp. 11-21.

Etgar, Michael Porter and Malhotra, "Determinants of Price Dependency: Personal and Perpetual Factors", *Journal of Consumer Research,* September 1981, pp. 217-222.

Frank, Alpert, "Consumer Market Beliefs and their Managerial Implications – An empirical Examination", *Journal of Consumer Research,* March 1993, pp. 56-70.

Gable, M., Fairhurst A. and Dickinson R., "The Use of Benchmarking to Enhance Marketing Decision Making", *Journal of Consumer Marketing*, Vol. 10, No. 1, 1993, pp. 52-60.

Government of Kerala, 'Report on Census of India', *Car industry*, Ministry of Finance, New Delhi, 2001.

Gupta, H.P. and Raghubir Singh, "Consumer Brand Choice Behaviour for Television", *Indian Journal of Marketing*, March 1989, pp. 17-32.

Gupta, Vivek and Avishek Suman, "Hyundai's Marketing Strategies in India" *Marketing Mastermind*, Vol. 5, No. 5, May 2005, pp. 69-81.

John, Deborah Roedder, "Consumer Socialization of Children", *Journal of Consumer Research*, December 1999, pp. 183-213.

Johnson, Chang, "The Comparison of Car Buying Behaviour between American and Chinese People Living in North America: An Exploratory Study", *Journal of Marketing Research*, Vol. 18, No. 7, August 2001, pp. 180-189.

Jones, David B., "Setting Promotional Goals: A Communication Relationship Model", *Journal of Consumer Marketing*, Vol. 11, No. 1, 1994, pp. 38-49.

Jones, Thomas O. and W. Earl Sasser Jr, "Why Satisfied Customers Defect", *Harvard Business Review*, December 1995, pp. 88-89.

Joseph, W. Newman and Richard Staelin, "Pre-purchase Information Seeking for New Cars and Major Household Appliances", *Journal of Marketing Research*, Vol. 9, No. 3, August 2002, pp. 249 - 257.

Kiel, Geoffrey C. and Roger A. Layton, "Dimensions of Consumer Information Seeking Behaviour Among New Car Buyer", *Journal of Marketing Research*, Vol. 18, No. 1, May 2000, pp. 233-239.

Krishna, Anandha, "The Effect of Deal Knowledge on Consumer Purchase Behaviour", *Journal of Marketing Research*, February 1999, pp. 76 - 91.

Krishna, Aradhana, Imran S. Currin and Robert W. Shumacher, "Consumer Perceptions of Promotional Activity", *Journal of Marketing*, April 1991, pp. 5-16.

Krishnakumar, K.M., "Consumer Perception about Promotional Strategies with reference to FMCG Goods in Kerala", *Ph.D. Thesis*, University of Calicut, Kerala, 2006.

Makkar, Urvashi, "Impact of the Phenomenon of Social Class Mobility on the Consumer Buying and Disposal Behaviour in Indian Perspective; A Case Study of White Goods Markets" *Indian Journal of Marketing*, Vol. 36, No. 2 February 2006, pp. 20-26.

Martilla, J.C., "Word of Mouth Communication in the Industrial Adoption Process", *Journal of Marketing Research*, Vol. 3, No. 2, 1971, pp. 173-178.

Maryline, Lavin, "Husband-Dominated, Joint Shopping Typology for Baby Boomer Couples", *Journal of Consumer Marketing*, September 1993, pp. 33-42.

Michel, G. Mueller and Peter de Haan "The Impact of Incentives on Car Purchase in Agent Based Micro Simulation of Consumer Choice of New Cars", *Energy Policy*, Vol. 37, No.3, March 2008, pp. 1072-1082.

Mohanan, P., "Marketing Problems of Small Enterprises in Kerala", *Ph.D. Thesis*, University of Calicut, Kerala, 1997.

Nathan, S.V., "Dimensions of Marital Roles in Consumer Decision Making", *Vikalpa*, March 1997, pp. 11-21.

Oberoi, Prathap and Michael J. Baker, "International Marketing Strategies in India: An Application of Mixed Method Investigation", *Vikalpa*, Vol. 30, No. 4, December 2005, pp. 11-23.

Oliver, Richard K., "A Cognitive Model of the Antecedents and Consequences of Satisfaction Decisions", *Journal of Marketing Research*, 1980, pp. 460-490.

Porter, Michael E., "How Competitive Forces Shape Strategy", *Harvard Business Review*, Vol. 57, No. 2, March 1979, pp. 137-145.

Purushottam, Papatta and Lakshman Krishna Murthi, "Measuring the Dynamic Effects of Promotions of Brand Choice", *Journal of Marketing Research*, February 1996, pp. 20-35.

Randolph, E. Bucklin and Silva Risso George, "Distribution Intensity and New Car Choice", *Journal of Marketing Research*, Vol. 45, No. 4, August 2008, pp. 473-486.

Sankaran, K., "Pure and Applied Research in Business - How Shall the Twain Meet?" *IIMB Management Review*, Vol. 17, No. 3, September 2005, pp. 115-124.

Saraswathy, B.C., "CRM - A New Dimension of Marketing", *Indian Journal of Marketing*, Vol. 36, February 2006, pp. 9-11.

Shapiro, B.P. et al., "Manage Customers for Profits (Not Just Sales)", *Harvard Business Review,* Vol. 65, No. 5, September 1987, pp. 101-108.

Simms, J., "Market or Die", *Marketing Business,* June 1995, pp. 12-13.

Suresh, A.M. and Raja K.G., "Measuring Customer Satisfaction for Small Cars - An Empirical Study", *Indian Journal of Marketing,* Vol. 36, No. 2, February 2006, pp. 3-8.

Thomas, Andrews and Cynthia Benzing, "The Determinants of Price in Internet Auctions of Used Cars", *Atlantic Economic Journal,* Vol. 35, No. 1, March 2007, pp. 43-57.

Waldrop, Judith and Thomas Exter, "What the 1990 Census will Show?", *American Demographics,* January 1990, p. 30.

William, P. Putsis and Narasimham Srinivasan, "Buying or Just Borrowing? The Duration of Purchase or Deliberation", *Journal of Marketing Research,* August 1994, pp. 103-114.

Yung, Shang Chan, "A Study on the Relationship between the Service Quality Elements and Customer Satisfaction with Reference to the Car Industry", *Journal of International Management,* Vol. 7, No. 2, March 2007, pp. 129-149.

Interview Schedule

Interview Schedule – I
(To Interview the Car Owners in Kerala)

Region	*District*	*Urban/Rural*

Please put tick (√) mark against the appropriate choice

1. Please mention the brand of your car:
2. Who among the following have influenced your purchase most? (Rank them)
   a. Friends b. Relatives
   c. Own family members d. Neighbours
   e. Own decision f. Others (Please specify)
3. If your family members have influenced your purchase, who among them have influenced the most?(Rank them)
   a. Wife/Husband b. Children
   c. Father d. Mother
   e. Siblings f. Others (Please specify)
4. Who drives the car most of the time?
   a. Self b. Driver
   c. Others (Please Specify)
5. The major use of the car is for?
   a. Official/Business purpose b. Personal purpose
   c. Both

6. How many cars do you have?

   a. 1 b. 2

   c. More than two

7. Have you made a comparison of cars before you owned the present one?

   a. Yes b. No

8. If yes, what are the other cars with which you have compared yours?

   a. Maruti 800 b. Maruti Alto

   c. Maruti Zen d. Maruti Swift

   e. Tata Indica f. Hundai Santro

   g. Other (Please specify)

9. Which of the following helped you purchase the car you presently possess? (Rank them accordingly)

   a. Advertisement in Newspaper
   b. Advertisement in Television
   c. Advertisement in Radio
   d. Advertisement in Internet
   e. Advertisement in Magazines
   f. Word of mouth
   g. Car shows & other melas
   h. Test drive
   i. Exchange melas / loan melas
   j. Others (Please specify)

10. Read the following statements and tick appropriately? (SA: Strongly Agree; A: Agree; UND : Undecided; DA : Disagree; SDA : Strongly Disagree)

	SA	*A*	*UND*	*DA*	*SDA*
a. Price is the most important factor while buying a car	5	4	3	2	1
b. Mileage/fuel efficiency matters the most	5	4	3	2	1
c. Brand Image stands tall among all the factors	5	4	3	2	1
d Resale value of the car should be given utmost importance	5	4	3	2	1
e Design & Style are the most important parameters	5	4	3	2	1

f	Efficient after sales service must be accorded top priority	5	4	3	2	1
g	Pressure from the family members is the key factor	5	4	3	2	1
h	Impressive advertisements are very important	5	4	3	2	1
i	Spare parts availability	5	4	3	2	1
j	Free sops available for the car as sales promotion	5	4	3	2	1

11. Rate the following aspects according to their importance while choosing a Car EI-Extremely Important; VI-Very Important : I-Important; LI-Less Important; NI-Not Important)

		EI	*VI*	*I*	*LI*	*NI*
a	Power steering	5	4	3	2	1
b	Attractive Colour	5	4	3	2	1
c	Power windows	5	4	3	2	1
d	Easy entry & Exit	5	4	3	2	1
e	Upholstery	5	4	3	2	1
f	Remote Control	5	4	3	2	1
g	Air conditioner	5	4	3	2	1
h	Body coloured bumpers	5	4	3	2	1
i	Easy shift gears	5	4	3	2	1
j	Comfortable seats	5	4	3	2	1
k	Good suspension	5	4	3	2	1
l	Comfortable seats	5	4	3	2	1
m	Ample leg space	5	4	3	2	1
n	Booster assisted brakes	5	4	3	2	1
o	Streamlined dash board	5	4	3	2	1
p	Audio system	5	4	3	2	1
q	Diesel/Petrol/LPG/CNG Car(fuel specific)	5	4	3	2	1
r	Sear belts/Air bags	5	4	3	2	1

12. Which of the following sales promotion tools has influenced your car purchase the most? (Rank them)

    a. Discounts　　b. Free Insurance

    c. Exemption from Road Tax　　d. Free Accessories

    e. Others

13. Kindly provide details regarding your previous ownership of vehicle?

    a. Which vehicle did you have before buying the car?

        1. Two wheeler　　2. Car

        3. Others (Please specify)

b. If it is a car, please mention the brand of the car:

c. When did you buy the previous car?

d. How was it purchased as?

1. New 2. Used

e. What was the price of the car?

f. Do you still have that car?

14. Kindly answer the following questions relating to the reasons for replacing the previous car?

(SA : Strongly Agree; A: Agree, UND : Undecided
DA : Disagree, SDA : Strongly Disagree)

	SA	*A*	*UND*	*DA*	*SDA*
a. Increased income led to the purchase of a costlier car	5	4	3	2	1
b. We needed a bigger car as the family size increased	5	4	3	2	1
c. Availability of financing schemes led to replacement	5	4	3	2	1
d. The useful life period of the car was over	5	4	3	2	1
e. The models launched were more attractive	5	4	3	2	1
f. The maintenance cost of the previous car started increasing	5	4	3	2	1
g. We changed the car because the service quality was not good	5	4	3	2	1
h. The exchange programme of the car company was attractive	5	4	3	2	1

15. Kindly answer the following questions relating to the reasons for shifting from two wheelers to cars?

(SA: Strongly Agree; A: Agree, UND: Undecided
DA: Disagree, SDA: Strongly Disagree)

	SA	*A*	*UND*	*DA*	*SDA*
a. Cars provide more safety than two-wheelers	5	4	3	2	1
b. Convenient for a family to travel	5	4	3	2	1
c. Status symbol	5	4	3	2	1
d. Neighbour possesses a car	5	4	3	2	1
e. Cars provide value for the money spent	5	4	3	2	1
f. Ca loan availability	5	4	3	2	1
g. Increased disposable income	5	4	3	2	1
h. Availability of good after sales service for cars	5	4	3	2	1
i. The desire for a change	5	4	3	2	1

16. What was your source of fund for the purchase of the car ?
    a. NBFC
    b. Commercial Bank
    c. Private Financiers
    d. Friends/Relatives
    e. Self
17. What is your opinion of the exchange offer provided by the Pre-Owned Car Outlets or True Value Outlets?
    a. Very good
    b. Good
    c. Bad
    d. Very bad
    e. No opinion
18. Do the car dealers provide you good after sales service?
    a. Yes
    b. No
19. If no, what are the reasons for it?
    a. Inadequate strength of service personnel
    b. Incompetent/unskilled service staff
    c. Few number of service centres
    d. Expensive after sales service
    e. Any other (Please specify)

Personal Details

20. Name :
21. Sex : Male/Female
22. Age in years :
    a. Below 25
    b. 26-35
    c. 36-45
    d. 46-55
    e. Above 55
23. Address :
24. Education
    a. School Education
    b. Degree/diploma
    c. Post Graduate
    d. Professional
    e. Others (Specify)
25. Employment :
    a. Govt. employee
    b. Private employee
    c. Self-Employed

d. Retired
e. Homemaker
f. Agriculture
g. Others (Please specify)

26. Profession :

27. Marital Status : 1. Single
2. Married
3. Others

28. If married, occupational status of the spouse
a. Employed
b. Homemaker
c. Business
d. Retired
e. Agriculture
f. Professional
g. Others (Please specify)

29. No. of family members :
Men :
Women :
Children :

30. No. of earning members in the family :
Men :
Women :
Children :

31. Average monthly income of the car owner
Rs. :

32. Average monthly income of the family
Rs. :

Interview Schedule – II

(To Interview the Car Dealers of Kerala)

Region *District*

1. Name of the car dealer :
2. Address :
3. Date of establishment :

Please put tick (√) mark against the appropriate Choice.

4. Which company's cars do you deal with?
   a. Maruti Udyog Ltd b. Tata motors
   c. Hyundai motors d. Others (please specify)
5. What are the models of cars you deal with?
   a. Maruti 800, Alto, Zen Estilo, Swift, WagonR, Baleno, Esteem, Omni
   b. Tata Indica, Indica V2, Indica V2 XETA, Indigo
   c. Hyundai Santro, Getz, Accent, Sonata, i10
   d. Others (please specify)
6. Which of the following cars has recorded the highest sale from your showroom during the last six years (2002-2008)? (Rank them)
   a. Maruti 800, Alto, Zen Estilo, Swift, WagonR, Baleno, Esteem, Omni
   b. Tata Indica, Indica V2, Indica XETA, Indigo
   c. Hyundai Santro, Getz, Accent, Sonata, i10
   d. Others (please specify)
7. Please mention the average annual sales of the cars you deal with (during the period from 2002 to 2008):
   a. Maruti 800, Alto, Zen Estilo, Swift, WagonR, Baleno, Esteem, Omni

b. Tata Indica, Indica V2, Indica XETA, Indigo
c. Hyundai Santro, Getz, Accent, Sonata, i10
d. Others (please specify)

8. Which promotional tool do you adopt the most to sell your cars? (Rank them)

a. Advertisement b. Sales promotion
c. Personal selling d. Direct marketing
e. Public-relations & Publicity f. Events and Experiences
g. Others (please specify)

9. If it is 'advertisement', in which do you advertise the most ?

a. Print media b. Electronic media
c. Both

10. If print media, in which of the following do you advertise the most? (Rank them)

a. Newspapers b. Magazines
c. Billboards d. Posters & leaflets
e. Brochures & booklets f. Banners

11. If electronic media, in which of the following do you advertise the most? (Rank them)

a. Television b. Radio
c. Internet d. Cinema theatres
e. Videotapes

12. If 'sales promotion' is used as a promotional tool, which of the following helps in increasing your sales the most (Rank them)?

a. Discounts b. Free insurance
c. Road tax exemption d. Free test drives
e. Free accessories f. Car loans
g. Extended warranty h. Others (please specify)

13. Rank the following promotional tools that help in promoting your car sales.

a. Exchange melas b. Car shows/Trade shows
c. Road shows d. Sponsoring events
e. Awareness campaign f. Others (please specify)

14. Do you receive complaints about 'after sales service'?

a. Yes b. No

15. If yes, what are the reasons for the poor after sales service?
    a. Inadequate strength of the service personnel
    b. Incompetent/unskilled service staff
    c. Few number of service centers
    d. Expensive after sales service
    e. Others (please specify)
16. Read the following statements and tick appropriately.
    (SA: Strongly Agree; A: Agree; UND: Undecided; DA:Disagree; SDA: Strongly Disagree)

	SA	*A*	*UND*	*DA*	*SDA*
a. Majority of your customers prefer small cars to large cars.					
b. Most of the customers are price conscious while buying a car.					
c. Most of the customers give preference to mileage in purchasing a car.					
d. Brad image is given priority while buying a car.					
e. Most of the customers prefer cars having high resale value.					
f. Design and style are given due consideration before a car is purchased.					
g. Customers give high priority to efficient after sales service while purchasing a car.					
h. A car purchase is made because of the pressure from the family members.					
i. Advertisement in the print media is more effective than in the electronic media for a car purchase.					
j. Spare parts availability is an important factor in purchasing a car.					
k. Availability of car loans greatly promotes car sale.					
l. A car is purchased because free sops are available as sales promotion.					
m. Car shows and Exchange melas are the only factors that influencedpeople to buy.					
n. Test-drives determine whether or not to finally purchase a car.					
o. The "Word of mouth" factor influences people in buying a car.					

17. Rate the following aspects according to their importance in promoting the sale of a car. (**EI**: Extremely Important; **VI**: Very Important; **I**: Important; **LI**: Less Important; **NI**: Not Important.)

	EI	*VI*	*I*	*LI*	*NI*
1. Providing car loans to customers					
2. Allowing long test-drives					
3. Training the sales executives to understand customer behaviour					
4. Making sales calls by the sales force					
5. Dealing with branded accessories inside the showroom					
6. Having an in-house spare parts center					
7. Having an in-house service center					
8. Having a stockyard near the showroom premises					
9. Having a toll-free number for the customers					
10. Having a prompt customer care service					
11. Making charitable donations					
12. Building community relations					
13. Demonstration of the working of the car					
14. Entertainment					
15. Conducting contests					
16. Conducting fairs and trade shows					
17. Conducting sales meetings					
18. Sponsoring events					

Interview Schedule – III

(To Interview the Car Manufacturers of Kerala)

Region *District*

1. Name of the car manufacturer :
2. Address :
3. Date of establishment :

Please put tick (√) mark against the appropriate Choice.

4. Which company's cars do you deal with?
   a. Maruti Udyog Ltd b. Tata motors
   c. Hyundai motors d. Others (please specify)
5. What are the models of cars you deal with?
   a. Maruti 800, Alto, Zen Estilo, Swift, WagonR, Baleno, Esteem, Omni
   b. Tata Indica, Indica V2, Indica V2 XETA, Indigo
   c. Hyundai Santro, Getz, Accent, Sonata, i10
   d. Others (please specify)
6. Please mention the average annual sales of the cars you deal with (during the period from 2002 to 2008):
   a. Maruti 800, Alto, Zen Estilo, Swift, WagonR, Baleno, Esteem, Omni
   b. Tata Indica, Indica V2, Indica XETA, Indigo
   c. Hyundai Santro, Getz, Accent, Sonata, i10
   d. Others (please specify)
7. Which promotional tool do you adopt the most to sell your cars? (Rank them)
   a. Advertisement b. Sales promotion
   c. Personal selling d. Direct marketing
   e. Public-relations & Publicity f. Events and Experiences
   g. Others (please specify)

8. If it is 'advertisement', in which do you advertise the most?
   a. Print media
   b. Electronic media
   c. Both
9. If print media, in which of the following do you advertise the most? (Rank them)
   a. Newspapers
   b. Magazines
   c. Billboards
   d. Posters & leaflets
   e. Brochures & booklets
   f. Banners
10. If electronic media, in which of the following do you advertise the most? (Rank them)
    a. Television
    b. Radio
    c. Internet
    d. Cinema theatres
    e. Videotapes
11. If 'sales promotion' is used as a promotional tool, which of the following helps in increasing your sales the most? (Rank them)
    a. Discounts
    b. Free insurance
    c. Road tax exemption
    d. Free test drives
    e. Free accessories
    f. Car loans
    g. Extended warranty
    h. Others (please specify)
12. Rank the following promotional tools that help in promoting your car sales.
    a. Exchange melas
    b. Car shows/Trade shows
    c. Road shows
    d. Sponsoring events
    e. Awareness campaign
    f. Others (please specify)
13. Do you receive complaints about 'after sales service'?
    a. Yes
    b. No
14. If yes, what are the reasons for the poor 'after sales service'?
    a. Inadequate strength of the service personnel
    b. Incompetent/unskilled service staff
    c. Few number of service centers
    d. Expensive after sales service
    e. Others (please specify)
15. Read the following statements and tick appropriately.
    (SA: Strongly Agree; A: Agree; UND: Undecided; DA: Disagree; SDA: Strongly Disagree)

	SA	A	UND	DA	SDA
a. Majority of your customers prefer small cars to large cars.					
b. Most of the customers are price conscious while buying a car.					
c. Most of the customers give preference to mileage in purchasing a car.					
d. Brad image is given priority while buying a car.					
e. Most of the customers prefer cars having high resale value.					
f. Design and style are given due consideration before a car is purchased.					
g. Customers give high priority to efficient after sales service while purchasing a car.					
h. A car purchase is made because of the pressure from the family members.					
i Advertisement in the print media is more effective than in the electronic media for a car purchase.					
j Spare parts availability is an important factor in purchasing a car.					
k Availability of car loans greatly promotes car sale.					
l A car is purchased because free sops are available as sales promotion.					
m Car shows and Exchange melas are the only factors that influenced people to buy.					
n Test-drives determine whether or not to finally purchase a car.					
o The "Word of mouth" factor influences people in buying a car.					

16. Rate the following aspects according to their importance in promoting the sale of a car. (**EI**: Extremely Important; **VI**: Very Important; **I**: Important; **LI**: Less Important; **NI**: Not Important)

	EI	VI	I	LI	NI
1. Providing car loans to customers					
2. Allowing long test-drives					
3. Training the sales executives to understand customer behaviour					
4. Making sales calls by the sales force					
5. Dealing with branded accessories inside the showroom					

6. Having an in-house spare parts center
7. Having an in-house service center
8. Having a stockyard near the showroom premises
9. Having a toll-free number for the customers
10. Having a prompt customer care service
11. Making charitable donations
12. Building community relations
13. Demonstration of the working of the car
14. Entertainment
15. Conducting contests
16. Conducting fairs and trade shows
17. Conducting sales meetings
18. Sponsoring events